D1289299

Architecture of the Gollins Melvin Ward Partnership

Architecture of the

Foreword by Sir Colin Anderson, KBE

Gollins Melvin Ward Partnership

Introduction by Tony Aldous

Traduction française par Jacques Engelmann
Deutsche Übersetzung von Nora von Mühlendahl

Lund Humphries London

First edition 1974
Published by
Lund Humphries Publishers Limited
12 Bedford Square London WC1

SBN 85331 368 7

Made and printed in Great Britain by
Lund Humphries, Bradford and London

Partners

Frank Gollins
James Melvin
Edmund Ward
Robert Headley
Brian Mayes
Robert Smith
Anthony Gregson
David Miller
Julian Ryder Richardson
Neil Southam

Contents/Table des matières/Inhalt

Foreword/Préface/Vorwort Sir Colin Anderson, KBE 7

Introduction/Introduction/Einführung Tony Aldous 9/19/26
Colour plates/Planches couleurs/Farbbilder 11–14, 17, 23, 24, 27–30

Buildings and projects/Bâtiments et projets/Bauten und Projekte:

1 University of Sheffield: Central Redevelopment and Library 36
2 The Polytechnic, Sheffield 42
3 New Cavendish Street, LondonW1 44
4 Radley College, Berkshire 46
5 174–204 Marylebone Road, London W1–Castrol House 48
6 University of Sheffield: Faculties of Arts, Economics and Social Studies 52
7 University of Sheffield: University House 55
8 College of Education, Loughborough, Leicestershire 56
9 Women's Royal Army Corps College, Camberley, Surrey 60
10 Sevenoaks Hospital, Kent: Outpatients' and Maternity Departments 66
11 District General Hospital, Hillingdon, Middlesex 70
12 Royal Military College of Science, Shrivenham, Wiltshire 74
13 Headquarter Offices, St Mellons, Monmouthshire 76
14 Headquarter Offices, Leadenhall Street, London EC3 80
15 House on Campden Hill, London W8 88
16 HMS *Caledonia* Naval Barracks, Rosyth, Scotland 90
17 Royal Air Force, West Drayton, Middlesex: Residential accommodation 92
18 Royal Military Academy, Sandhurst, Camberley, Surrey 96
19 Upper School, Desford, Leicestershire 102
20 International Airport Terminal J F Kennedy Airport, New York 106
21 Upper School, Syston, Leicestershire 114
22 University of Sheffield: Biological Sciences 120
23 University Library Extension, Grange Road, Cambridge 122
24 Headquarter Offices, Stevenage, Hertfordshire 126
25 Woking Centre Pool, Surrey 130
26 Headquarter Offices, Fulham Road, London SW3 134
27 Munich 2 Airport, West Germany 136
28 Mombasa Airport Development, Kenya, East Africa 138
29 Holiday Resort and Hotel, Cesme Peninsula, Turkey 140
30 Westminster City School, Nine Elms, London SW8 142
31 Headquarter Offices, Brighton, Sussex 144
32 Royal Opera House, Covent Garden, London WC2 146

Foreword by Sir Colin Anderson, KBE

Unlike some of those public personalities who draw our attention to goods in advertisements, I can declare myself a real client, a real user, of the firm of Gollins Melvin Ward – and a well-satisfied one at that.

It falls to me to see a great deal of today's architecture, in drawing and plan form, as well as completed; and I could not but acquire through this a comparative sense as to which is more and which less admirable – just as a tea-taster or wine-taster can. This choice has to be instinctive, for there is no rulebook: we have been born into an age of revolution in the arts and we have to take part in the formation of the new pattern. No wonder we find ourselves faced with all sorts of choices as between untried and unknown alternatives. In this exciting field I have found myself much drawn towards architectural projects put forward by Gollins Melvin Ward until – at last – there came the chance to put this hunch to the test. The splendid outcome seemed to surprise many observers. They seemed to me to be expecting to submit, rather than to admire, and I was reminded once more of the sad ignorance, even among enlightened members of the community, about our architects and their work.

This is why I am so glad to be able to wish this book well and to add my own commendation to the visual evidence of a most distinguished achievement, which it provides.

Préface

A la différence de nombre de ces personnages publics qu'on voit, dans les publicités, vanter les mérites de tel ou tel produit, je suis bel et bien un utilisateur réel, un client de l'Agence d'architectes Gollins Melvin Ward et, je l'atteste, un client satisfait.

Je me trouve avoir professionnellement à connaître des travaux de l'architecture contemporaine, tant sous la forme d'esquisses ou de plans que de réalisations; ce qui n'a pas manqué de développer chez moi un certain sens du relatif, une faculté d'appréciation du plus ou moins remarquable – assez analogue au discernement des dégustateurs de thé ou de vin. Ce choix ne peut qu'être instinctif, car il n'existe pas de code ni de manuel de référence: nous vivons une époque de révolution dans les arts, où nous sommes appelés à contribuer à la formation de modèles nouveaux. Il n'est donc pas étonnant que nous nous trouvions confrontés à toutes sortes de choix, portant sur des alternatives non expérimentées et inconnues, Dans ce domaine passionnant, je me suis découvert une prédilection marquée pour les projets architecturaux élaborés par Gollins Melvin Ward, jusqu'à ce que l'occasion se présentât – enfin – d'éprouver, dans le cadre d'une commande, le bien-fondé de cette inclination. Le splendide résultat a paru surprendre beaucoup d'observateurs. On aurait dit qu'ils s'étaient attendus à avoir à se résigner plutôt qu'à admirer, et cela m'a rappelé une fois de plus le triste état d'ignorance dans lequel se trouvent jusqu'aux membres éclairés de notre société à l'égard de nos architectes et de leurs travaux.

C'est pourquoi je suis particulièrement heureux de pouvoir apporter mon soutien à ce livre, et d'ajouter la caution de mes éloges personnels à la haute qualité des réalisations dont il fournit visuellement l'évidente démonstration.

Vorwort

Im Gegensatz zu jenen Personen der Öffentlichkeit, die unsere Aufmerksamkeit durch Anzeigen auf Waren lenken, kann ich mich als wirklicher Klient und Nutznießer der Firma Gollins Melvin Ward bezeichnen – und als ein zufriedengestellter obendrein.

Ich sehe von Berufs wegen sehr viel neue Architektur sowohl in Form von Zeichnungen und Plänen als auch ausgeführte; dadurch habe ich notgedrungen ein vergleichendes Gefühl dafür erworben, was gut und was weniger gut ist, etwa wie ein Tee- oder Weinprüfer. Diese Entscheidung muß instinktiv erfolgen, denn es gibt keine Richtlinien dafür. Wir sind in ein Zeitalter der Revolution der Künste geboren und gezwungen, an der Bildung einer neuen Ordnung teilzuhaben. Kein Wunder, daß wir uns allen Arten von Wahlmöglichkeiten sowie unausprobierten und unbekannten Alternativen ausgesetzt sehen. In diesem erregenden Bereich fühlte ich mich von den Projekten von Gollins Melvin Ward sehr angesprochen, bis ich schließlich die Gelegenheit erhielt, dieses Gefühl zu testen. Das hervorragende Ergebnis hat offenbar manche Beobachter überrascht. Sie schienen von mir zu erwarten, daß ich nachgeben, aber nicht bewundern würde. Wieder einmal wurde mir die bedauerliche Ignoranz selbst gebildeter Mitglieder der Gesellschaft über unsere Architekten und ihr Werk bewußt.

Deshalb ist es mir eine solche Freude, diesem Buch Erfolg wünschen und meine Empfehlung für das visuelle Zeugnis einer großartigen Leistung hinzufügen zu können.

Some firms of architects make a strong impact on public consciousness because their buildings have a strong common personality, use the same visual idioms again and again. The song has a catchy chorus; though we may sometimes think the words vulgar or uncommonly ill-chosen, the refrain is certainly familiar. Other firms (sometimes disparagingly called 'developers' architects') produce an architecture which seems to many people to amount to little more than a tidy packaging of the client's requirements: so many thousand square feet of office space, automatically cut to order, ingeniously arranged to meet planning authority and office development permit requirements, and wrapped in whatever external cladding seems appropriate to the market and the moment.

Between these two extremes – the *prime donne* asserting their own idiosyncratic vision on a protesting public and a resentful townscape, and the automatic architecture of mere suppliers of office space – is another kind of architectural practice which cannot be so easily categorized. It has no preconceived solutions and no stomach for purchasing glory at the visual expense of what is there already. Such a firm is the Gollins Melvin Ward Partnership. Their chosen path is a harder one, and much less clear. The rewards are more often than not tinged with disappointment, because the task they set themselves is complex and their standards tough ones.

Some new buildings are like the man who enters a party never doubting that everyone will be overjoyed at his arrival: 'Hullo, everybody. I've come at last' they seem to be saying. The GMW approach (though far from being timid) is more diffident. Instead it seems to be saying: 'We think this building is just about right for its purpose and its surroundings. We hope you agree.'

That is one reason why some of the practice's best known buildings do not at first sight appear to have much family resemblance to one another. Its much admired award-winning pair, Commercial Union and P & O in the City of London, **14**, are no more 'typically' GMW buildings than the long, low, grey battleship of its new college buildings at Sandhurst, **18**; its early curtain-wall office block, Castrol House, in Marylebone Road, **5**, is no more 'typical' than its squat, round nuclear-reactor buildings at Shrivenham, **12**, its BOAC terminal at Kennedy Airport, **20**, than the many-windowed, precast concrete tower of Loughborough College, **8**, or the tall, white slab of Hillingdon Hospital, **11**. And this also has something to do with the way in which this twenty-five-year-old practice is run. GMW on the whole shuns the notion of 'partners-in-charge' of jobs. Ever since Frank Gollins, James Melvin, and Edmund Ward started the practice with a handful of staff in a house in Russell Square, a strong sense of collective decision and collective responsibility has ruled. Each client, of course, has one partner he deals with and who will answer for the firm; but, with rare exceptions, design is the result of team discussion and experiment. This holds good as strongly today at Manchester Square as in the practice's early days. There are now ten partners, seventeen associates and a staff of around 200.

Because the GMW approach is thus exploratory and empirical, it is hard to pin down a coherent design philosophy. It exists, is in practice well understood, but cannot easily be defined. The best I can do, beyond discussing my own selection of representative buildings, is to state two very broad principles: fitness for purpose, and fitness for setting. Pious purposes to which most architects might be thought to subscribe. By their fruits ye shall know them . . .

Two events changed Gollins Melvin Ward from an obscure small firm doing housing conversion work for some of the old Metropolitan boroughs into a major and creative architectural practice. One was a commission to do new housing work for Lambeth Borough Council, soon followed by schools for Hertfordshire and Kent. The other, in 1953, was the winning of the first prize in an open competition for the development of Sheffield University's central area, **1**. They are still architects for this, and have to date designed some ten new buildings there. Yet, through no fault of GMW's, they have to some extent been disappointed in their early hopes and aspirations. Delays, a drastically changing brief, exploding student numbers, and tighter and tighter cost limits, have robbed the campus of something of the architectural consistency it might have had.

That said, it is remarkable how well the buildings do relate to each other and to their neighbours. The University Library (1959), **1**, large by British standards with more than a million books, is calculated to make university architects of the 1970s gasp with envy. Its use of materials (white and black marble and wood floors, for instance) and of space are lavish. Outwardly, the Portland stone facing above and below the main curtain of glass blunts its outline somewhat. Its glory is the interiors – a sense of place and space which today's cost limits initially forbid – and its views outwards, particularly from the main reading room on to a public park with lake and trees. That outlook has been exploited to maximum effect.

The 1962 Physics and Mathematics Building, to the south across a dual carriageway road, stands on the same steeply falling site as University House (same year), **7**, which houses the student union and senior common rooms. Physics and Maths consists of two distinct elements: the larger is a curtain-wall office and laboratory block, the smaller an aggregate-panelled lecture theatre block. They are linked by a three-storey glass bridge over a public footpath, and the colour of the main block's glass spandrel panels – a smoky blue – helps to give it just the required crispness of outline without stressing its bulk. Visually, it 'rhymes' with other curtain-wall buildings on the site: University House; the neat and decent west extension to an earlier architect's chemistry block; and, above all, the twenty-three storey Arts Tower, **6**. A dominant feature of the campus, this is as clear-cut and unfussy a tall cube as the better-known Commercial Union building in London, with the same effective use of the space occupied by lift machinery and plant room to crown it with a solid band of colour.

The Arts Tower is meant to be the focus of the campus, and indeed it is from any distant view. From closer to, what currently draws one's attention most strongly is the Biological Sciences Building (1971), **22**: a large slab of a building in shiny red-brick sitting at first-floor level on concrete piers. From the south it appears as a huge brick wall with four-and-a-half rows of rather squarish fixed windows topped by a deeper band of brick. It comes over immediately as a warm and pleasing building, but one wonders at first 'Why brick?' Closer inspection reveals the subtlety of the solution. Biological Sciences is red-brick because it extends and sits adjacent to earlier red-brick buildings, Edwardian in date and more or less Gothic in style. The architects, after some soul searching, decided it would be neither 'phoney' nor dishonest to build a little more Edwardian Gothic so as to smooth the links between old and new. Where the previous architects left a half-built Gothic tower, GMW finished it off, crenellations and all.

The remaining major building on the Sheffield campus featured in this book is University House (1962), **7**, in that same steep slope as Maths and Physics but designed to a brief that allowed a somewhat more lavish treatment. Though there is a broad band of brick at podium level, visually University House is in the same large-glass-window, curtain-wall idiom as the library, and 'rhymes' with it, the Arts Tower and the neighbouring Physics and Mathematics Building.

The 'union' part of the building has taken a pounding in the past twelve years from a student population both more numerous and more boisterous than its designers expected, and internally the staff common rooms on the top floor have preserved very much better the look and feel originally intended. The building has some gay, even playful features such as the orange mosaic-faced lift shaft visible through clear glass curtain-walling at the north-west corner. But it is, one suspects, even more than the library, a building which takes its character chameleon-like from what is going inside and what surrounds it. Its link with the original student union building (in weak classical style from the 1930s) is a cleverly serpentine curtain-wall building housing the union offices. A paved garden with ivy and trees lies between that and a well-detailed brick retaining wall, to the north of which opens out the main area of purplish brick paving extending between the buildings and on under Arup's ingenious dual-carriage-way road bridge. Somehow, in spite of all the difficulties, in spite of the patch-and-extend nature of the changing later brief, the architects have, against the odds, to a considerable extent managed to make this campus fit together in a meaningful way.

The Royal Military Academy at Sandhurst (1970),**18**, posed a very different set of problems. The brief was, basically, to provide university-type buildings at not much more than University Grants Committee cost levels, but answering to the Army's special requirements both functionlly and in respect of army tradition and hierarchy. The solution was, moreover, to be one which would respect a sensitive site, open parkland edged by pine woods, its shallow amphitheatre already partly backed by a string of historic or 'grand' buildings, the Regency 'Old College' and the Edwardian 'New' and 'Victory' Colleges.

The Army's brief in practice left the architects with little choice but to range their new buildings as an extension of the crescent formed by these existing buildings. The solution adopted – a long, relatively low profile in concrete faced with panels of dark grey aggregate – manages to balance the scenic weight of Old College (a fine set-piece dating from 1812) without challenging or attempting to outface its architectural quality. The residential and teaching blocks look, from a distant view on a grey day, like a fleet of battleships at anchor on the far edge of the harbour. In fact they extend back behind this profile, cutting into the edge of the woodlands that separate RMA Sandhurst from that distinct and independent establishment, the Staff College. (Though felling was kept to a minimum, some 2,000 trees had to be cleared to make way for the new buildings.) A stream originally running through the site was diverted to run between the buildings and the main expanse of parkland. The concrete bases of the buildings are splayed down towards the water, at once giving an impression of sloping banks and helping to reduce the apparent bulk of the frontages.

Behind the main range of buildings, other (generally lower) blocks run back at right-angles, so placed as to leave some fine, tall fir trees and shrubberies preserved to grace the garden quadrangles thus created. The plan pushes car parks and delivery bays to the back of the buildings where they are served by a new perimeter road and are largely hidden from the park by the front range of buildings.

This range of the residential and teaching blocks are terminated towards the end of the 'crescent' by the Headquarters building, compact and somehow contriving to be both robustly no-nonsense military and an elegant structure in its own right. As with the main range of college buildings, its large dark grey aggregate panels often reflect the presence behind them of windowless briefing or seminar rooms (in the college buildings, quaintly called 'halls of study', though designed for tutorial groups of no more than a dozen). The use of these large aggregate panels on the residential blocks means narrow windows and relatively sombre study-bedrooms. Perhaps that is thought appropriate to the life of the young officer cadet. Daylighting is, however, up to the required standard; and externally it is certainly effective as an elevational treatment.

The 1,200-seat assembly hall suffers somewhat in external appearance from the spindly proportions of the columns supporting the back of its raked auditorium – the side facing into the central area of parkland; although this building is set back from the main line of the 'crescent'. The thinness of these columns was, it seems, the result of enforced economies. Inside, however, the hall achieves admirably that combination of robust utilitarianism and elegance which GMW seem to aim at in their military buildings generally .The elegance and excitement come to a large extent from the space-frame roof spangled with aluminium light fittings and focusing on a huge black suspended cylinder which houses the extract fan. That ceiling is a *tour de force.*

Two other sets of military buildings merit special mention. At the Royal Military College of Science, Shrivenham, **12**, the three squat Camber Castle-like circular buildings of the Rutherford Laboratory (1968) now looks so inevitable that one wonders how anyone could ever envisage a nuclear and its associated laboratories as any other shape.

The Women's Royal Army Corps' school of instruction at Camberley, **9**, posed in some respects similar problems to RMA Sandhurst: an attractive wooded site which new buildings should respect; tight cost limits; and the peculiar requirements of a military establishment, with its still rigid demarcation between officers, NCOs and other ranks. The 13-acre site had been that of an orphanage and though the dormitory block was not usable and effectively beyond restoration, the architects persuaded their client to retain the attractive 1860s assembly hall, to which they skilfully attached a small new chapel, intercommunicating, clad externally in a golden Columbian pine, with angles mostly at diagonals thus making it seem much smaller than it is, and set on a plinth whose proportions and moulding continue those of the ground floor of the Victorian building.

The new buildings at Camberley are of three kinds: single storey in timber and white-painted fletton brick; two- and three-storey in a purplish load-bearing brick with concrete floors visible; and the concrete 'post-and-rail' construction of the officers' mess. The creation of a sunken garden in what was the cellar of the demolished dormitory block and the skilful retention of trees and rocks to make garden courtyards within and behind the officers' mess are noteworthy. But though officers, officer cadets and NCOs enjoy plum sites and better space allocations, the way in which Other Ranks' residential and social blocks have been arranged and designed is, in its way, quite as effective.

The British terminal at Kennedy Airport, New York (1970), **20**, posed problems quite as much by way of physical and operational constraints as of cost. The only separate terminal to be occupied by a foreign airline, it was expected to make a distinctive national statement architecturally, but at the same time it occupied virtually the last and least easy site available for this purpose. Its shape was to a large extent dictated by sight lines from the airport control tower, and by the requirement of a roof strong enough and sufficiently well screened to take helicopter landings. (It is a galling and ironic fact that changes in the safety regulations have prevented it being used for

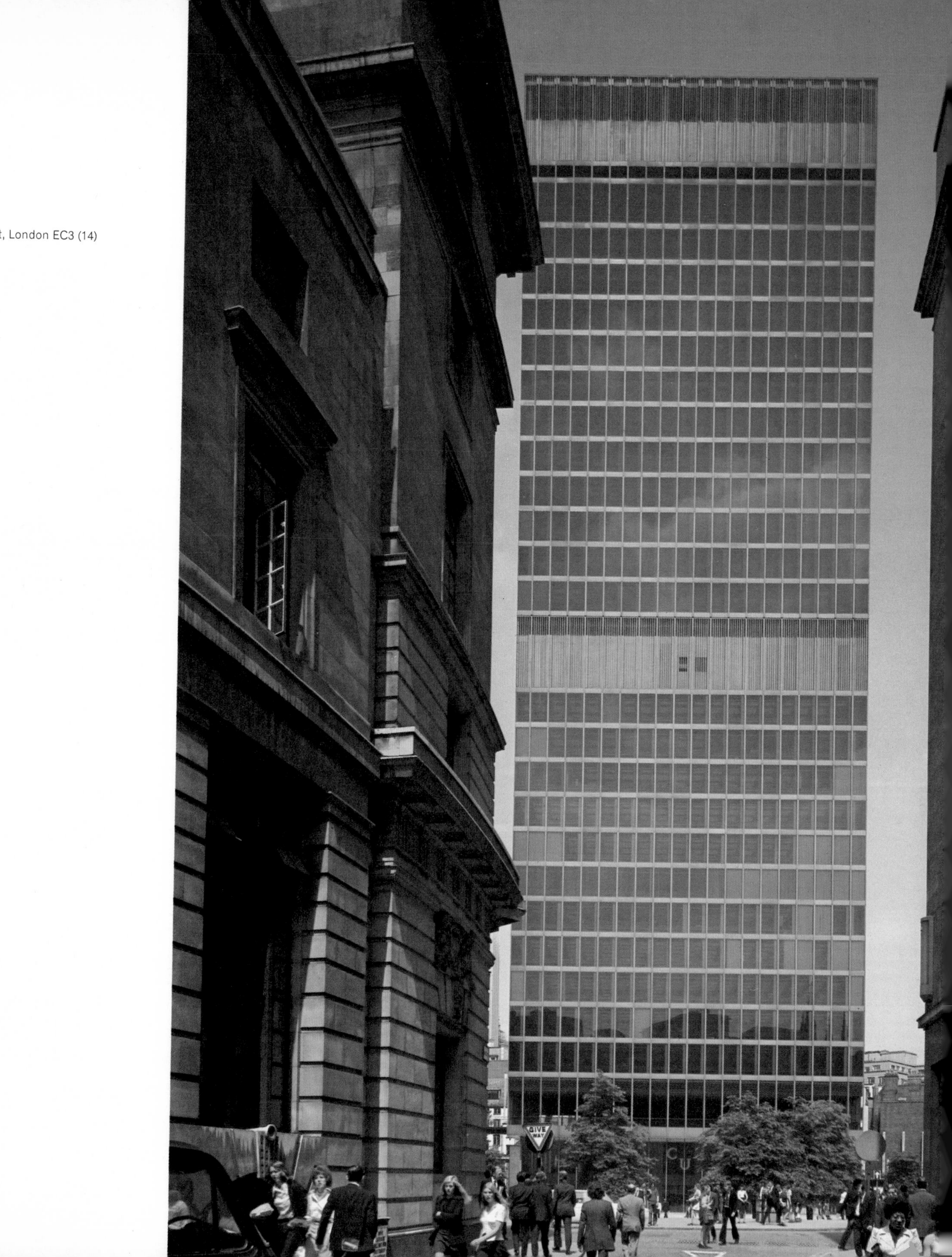

Headquarter Offices, Leadenhall Street, London EC3 (14)
Commercial Union

Royal Military Academy, Sandhurst, Camberley, Surrey (18)

Headquarter Offices, Leadenhall Street, London EC3 (14)
P&O, Commercial Union (on the right/à droite/ rechts)

this purpose.) In spite of all this, and complex technical requirements, the building does 'speak for Britain' in a way that does it and its designers much credit. It is one of the few British-designed buildings to have gained major awards in the United States.

The Kennedy terminal was, however, also important as a further turning point in the development of the practice. It firmly established GMW's reputation as airport architects, and other airport commissions followed: from the same client, Boadicea House, the BOAC computer centre at Heathrow (1967), and a flight catering centre (1968); then in 1970, also at Heathrow, a services building for Air Canada. Further afield it brought commissions, with aviation consultants Studiengruppe Luftfahrt, for a second airport at Munich, **27,** and for the development of Mombasa Airport, **28,** now in progress.

Woking swimming pool (1973), **25**, on a more modest scale, shows how an architect's best intentions may be in part thwarted by changes in the context of his building. As consultants to the urban district council for its new civic complex, GMW placed it in what they thought was the best position functionally and visually in relation to the rest of the town centre. A central government decision on roads has left it stranded in the middle of a roundabout which originally would not have existed, dwarfed by excessively tall lamp columns that come with it. But the building – in which the main pool had to be in the form of a tank at ground level rather than excavated – nonetheless remains an attractive one, with pitched tops to its bush-hammered concrete walls helping to break up surfaces and reduce its sense of bulk.

Probably the most widely acclaimed Gollins Melvin Ward buildings of recent years have been the Commercial Union and P & O Towers, **14**, at the junction of Leadenhall Street and St Mary Axe in the City of London. Here two sites which could not have been developed satisfactorily separately were put together and turned into a single composition with two complementary but distinctive office towers, both opening on to a newly created open space.

Commercial Union, at 387 ft much the taller of the two, is from the podium upwards a pure elongated cube much in the spirit of Mies van der Rohe. Eleven storeys of office space with tall oblong windows are topped by the double-storey louvred band of the halfway-up plant room. Above it rise eleven more office floors, crowned by a second double-storey louvred plant room which tops the structure. These divisions are also significant in terms of structure: the office floors are hung from steel 'umbrella spokes' which project from the central concrete core at roof and halfway levels.

Below the lowest office floor the 'cube' is broken by an open podium, enforced on an unwilling architect and client by the dictates of the City of London's ambitious but unloved upper pedestrian walkway ('Pedway') system. Visually, it does nothing for the building; as far as the pedestrian is concerned, it is a dead end; for Commercial Union it is so much dead space. Below this open deck, the building pinches in slightly to the glass box that is its foyer. Opinions differ whether or not that smaller ground floor is visually a success. Should the curtain have continued straight down into the ground? Some otherwise distinguished buildings that do so, contrive to look in that respect somehow lacking or unfinished. Yet that glass box is perhaps the building's one real weakness.

Windows apart (and glass is a high proportion of its curtain walling), the CU building is clad in anodized aluminium. Its colour varies remarkably with light and distance. Even the drawing of blinds behind the tinted glass of some of the windows produces strange ripples and sheens over whole sections of the 'curtain'. Close to, the metal looks (as it was intended to) a dark grey; but from any distance it takes on the dark bronze colour which is, to my mind, one of the building's most attractive qualities.

The other building on the site, the Peninsular & Oriental shipping company's headquarters, is deliberately different both in colour and shape. 191 ft high compared with CU's 387 ft (160,000 sq.ft of usable office space compared with 280,000 sq.ft in Commercial Union), it also has a smaller area on each floor. But because of its wider podium, its lower height, the squareness of its windows and the projecting sill to each floor, it somehow appears squatter, more solid than its taller neighbour. Its distinctiveness gains from the absence of any metal frame to the windows at the corner of each floor, the two clear glass sheets fitting directly together at right-angles, and from a deliberately different colour scheme. Natural coloured aluminium fascias (designed, incidentally, to prevent pigeon droppings spoiling the building's good looks) stand out from the projecting sills; the panels below the windows are of bronze-coloured aluminium; and the mullion casings between them are black.

The two buildings are connected at podium level by the upper walkway system, which neatly turns round the ribbed concrete ventilation shaft from the underground garage. The new piazza in the right-angle between the two buildings benefits from some semi-mature lime trees; and in the treads of the steps that lead down to it are to be found the intake louvres for ventilating the CU building's five underground storeys: staff restaurant, garage, and three floors of storage and strongrooms. The boiler room high up in the Commercial Union tower also serves P & O. Wind tunnel tests at the Royal Military College of Science, Shrivenham, showed that fumes from almost anywhere in the smaller building would be likely, in certain wind conditions, to hang about the face of one or other of the buildings.

But if Commercial Union is GMW's tallest building to date, it is not, screened from many angles by the increasing forest of tall buildings in the City of London, its most prominent. That title may go to Loughborough College's tall white tower of precast concrete units, **8**; perhaps to the great white slab of Hillingdon Hospital, **11**, rising above the flat plains of half-urban, half-rural west Middlesex that lie to the north of London Airport. There had been a hospital at Hillingdon since 1747. It had grown, since the First World War, mainly through the accretion of unplanned hutments and other *ad hoc* buildings.

GMW's 1966 buildings gave it at one blow new operating theatre and laboratory facilities in a low block to the north containing also out-patients departments (and some attractive garden courtyards with pools); a slab block containing seven thirty-bed wards designed on the then fashionable Nuffield plan; a single-storey new restaurant and kitchen block; and a lift tower attached to the ward block designed to cater for two other ward wings to be added later. But it did more. Its eight-storey ward block, topped by a white clad box containing water tanks and lift machinery, stood out as a landmark in a flat no-man's land short of vertical features. What was a non-place in a wasteland of superannuated market gardens and depressed pebble-dashed semis, now has a clear, strong identity. The extra ward wings have, incidentally, not yet been built, and the fashionable size and shape of nursing floors are now quite different.

Another Gollins Melvin Ward hospital building in this book, at Sevenoaks, **10**, though also curtain walled, is very different in scale and character. Set back from the road opposite a muddle of drab brick buildings that are the rest of the hospital, it is a modest white-walled two-storey building providing a twenty-six-bed maternity unit above, a new outpatients' department below. The steel frame, painted grey, stands out on the surface of the building; the opaque white glass panels and black neoprene gaskets give it an appropriately clinical but not unfriendly character. It is a modest, no-nonsense building which makes an attractive impression and (apart from some complaints of over-glazing) has pleased those who use it.

Cambridge University Library extension (1971), **23**, is one of the practice's most self-effacing buildings. It respects Giles Gilbert Scott's 1934 library which, though not particularly efficient as a group of buildings, has considerable presence and character. The GMW extension, though rightly not attempting any spurious classicality, is in brick like Scott's building, with concrete floors often lining up with the stone string courses of the original building. But from under its square-box arches shines out a strong personality of its own, of brown anodized aluminium and large expanses of glass. As a functional building, it offers a productivity several hundred per cent greater per cubic foot than the original, to which it is linked by recessed glass 'bridge' sections. And it has the great virtue of being readily expandable when its 200,000 linear ft of shelving are exhausted.

So far we have discussed here buildings finished and in use. Others in this book are still being built, still only on paper or in some cases dreams which may never be realized. One set of designs, however, the latest in an (until now) constantly evolving effort to find a right and acceptable solution to a difficult problem – deserve some comment. They are the latest designs for an extension to the Royal Opera House, Covent Garden, **32**.

For at least three decades Covent Garden Opera has achieved its high artistic standards and international reputation in spite of, rather than because of, the building which houses it. The brief given to Gollins Melvin Ward by the board of the opera house was to provide a second auditorium; space for the opera school (now housed in a building due to be demolished in Hammersmith) and for the ballet school (operating in an old cinema in the East End); adequate room behind and to the side of the stage of the present auditorium (the lack of which greatly hampers large-scale productions); two rehearsal rooms able to take scenery (and therefore 33 ft high); other additional rehearsal space; new dressing rooms to replace the inadequate ones in the ugly extension stuck on to the west end of the original building in the 1930s; and more spacious and better facilities for the opera-goer, including a public restaurant. All this was to be achieved in a way which not only enhanced Barry's original 1858 Opera House, but dove-tailed with the Greater London Council's plans for restoring Fowler's 1830s market buildings to the south and their surrounding piazza on the removal of the vegetable market south of the Thames to Nine Elms during 1974. The market's move meant that original plans to extend the opera house northward as well as west and south had to be abandoned in favour of extensions only to the south and west on land which would be in public ownership.

At first the architects regarded the additional constraints imposed by the planners and official conservationists, on top of the already difficult task of extension of an historic building to function efficiently as a modern opera house, as a heavy cross to bear – an almost impossible brief aesthetically. The way in which their attitude changed is characteristic at once of the humility and the creativeness of the GMW approach. Instead of either accepting or rejecting outright demands that they should extend the 1870s neo-classical arcades on the north side of the piazza, they fretted away searching for a solution that would respect Fowler and the character of the spaces to the south, but be less 'phoney' aesthetically and more efficient functionally as space for the opera house as well as a curtain to the bigger spaces it needed. The answer on which they have finally pinned their faith, though it came far from easily, is little short of brilliant. It honours the spirit of the piazza without any slavish or weak imitation of the past. It takes the widths and proportions of the existing arcades and re-creates them not in stone or brick, but in the modern aluminium equivalent of Paxton's Crystal Palace cast-iron. The ground floor nods with respect rather than undue deference to the Clutton arcades; the next floor is set back a whole module and is halved to produce narrower gaps between the columns. Some of the spaces are arcades (ground floor), some windows, some open galleries. The pattern runs right through, from James Street on the east to the back of the Floral Hall, then south and east again, then north to meet a skilful though not slavish restoration of the damaged Floral Hall itself. Cars and taxis will run under the bottom level into what is in effect the most spacious and brilliantly lit of *porte-cochères*.

The east part of the re-built Floral Hall thus becomes a new main foyer, with the Opera House's present foyer reserved as a 'Royal' or 'Gala Night' entrance. For the most prominent vertical feature of the scheme, the very much larger 100 ft fly-tower to be erected above the present building, the architects have adopted an unrepentently 'backward-looking' solution. There is only one way a big box on top of an 1850s classical opera house can be clad, they say: in stucco, with cornice, decoration and all. Curtain walling with a vengeance. And yet they are surely in this case right. Will the scheme be implemented? At the time of writing, it seems less threatened by opposition from planners or preservationists than by economic stringency. I hope it will be built. The opera house authorities have sometimes been accused of special pleading. But then Covent Garden *is* a special case.

So much for discussion and opinion. Now for the buildings. Let the architecture of Gollins Melvin Ward speak for itself.

Headquarter Offices, Leadenhall Street, London EC3 (14)
Entrance from the piazza/Entrée vue de la piazza/Eingang, Blick von der Piazza

Headquarter Offices, Leadenhall Street, London EC3 (14)
P&O Entrance lobby/Vestibule d'entrée/Eingangshalle

Il y a des agences d'architecture qui font une forte impression sur la conscience publique parce que leurs ouvrages sont fortement personnalisés, qu'ils présentent tous « un air de famille », dû à l'utilisation répétée, inlassable, du même langage visuel. La chanson a un refrain accrochant; même s'il nous arrive parfois de trouver les paroles vulgaires ou singulièrement mal choisies, il reste que le refrain nous est familier. D'autre agences (qu'on qualifie parfois péjorativement d'architectes « à la solde des promoteurs ») produisent une architecture qui paraît à beaucoup n'être guère plus qu'un conditionnement ordonné des exigences du client: tant de milliers de mètres carrés d'espace de bureaux, découpés automatiquement à façon, disposés ingénieusement pour satisfaire aux exigences des services de l'urbanisme et du permis de construire, et emballés dans le type de revêtement extérieur qui correspond au marché et à la mode du moment.

Entre ces deux extrêmes – la primadonna assénant sa vision idiosyncratique à un public qui proteste et à un paysage urbain qui en souffre, et l'architecture mécanique des simples fournisseurs d'espace de bureaux – prend place une autre espèce d'architecture qu'il est beaucoup moins aisé de caractériser. Elle ne possède pas de solutions préconçues et n'a pas de goût pour s'acquérir de la gloire aux dépens (visuels) de ce qui se trouve déjà exister. C'est ce genre d'architecture que pratiquent Gollins Melvin Ward Partnership. Le chemin qu'ils ont ainsi choisi est plus difficile, et beaucoup moins évident. Les récompenses, les satisfactions qu'ils obtiennent sont, plus souvent que l'inverse, nuancées de déception, car la tâche qu'ils se sont assignée est complexe, et leurs propres critères de qualité sont exigeants.

Il y a des constructions nouvelles qui ressemblent à cet homme arrivant à une réception absolument persuadé que tout un chacun sera enchanté de son arrivée, et qui semblent vouloir dire: «Salut tout le monde. Me voici enfin. » L'approche de GMW, bien que loin d'être timide, est plus réservée. Elle semble plutôt dire: «Nous pensons que ce bâtiment est tout à fait approprié à son objet et à son environnement. Nous espérons que vous partagerez cette opinion. »

C'est la raison pour laquelle certains des ouvrages les plus connus de ces praticiens paraissent à première vue ne guère avoir entre eux d'air de famille. La paire tant admirée (et lauréate de distinctions professionnelles) des immeubles de la Commercial Union et de P & O dans la Cité de Londres, **14**, ne constitue pas un œuvre plus « typiquement » GMW que le long et bas cuirassé gris des nouveaux bâtiments de l'Académie Militaire Royale de Sandhurst, **18**; la Castrol House, le long de Marylebone Road, **5**, l'un des tout premiers immeubles de bureau à mur-rideau, n'est pas plus « typique » d'une manière que les bâtiments circulaires trapus du réacteur nucléaire de Shrivenham, **12**, le terminal de la BOAC à l'Aéroport John F. Kennedy, **20**, que la tour en béton précontraint et pleine de fenêtres du Loughborough College, **8**, ou la blanche haute silhouette tranchante de l'hôpital d'Hillingdon, **11**. Il y a sans doute là quelque rapport avec la manière dont cette pratique, forte de vingt-cinq ans d'expérience, s'exerce. GMW fuit par dessus tout la notion de « l'associé en charge d'un projet ». Toujours, depuis l'époque où dans une maison de Russell Square, Frank Gollins, James Melvin et Edmund Ward se lançaient dans le métier avec une poignée de collaborateurs, a régné dans leur équipe un sentiment très fort de la décision collective et de la responsabilité collective. Naturellement chaque client a en face de lui un associé avec lequel il discute et qui répond au nom de la firme; mais, sauf rares exceptions, la conception résulte d'un travail d'équipe et d'une mise en commun de l'expérience. Cette règle vaut aussi solidement aujourd'hui à Manchester Square que dans les jours d'antan à Russell Square. Et il y a aujourd'hui dix associés principaux, dix-sept associés et environ 200 autres personnes.

D'une approche ainsi exploratoire et empirique, il est difficile de dégager une philosophie très cohérente de la conception architecturale. Cette philosophie existe, est bien saisie et appliquée dans la pratique, mais elle ne peut être aisément définie. Le mieux que je puisse faire, au delà d'une justification de ma sélection personnelle d'œuvres représentatives, est d'énoncer deux principes très larges: adaptation de la conception au but, adaptation du projet à son cadre. Pieux objectifs auxquels on pensera que la plupart des architectes pourraient souscrire. Vous les reconnaîtrez à leurs fruits...

Deux événements ont permis à Gollins Melvin Ward, modeste petite firme qui faisait des études de rénovation de certains vieux faubourgs londoniens, de devenir une agence d'architecture créative comptant parmi les plus grandes. Ce fut d'abord la commande de l'étude d'un nouveau quartier d'habitat pour le Conseil Municipal de Lambeth, suivie peu après par celle d'écoles pour le Hertfordshire et le Kent. Ce fut d'autre part, en 1953, l'obtention du premier prix du concours pour l'aménagement de la zone centrale de l'Université de Sheffield, **1**. GMW sont encore les architectes de l'Université, et ont à ce jour conçu quelque dix bâtiments nouveaux dans le cadre de ce projet. Cependant, et sans qu'il y entre le moins du monde de leur faute, celui-ci les a d'une certaine manière déçus par rapport à leurs aspirations et à leurs espoirs initiaux. Des retards, des modifications rigoureuses du programme, un accroissement excessif du nombre d'étudiants, des limitations de coût de plus en plus sévères, ont privé le campus d'une part de la force architecturale qu'il aurait pu présenter.

Cela dit, remarquable est la manière dont sont établis des rapports entre les différents bâtiments, de même qu'entre ces « nouveaux venus » et les bâtiments préexistant. La Bibliothèque Universitaire (1959), **1**, qui avec plus d'un million de livres a une capacité considérable pour les canons britanniques, fait encore haleter d'envie les architectes universitaires des années 1970. L'utilisation des matériaux (le marbre blanc et noir, le bois des planchers) et de l'espace y est somptueux. Extérieurement la pierre de Portland apparaissant au dessus et en dessous du grand rideau de verre émousse quelque peu la vivacité de la silhouette. La grande réussite est l'intérieur – où se manifeste un sens des emplacements et de l'espace que les limitations budgétaires rendraient aujourd'hui impossible – et les vues qu'il ménage vers l'extérieur, en particulier celle que l'on a de la salle de lecture principale sur le lac et les arbres d'un jardin public. On a su exploiter cette perspective pour en tirer le plus grand effet.

Le bâtiment de la Physique et des Mathématiques (1962), situé au Sud de l'autre côté d'une artère à double voie, est installé sur le même terrain à la pente accusée que la Maison Universitaire (construite la même année), **7**, qui abrite l'Union des étudiants et l'association des professeurs. L'ensemble Physique-Mathématiques est composé de deux éléments distincts: le plus grand est un bloc à mur-rideau contenant bureaux et laboratoires, le plus petit un bloc d'amphithéâtres, aux façades recouvertes de panneaux d'agrégat. Ils sont reliés par une passerelle vitrée de trois étages enjambeant un chemin de piétons, et la couleur des panneaux vitrifiés de la façade du bloc principal – un bleu fumé – contribue à marquer juste ce qu'il faut la netteté de sa silhouette sans accentuer sa masse. Visuellement il « rime » avec les autres bâtiments à mur-rideau disposés sur le site: la Maison Universitaire; l'extension Ouest, nette et adéquate, du bloc de la chimie dont le corps principal est dû à un précédent architecte; et par dessus tout, la tour de vingt-trois étages de la Faculté des Lettres. Trait dominant du campus, cette tour est un parallélépipède rectangle découpé avec autant de netteté et d'évidence que l'immeuble beaucoup plus connu de la Commercial Union dans la Cité de Londres; on y a utilisé de la même manière efficace l'espace nécessaire à la machinerie et aux locaux techniques pour couronner la tour d'une solide bande de couleur.

On a voulu que la tour des Lettres, **6**, soit le point focal du campus, et de tout point d'observation un peu éloigné elle joue effectivement ce rôle. De plus près c'est couramment le bâtiment des Sciences Biologiques (1971), **22**, qui attire le plus fortement l'attention: un grand corps de bâtiment en briques rouges luisantes assis à hauteur du premier étage sur des piliers de béton. Vu du Sud, il apparaît comme un grand mur de briques éclairé de quatre rangées et demie de fenêtres d'aspect carré surmontées d'un large bandeau de briques. On a immédiatement l'impression que c'est un bâtiment chaud et plaisant, mais l'on se demande au premier abord pourquoi ces briques. Un examen plus attentif révèle la subtilité de cette solution. C'est que le bâtiment des Sciences Biologiques prolonge des bâtiments adjacents plus anciens construits en brique rouge, bâtis à l'époque édouardienne dans un style plus ou moins gothique. Les architectes, après quelques débats d'ordre esthétique et déontologique, convinrent que ce ne serait pas « faire du toc » ni être déloyal que de rajouter un peu de gothique édouardien de façon à adoucir la transition de l'ancien au moderne. Là où les architectes précédents avaient laissé à demi – construite une tour gothique, ils l'achevèrent, créneaux compris.

Le dernier immeuble important du campus de Sheffield que présente ce livre est la Maison Universitaire, **7**, implantée sur la même pente accentuée que le bâtiment de la Physique et des Mathématiques, mais répondant à un programme qui permettait un traitement un peu plus somptueux. Malgré le large bandeau de brique au niveau du podium, la Maison Universitaire utilise le même langage visuel (mur-rideau et larges panneaux vitrés) que la bibliothèque et « rime » avec celle-ci, la tour des Lettres et le bâtiment voisin de la Physique et des Mathématiques.

La partie du bâtiment utilisée par l'Union des étudiants a été quelque peu malmenée au cours des douze dernières années par une population étudiante à la fois plus nombreuse et plus tapageuse que ne l'avaient prévu les concepteurs, et intérieurement ce sont les locaux de l'association des professeurs qui ont le mieux conservé l'aspect et l'atmosphère qui leur avaient été initialement conférés. Le bâtiment présente quelques particularités gaies et même joyeuses, telles que la cage d'ascenseur revêtue d'une mosaïque orange que l'on voit à travers le mur-rideau vitré dans l'angle Nord-Est du bâtiment. Mais l'on sent bien que ce bâtiment, plus encore que la bibliothèque, est un bâtiment-caméléon qui tire son caractère des activités qu'il abrite et de son environnement. Il est relié au bâtiment initial de l'Union des étudiants (construction des années 1930 d'un style classique assez faible) par un bâtiment à mur-rideau, adroitement sinueux, qui abrite les bureaux de l'Union. Un jardin dallé avec des arbres et du lierre s'étend jusqu'à un mur de soutènement bien dessiné et revêtu de briques, au Nord duquel s'ouvre la cour principale, pavée de briques violacées, qui s'étend entre les bâtiments et passe sous le pont de l'artère à double voie, ingénieusement dessiné par Ove Arup. D'une manière ou d'une autre, en dépit de toutes les difficultés, en dépit du caractère de rapiéçage et de surcharge d'un programme tardivement modifié, les architectes sont parvenus dans une large mesure, alors que les chances étaient contre eux, à ce que les éléments de ce campus soient cohérents et adaptés les uns aux autres d'une manière significative.

L'Académie Militaire Royale de Sandhurst (1970), **18**, posait des problèmes très différents. L'objectif fondamental était de réaliser à des niveaux de prix peu supérieurs à ceux appliqués par la Commission des budgets universitaires des bâtiments de type universitaire, mais devant répondre en outre aux besoins particuliers de l'armée tant du point de vue fonctionnel que du point de vue des traditions militaires et de la hiérarchie. Qui plus est, la solution retenue devait respecter un site très sensible, vaste parc ouvert bordé de bois de pins formant une espèce d'amphithéâtre peu profond déjà partiellement ceinturé par de « grandioses » bâtiments historiques: « l'Old College » datant de la Régence, les « New College » et « Victory College » édouardiens.

Le programme de l'armée ne laissait en fait guère d'autre choix aux architectes que de disposer les nouveaux bâtiments comme une extension du croissant formé par les bâtiments existants. La solution adoptée – une silhouette longue et relativement basse en béton recouvert de panneaux d'agrégat gris foncé – parvient à équilibrer le poids scénique de l'Old College (un beau chef d'œuvre datant de 1812) sans chercher à défier ou troubler sa qualité architecturale. Les blocs de logement et d'enseignement, vus à distance par un jour gris, ont l'air d'une escadre de cuirassés à l'ancre au bout de la rade. En fait ils s'étendent largement vers l'arrière du site, coupant l'angle des bois qui séparent le Collège Militaire Royal de l'établissement distinct et indépendant qu'est l'Ecole d'Etat-Major. (Quoiqu'on ait réduit l'abattage au strict minimum, quelque 2.000 arbres ont été coupés pour l'implantation des nouveaux bâtiments.) Une rivière qui parcourait le terrain a été détournée pour passer entre les bâtiments puis dans la partie centrale du parc. Les fondations en béton des bâtiments descendent en biais vers l'eau, ce qui donne au premier abord l'impression de rives inclinées et réduit apparemment la masse des façades.

Derrière la principale ligne de bâtiments, d'autres (généralement plus bas) sont disposés à angle droit et placés de manière à ménager des jardins rectangulaires que les quelques beaux sapins et buissons qui ont été préservés embellissent. Le plan-masse a repoussé les zones de stationnement et de livraison à l'arrière des bâtiments, de manière à ce qu'elles soient desservies par la nouvelle route périphérique qui a été créée, et cachées du parc par la première rangée de bâtiments.

Cet ensemble de blocs de logement et d'enseignement se termine, au bout du « croissant », par le bâtiment du Quartier-général, bâtiment compact et qui réussit à être robustement pragmatique tout en constituant une structure élégante par elle-même. Au même titre que dans la rangée principale de bâtiments, ses vastes panneaux d'agrégat gris foncé révèlent souvent la présence de salles d'instruction ou de séminaire sans fenêtres (bizarrement appelés « halls d'études » bien qu'elle soient conçues pour des groupes d'instruction ne dépassant pas la douzaine d'élèves). L'utilisation de ces grands panneaux d'agrégat dans les blocs résidentiels signifie des fenêtres étroites et des chambres relativement sombres. Peut-être a-t-on considéré cela comme approprié à la vie du jeune officier. Le niveau d'éclairement reste néanmoins conforme à la norme requise; et extérieurement c'est un parti certainement efficace pour le traitement architectural de l'élévation des bâtiments.

La salle de réunion de 1.200 sièges souffre quelque peu dans son apparence extérieure des proportions fusiformes des colonnes supportant l'arrière de son auditorium incliné (c'est-à-dire le côté regardant la partie centrale du parc), bien que ce bâtiment soit placé un peu en arrière de la principale ligne de force du « croissant ». La minceur de ces colonnes est, semble-t-il, le résultat d'économies imposées. Intérieurement, par contre, cette salle parvient admirablement à cette combinaison d'un utilitarisme robuste et d'élégance, qui semble être l'objectif général recherché par GMW dans les bâtiments militaires qu'il conçoit. Ici l'élégance et la sensation proviennent, dans une large mesure, de la structure spatiale du toit, constellé de luminaires d'aluminium, et dont le foyer est un grand cylindre suspendu, noir, qui abrite le ventilateur d'évacuation de l'air vicié. Ce plafond est un tour de force.

Deux autres ensembles de constructions militaires méritent une mention spéciale. Au Collège Militaire Royal des Sciences, de Shrivenham, **12**, les trois bâtiments circulaires du Laboratoire de Rutherford (1968), ramassés sur eux-mêmes à l'image du château de Camber Castle, paraissent maintenant tellement inévitables que l'on se demande comment quelqu'un aurait jamais pu envisager un laboratoire nucléaire et ses laboratoires d'accompagnement sous quelque forme différente.

L'école d'instruction des auxiliaires féminines de l'armée (WRAC), **9**, à Camberley, posait à certains égards des problèmes semblables à ceux rencontrés à Sandhurst: un site boisé attrayant que les nouveaux bâtiments devaient respecter; de sévères limitations de coût; les exigences particulières à un établissement militaire, avec la démarcation encore stricte faite entre les officiers, les sous-officiers et la troupe. Le terrain (un peu plus de 5 hectares) avait été celui d'un orphelinat et bien qu'il fût impossible d'utiliser les bâtiments détériorés des dortoirs non plus que de les restaurer, les architectes persuadèrent le maître d'ouvrage d'en conserver la séduisante salle de réunion, datant des années 1860. Ils y adjoignirent ingénieusement, communicant avec elle, une nouvelle petite chapelle, revêtue extérieurement de pin doré de Colombie; ses murs disposés en diagonale par rapport à ceux de la salle de réunion la font paraître plus menue qu'elle n'est, et elle est assise sur un socle dont les proportions et le gabariage continuent ceux du rez-de-chaussée du bâtiment victorien.

Les nouveaux bâtiments de Camberley sont de trois types: à un niveau, en bois et brique peinte en blanc; à deux ou trois niveaux avec murs de briques porteuses violacés et dalles de niveau en béton visibles; enfin la construction du mess des officiers, présentant un « grillage » apparent de poutres et poteaux en béton. Sont à remarquer le jardin installé en contrebas dans ce qui était la cave du bloc de dortoirs démoli, et l'adroite conservation d'arbres et de rochers pour décorer des cours – jardins à l'intérieur et en arrière du mess des officiers. Mais si les officiers, élèves-officiers et sous-officiers bénéficient de sites remarquablement traités et d'une meilleure attribution d'espaces, la manière dont les locaux de logement et d'activités sociales de la troupe ont été conçus et disposés est, dans une manière différente, tout aussi réussie.

Les problèmes que posait le terminal britannique de l'Aéroport John F. Kennedy à New-York (1970), **20**, étaient dus presque autant aux contraintes physiques et opérationnelles qu'à celles de coût. Seul terminal indépendant à être occupé par une compagnie aérienne étrangère, on attendait de lui qu'il constitue sur le plan architectural une affirmation nationale distinctive, mais en même temps le terrain était le dernier site disponible pour un terminal, et le moins commode à aménager. La forme a été dictée dans une large mesure par l'obligation de préserver les lignes de vue de la tour de contrôle de l'aéroport, et par celle de construire un toit suffisamment solide et abrité pour permettre les atterrissages d'hélicoptères. (Irritante ironie du sort: des modifications des réglements de sécurité interdisent en fait cette utilisation.) En dépit de ces éléments défavorables et de complexes exigences techniques, le bâtiment « témoigne pour la Grande-Bretagne » d'une manière qui lui fait honneur, ainsi qu'à ses concepteurs. C'est l'une des rares constructions conçues par des Britanniques à avoir reçu aux Etats-Unis les principales distinctions professionnelles.

Cependant le terminal de l'Aéroport Kennedy a également été important pour GMW, en ce qu'il a marqué un tournant du développement de la firme. Il a solidement établi sa réputation d'architectes d'aéroports, et d'autres commandes ont suivi: du même client, Boadicea House, le centre informatique de la BOAC à Heathrow (1967) et un centre d'approvisionnement des vols passagers (1968); puis en 1970, à Heathrow également, un bâtiment de bureaux pour Air Canada. Plus loin, GMW en association avec les ingénieurs-conseils en problèmes aéronautiques Studiengruppe Luftfahrt, ont été chargés d'étudier le deuxième aéroport de Munich, **27**, et l'aménagement de l'aéroport de Mombasa, **28**, actuellement en cours.

Sur une échelle plus modeste, les piscines de Woking (1973), **25**, montrent comment les meilleures intentions, d'un architecte peuvent être en partie mises en échec par des changements intervenant en cours de construction. Etant ingénieurs-conseils du Conseil du district urbain pour le nouveau « complexe civique », GMW y avaient placé la piscine dans ce qu'ils estimaient être, fonctionnellement et visuellement, la position la meilleure par rapport au reste du centre ville. Une décision ultérieure du gouvernement central sur des tracés de voirie la laisse échouée au milieu d'un rond-point qui initialement n'aurait pas dû exister, et rapetissée par les candélabres excessivement hauts qui équipent ce rond-point. Mais le bâtiment lui-même – où le bassin principal n'est pas en excavation mais a la forme d'un réservoir dont la base est au niveau du sol – n'en reste pas moins attrayant, avec des murs en béton bouchardé, inclinés dans le haut pour rompre la monotonie des surfaces et réduire l'aspect massif du bâtiment.

Les bâtiments sans doute les plus largement applaudis des ouvrages réalisés ces dernières années par Gollins Melvin Ward sont les tours de la Commercial Union et de la P & O, **14**, au carrefour de Leadenhall Street et St Mary Axe dans la Cité de Londres. Là deux terrains dont chacun n'aurait pu être exploité isolément d'une manière satisfaisante ont été réunis et ont fait l'objet d'une composition unique comprenant deux tours de bureaux complémentaires mais bien individualisées, ouvrant toutes deux sur un nouvel espace libre.

Le parallélépipède rectangle de la Commercial Union, de beaucoup la plus haute des deux tours avec ses 118 m, s'élève avec élan au-dessus du podium et rappelle beaucoup l'esprit de Mies van der Rohe. Onze étages d'espace de bureaux avec de hautes fenêtres rectangulaires sont coiffés par le bandeau, percé de minces volets verticaux, de la galerie technique installée sur deux niveaux à mi-hauteur de la tour. Au-dessus s'élèvent onze autres étages de bureaux, couronnés par une seconde galerie technique occupant également deux niveaux, d'aspect analogue à la première (bandeau percé de volets verticaux). Ces divisions sont significatives en termes de structures: les étages de bureaux sont suspendus à des « baleines de parapluie » en acier qui font saillie du noyau central de béton au sommet et à mi-hauteur de celui-ci.

Sous l'étage de bureaux le plus bas, le « cube » est rompu par un vaste podium ouvert, qui a été imposé à un architecte et à un maître d'ouvrage récalcitrants par les diktats de la Cité de Londres, qui prévoit dans tout le quartier l'installation d'un ambitieux système surélevé de circulation pédestre (le « Pedway »). Visuellement, cela ne gâte en rien le bâtiment; dans la mesure où le piéton est concerné, ce podium sera un cul-de-sac; et pour la Commercial Union c'est autant d'espace perdu. En dessous de ce plateau ouvert, le bâtiment se rétrécit légèrement au niveau de l'espèce de boîte de verre qui est son hall d'entrée. Ce rez-de-chaussée plus étroit est-il une réussite visuelle? Là-dessus les opinions divergent. Le mur-rideau aurait-il dû continuer tout droit jusqu'au sol? Mais dans certains bâtiments par ailleurs remarquables où il en est ainsi, il semble que cette solution donne l'impression d'un manque ou d'un défaut de finition. Pourtant cette boîte de verre est peut-être la seule faiblesse réelle du bâtiment.

Fenêtres mises à part (et le verre constitue une part importante de son mur-rideau), l'immeuble de la Commercial Union est revêtu d'aluminium anodisé. Sa couleur en varie d'une manière remarquable selon l'éclairage et la distance d'où on l'observe. Le fait même de tirer des stores derrière les vitres teintées de quelques fenêtres produit d'étranges ondulations et chatoiements sur des sections entières du « rideau ». De près (comme on l'avait recherché) le métal parait gris foncé; vu de quelque distance, il tire sur le bronze fumé, couleur qui à mes yeux constitue l'une des qualités les plus attirantes de ce bâtiment.

L'autre bâtiment construit sur le site, le siège social de la compagnie maritime Peninsular & Orient (P & O), est délibérément différent dans sa couleur comme dans sa forme de celui de la Commercial Union. Il n'a que 58 m de haut (au lieu de 118) et quelque 14.900 m^2 de surface de bureaux utile (contre plus de 26.000 m^2 pour la Commercial Union), et la surface de chaque niveau est moins vaste. Mais du fait de son podium plus large, de sa moindre hauteur, de l'aspect carré de ses fenêtres et des saillies qu'elle présentent à chaque niveau, cet immeuble apparaît en quelque sorte plus trapu, plus solide que son voisin élancé. Il tire son caractère distinctif de l'absence de tout encadrement métallique à ses fenêtres d'angle, les deux vitres s'ajustant directement l'une à l'autre à angle droit, et d'un coloris volontairement différent. Des bandelettes en aluminium de teinte naturelle font saillie sur les rebords d'étage (soit dit en passant, elles sont destinées à éviter que les excréments des pigeons ne gâtent la bonne apparence du bâtiment); les panneaux sous les fenêtres sont teintés bronze et les meneaux qui les séparent sont noirs.

Les deux immeubles sont reliés au niveau des podiums par le système de circulation piétonnière surélevé, qui tourne à la hauteur du puits de ventilation (en béton cannelé) des sous-sols de garage. La nouvelle « piazza » située entre les deux immeubles dans l'angle droit du terrain tire parti de quelques tilleuls encore jeunes; et les marches qui y conduisent contiennent les grilles des volets de prise d'aération pour la ventilation des cinq niveaux de sous-sol du bâtiment de la CU: restaurant du personnel, garage, et trois niveaux de réserves et de chambres-fortes. La chaufferie installée au sommet de la tour de la Commercial Union dessert également l'immeuble P & O. Des tests en tunnel à vent effectués au Collège Militaire Royal des Sciences de Shrivenham ont montré que, dans certaines conditions de vent, les émanations issues d'à peu près n'importe quelle partie du plus petit bâtiment, étaient susceptibles de rester plaquées contre la façade de l'un ou l'autre des immeubles.

Mais si Commercial Union est, à ce jour, le plus haut des bâtiments conçus par GMW, il n'en est pas, visuellement parlant, le plus saillant – caché qu'il est sous beaucoup d'angles par la forêt croissante de grands immeubles de la Cité de Londres. Ce titre pourrait revenir à la grande tour blanche, construite d'éléments de béton préfabriqué, de Loughborough College, **8**; ou peut-être à la grande silhouette blanche et tranchante de l'hôpital de Hillingdon, **11**, dominant la plaine plate de ce Middlesex de l'Ouest, mi-urbain mi-rural, qui s'étend au Nord de l'aéroport de Londres. Il y a un hôpital à Hillingdon depuis 1747. Il s'est agrandi, depuis la première guerre mondiale, par l'addition de baraquements et divers bâtiments de circonstance.

Les bâtiments conçus en 1966 par GMW l'ont doté d'un seul coup d'un nouveau bloc opératoire et de laboratoires dans un bâtiment bas, au Nord, contenant également les départements des consultations externes (et quelques plaisantes cours-jardins ornées de bassins); d'un bloc en hauteur contenant sept unités de soins de trente lits conçues d'après le plan Nuffield qui était alors à la mode; d'un bloc à un seul niveau contenant un nouveau restaurant et ses cuisines; et d'une tour d'ascenseurs flanquant le bloc des unités de soins et destinée à desservir également deux autres ailes d'unités de soins devant être ajoutées ultérieurement. Mais il y a plus. Ce bloc d'hospitalisation de huit étages, couronné par le bandeau blanc des locaux contenant les réservoirs d'eau et la machinerie des ascenseurs, s'est élevé comme un point de repère dans un no-man's land plat qui manquait singulièrement de caractéristiques verticales. Ce qui n'était qu'un secteur anonyme d'une zone de terrains vagues peuplés de jardins maraîchers surannés et de déprimantes maisons jumelles au crépi moucheté, possède maintenant une claire et forte identité. Soit dit en passant, les ailes d'unités de soins supplémentaires n'ont pas encore été construites, et la mode a considérablement évolué en ce qui concerne les dimensions et la forme de l'étage-type d'hospitalisation.

Un autre hôpital étudié par Gollins Melvin Ward et présenté dans ce livre, lui aussi à mur-rideau, est très différent d'échelle et de caractère. Le nouvel hôpital de Sevenoaks, **10**, situé en retrait de la route face à un fouillis de bâtiments de briques grisâtres qui sont le reste de l'ancien hôpital, est un modeste bâtiment de deux niveaux, aux murs blancs, avec en haut un service de maternité de vingt-six lits et en bas un service de consultations externes. La structure d'acier peint en gris ressort visiblement à l'extérieur du bâtiment; les panneaux de verre blanc opaque et les joints de néoprène noirs lui confèrent avec à-propos un caractère clinique mais aucunement répulsif. C'est un bâtiment modeste, terre à terre, qui fait une impression séduisante et qui (mises à part quelques critiques sur une surabondance de vitrage) a plu à tous ceux qui l'ont pratiqué.

L'extension de la Bibliothèque Universitaire de Cambridge (1971), **23**, est l'un des bâtiments où l'architecte s'est imposé la plus grande discrétion. Il respecte la bibliothèque de Giles Gilbert Scott, datant de 1934, groupe de bâtiments qui s'il n'a qu'une efficacité fonctionnelle très relative, a beaucoup de présence et de caractère. L'extension de GMW, sans rechercher du tout un classicisme artificiel, est en brique comme l'édifice de Scott, avec des planchers de béton qui sont le plus souvent de niveau avec les assises de pierre du bâtiment originel. Mais de sous ses arcades rectangulaires se dégage une personnalité propre, à base d'aluminium anodisé brun et de larges étendues de verre. Sur le plan fonctionnel, la productivité au mètre carré de l'extension est de plusieurs fois cent pour cent supérieure à celle de la bibliothèque principale, à laquelle elle est reliée par des passerelles vitrées en retrait des façades. Elle présente en outre le grand mérite de permettre facilement de nouvelles extensions le jour où ses 61.000 m linéaires de rayonnage seront remplis.

Nous avons jusqu'ici commenté des bâtiments achevés et déjà en cours d'utilisation. Ce livre en présente d'autres qui sont seulement en cours de construction, ou qui n'existent encore que sur le papier, quelques-uns même qui resteront des rêves jamais réalisés. Il y a cependant un ensemble de plans qui méritent quelque développement, car ils représentent le dernier état (à ce jour) d'un long et constant effort de recherche d'une solution correcte

Headquarter Offices, Leadenhall Street, London EC3 (14)
P&O Directors' conference room/Salle de conférence/Direktion

University Library Extension, Grange Road, Cambridge (23)

et acceptable à un problème difficile. Il s'agit des derniers plans de l'extension de l'Opéra Royal de Covent Garden, **32**.

Voici au moins trois décades que le Covent Garden Opera maintient son haut niveau de qualité artistique et sa réputation internationale malgré le bâtiment qui l'abrite. Le programme remis par le Conseil d'administration à Gollins Melvin Ward demandait de prévoir les éléments suivants: un nouvel auditorium; la place nécessaire pour l'école d'opéra (actuellement logée à Hammersmith dans un bâtiment qui doit être démoli) et l'école de ballet (qui fonctionne actuellement dans un vieux cinéma de l'East End); le dégagement d'un espace suffisant derrière et sur les côtés de la scène de l'auditorium actuel (espace dont l'absence gêne considérablement le montage de grandes productions); deux salles de répétitions pouvant recevoir des décors (et donc hautes de 10 m); des espaces de répétition complémentaires; de nouvelles loges-vestiaires pour remplacer les loges malcommodes installées dans la vilaine extension en stuck construite dans les années 1930 sur le côté Ouest du bâtiment primitif; enfin des installations générales plus confortables et plus spacieuses pour les habitués, en particulier un restaurant public. L'implantation de tout ce programme devait non seulement mettre en valeur le bâtiment original de l'Opéra construit en 1858 par E. M. Barry, mais aussi s'accorder au Sud avec les plans du Greater London Council pour la restauration des halles de Charles Fowler des années 1830 et de la « piazza » qui les entoure, une fois effectué le déménagement du marché des légumes à Nine Elms, au Sud de la Tamise, en 1974. Ce déménagement signifiait qu'il fallait abandonner les premiers projets envisageant une extension de l'Opéra vers le Nord aussi bien que vers l'Ouest et le Sud, en faveur de solutions concentrant les extensions sur le Sud et l'Ouest, sur les terrains relevant du domaine public.

Au début les architectes considérèrent les contraintes additionnelles imposées par les planificateurs et les conservateurs des monuments nationaux, se surajoutant à la tâche déjà ardue de concevoir une extension d'un bâtiment historique qui soit adaptée aux fonctions d'un opéra moderne, comme une lourde croix à porter – esthétiquement parlant, un programme presqu'impossible. La façon dont leur attitude changea progressivement me paraît caractéristique à la fois de l'humilité et de la créativité de l'approche de GMW. Comme il leur était demandé d'étendre au Nord de la « piazza » les arcades néo-classiques de 1870, ils ne rejetèrent ni n'acceptèrent cette exigence; ils la «ruminèrent» en cherchant une solution qui respecterait Fowler et le caractère des espaces libérés au Sud, tout en étant moins fausse esthétiquement et plus efficace fonctionnellement (en dégageant l'espace nécessaire à l'Opéra considéré comme un monument et en délimitant en même temps comme un rideau ou une enceinte les espaces correspondant à son extension). La solution qu'ils se sont finalement attachés à promouvoir, bien que son élaboration ait été laborieuse, me parait presque brillante. Elle honore l'esprit architectural de la « piazza » sans risquer d'être une faible ou servile imitation du passé. Elle reprend les largeurs et les proportions des arcades existantes et les reproduit, non pas en pierre et en brique, mais dans un aluminium moderne qui constitue l'équivalent de la fonte du Crystal Palace de Joseph Paxton. Le rez-de-chaussée fait ainsi écho, avec un respect dénué de tout excès de déférence, aux arcades de Henry Clutton; le premier étage est en retrait de la valeur d'un module et les proportions sont restreintes de moitié pour réduire les écarts entre les colonnes. Les espaces sont traités soit en arcades (rez-de-chaussée), soit avec des fenêtres, soit en galeries ouvertes. Ce dispositif court tout au long de la « piazza », de James Street à l'Est jusqu'à l'arrière de la Halle aux fleurs, puis au Sud et de nouveau à l'Est, puis vers le Nord où elle vient constituer une restauration habile mais non servile de la Halle aux fleurs elle-même. Voitures et taxis circuleront en dessous du niveau du sol dans ce qui constituera en fait la plus vaste et la plus brillamment éclairée des portes cochères qu'on peut rêver pour un Opéra.

La partie Est de la Halle aux fleurs reconstruite devient ainsi un nouveau foyer, et l'on fera du foyer actuel de l'Opéra une entrée « royale » qui servira aussi pour les nuits de gala. Pour la caractéristique verticale la plus saillante du projet, une très vaste tour-coupole qui s'élèvera de 30 m au-dessus du bâtiment actuel, les architectes ont adopté une solution d'un passéisme impénitent. Il n'y a, disent-ils, qu'une manière d'habiller une grande boîte disposée sur le toit d'un opéra construit dans le style classique des années 1850: c'est d'utiliser le stuc, les corniches, et tout ce système de décoration. Nous devrions nous récrier: le mur-rideau à tous crins! Et pourtant dans ce cas ce sont sûrement eux qui ont raison. Est-ce que ce projet verra le jour? A l'heure où j'écris il paraît moins menacé par l'éventuelle opposition des fonctionnaires planificateurs ou conservateurs des monuments nationaux, que par des restrictions budgétaires. J'espère qu'il sera réalisé. Les autorités de l'Opéra ont parfois été accusées d'avoir des positions de parti-pris. Mais Covent Garden *est* un cas spécial, qui justifie le parti-pris.

Mais j'ai bien assez argumenté et présenté mes opinions. Place aux bâtiments. Laissons l'architecture de Gollins Melvin Ward parler pour elle-même.

Manche Architekturbüros üben einen starken Einfluß auf das öffentliche Bewußtsein aus, weil ihren Bauten eine starke Ausdruckskraft gemeinsam ist und sie immer wieder die gleichen visuellen Idiome anwenden. Das Lied hat einen packenden Refrain; obgleich uns die Worte manchmal vulgär oder ungewöhnlich schlecht gewählt erscheinen, ist der Kehrreim zweifellos vertraut. Andere Büros (manchmal verächtlich als „Entwicklungs"-Architekten bezeichnet) produzieren eine Architektur, die für manche Leute aus wenig mehr als einer sauberen Erfüllung von Wünschen des Bauherrn zu bestehen scheint: soviel Tausend Quadratmeter Bürofläche, automatisch in eine Ordnung geschnitten, sinnvoll angeordnet in Übereinstimmung mit den Forderungen der Planungsbehörden und dem Stand der Entwicklung des Bürohausbaues und in irgendeine Verkleidung gehüllt, die dem Markt und dem Augenblick entspricht.

Zwischen diesen beiden Extremen – der Primadonna, die ihre eigene, übersensible Auffassung gegen eine protestierende Öffentlichkeit und eine ablehnende Stadtlandschaft durchsetzt, und der automatisierten Architektur bloßer Produzenten von Bürofläche – gibt es eine andere Art der architektonischen Praxis, die sich nicht so leicht kategorisieren läßt. Diese Architekten bieten keine vorgefaßten Lösungen und wollen keinen Ruhm erwerben auf visuelle Kosten des Bestehenden. Ein solches Büro ist die Gollins Melvin Ward Partnership. Der von ihnen gewählte Weg ist härter und weniger eindeutig. Die Ergebnisse sind häufiger von Enttäuschungen begleitet als umgekehrt, weil die sich selbst gestellten Aufgaben komplex und ihre Maßstäbe streng sind.

Einige Neubauten gleichen dem Mann, der eine Party betritt ohne den geringsten Zweifel, daß jedermann über sein Erscheinen entzückt sein wird. „Hallo, da bin ich", scheinen sie zu sagen. Die Lösungen von Gollins Melvin Ward sind selbstkritischer (obgleich keineswegs schüchtern). Sie scheinen statt dessen zu sagen: „Wir glauben, daß dieser Bau genau das Richtige ist für seine Bestimmung und seine Umgebung. Wir hoffen, Sie sind der gleichen Meinung."

Das ist ein Grund, weshalb einige der bekanntesten Bauten dieses Büros auf den ersten Blick keine Familienähnlichkeit zu haben scheinen. Commercial Union und Peninsular & Oriental, das vielbewunderte, preisgekrönte Gebäudepaar in der City of London, **14**, sind keine „typischeren" GMW-Bauten als das langgestreckte, niedrige, graue Kriegsschiff: der neue Collegebau in Sandhurst, **18**. Das frühe Curtain-Wall-Gebäude, das Castrol Building in der Marylebone Road, **5**, ist nicht weniger „typisch" als die untersetzten, runden Reaktorbauten in Shrivenham, **12**, das BOAC-Abfertigungsgebäude auf dem Kennedy Airport, **20**, ebenso wie das vielfenstrige, vorgefertigte Betonhochhaus des Loughborough College, **8**, oder die hohe, weiße Scheibe des Hospitals in Hillingdon, **11**. Und das hat etwas mit der Art zu tun, wie das fünfundzwanzig Jahre bestehende Büro geleitet wird. Gollins Melvin Ward vermeiden im allgemeinen das Prinzip eines Alleinverantwortlichen. Seit Frank Gollins, James Melvin und Edmund Ward ihr Büro mit einer Handvoll Mitarbeitern in einem Haus am Russell Square gründeten, hat dort ein starkes Bewußtsein für kollektive Entscheidungen und kollektive Verantwortlichkeit geherrscht. Natürlich hat jeder Bauherr einen Partner, mit dem er zu tun hat und der für die Firma Rede und Antwort steht, aber der Entwurf ist – mit wenigen Ausnahmen – das Ergebnis von Teamdiskussion und Experiment. Das trifft heute für das Büro am Manchester Square in gleichem Maße zu wie auf die frühen Zeiten des Büros. Gegenwärtig hat es 10 Partner, 17 Assoziierte und etwa 200 Mitarbeiter.

Da die Arbeitsweise von GMW exploratorisch und empirisch ist, ist es schwer, eine einheitliche Entwurfsmethode abzuleiten. Sie existiert, ist den Mitarbeitern im Büro sehr wohl bewußt, läßt sich aber nicht leicht definieren. Das Beste, was ich tun kann – außer meine eigene Auswahl repräsentativer Bauten zu erläutern – ist, zwei sehr allgemeine Prinzipien zu nennen: Eignung für den Zweck und Eignung für die städtebauliche Situation. Fromme Absichten, denen sich die meisten Architekten verschrieben zu haben glauben. An ihren Früchten sollt ihr sie erkennen ...

Zwei Ereignisse verwandelten Gollins Melvin Ward von einer unbekannten kleinen Firma, die Umbauten in einigen alten Londoner Stadtteilen durchführte, in ein großes und kreatives Architekturbüro. Eins war der Auftrag zur Planung neuer Wohnbauten für den Stadtteil Lambeth, dem bald Schulbauten in Hertfordshire und Kent folgten. Das andere war 1953 die Verleihung des ersten Preises in einem offenen Wettbewerb für den zentralen Bereich der Universität Sheffield, **1**. Dieser Auftrag besteht immer noch; bis jetzt sind zehn neue Bauten dort entstanden. Jedoch auf Grund nicht durch GMW beeinflußbarer Umstände sind die früheren Erwartungen und Bemühungen der Architekten bis zu einem gewissen Grade enttäuscht worden. Durch Verzögerungen, ein drastisch geändertes Programm, die Explosion der Studentenzahlen und immer engere Kostenbeschränkungen hat der Campus einen Teil seiner architektonischen Konsequenz eingebüßt, die er hätte erreichen können.

Unter diesen Umständen ist es um so bemerkenswerter, wie gut die Beziehung der Neubauten zueinander und zu den benachbarten Gebäuden ist. Die nach britischen Maßstäben mit mehr als einer Million Bänden große Universitätsbibliothek (1959) **1**, ist so bemessen, daß Hochschularchitekten der siebziger Jahre vor Neid erblassem. Die Anwendung der Materialien (zum Beispiel weißer und schwarzer Marmor und Holzböden) und die Nutzung des Raumes sind außerordentlich großzügig. Die Außenverkleidung aus Portlandsteinplatten als Streifen über und unter der Verglasung beeinträchtigt das Erscheinungsbild etwas. Das Beste an der Bibliothek sind die Innenräume – ein Gefühl für den Ort und für den Raum, den die heutigen Kostenbeschränkungen von vornherein verbieten würden – und der großartige Ausblick, vor allem vom großen Lesesaal in den Park mit einem See und Bäumen. Diese Situation ist optimal genutzt worden.

Das Physik- und Mathematikgebäude aus dem Jahre 1962, südlich der Schnellstraße gelegen, steht auf dem gleichen, steil abfallenden Gelände wie das University House (aus dem gleichen Jahr), **7**, das die studentischen Gemeinschaftsräume und die Aufenthaltsräume für den Lehrkörper enthält. Der Physik-Mathematikbau besteht aus zwei deutlich getrennten Elementen: das größere ist ein Büro- und Institutstrakt mit Curtain-Wall-Verkleidung, das kleinere ein mit Waschbetonplatten verkleideter Vorlesungstrakt. Sie sind durch eine dreigeschossige, verglaste Baubrücke über einem öffentlichen Fußweg miteinander verbunden. Die rauchblaue Verglasung des größeren Traktes verleiht ihm die notwendige äußere Klarheit, ohne seine Masse zu verschleiern. Visuell „reimt" er sich mit den anderen Curtain-Wall-Bauten auf dem Gelände: dem University House, der klaren und anständigen westlichen Erweiterung des früher von anderen Architekten errichteten Chemiegebäudes und, vor allem, dem dreiundzwanziggeschossigen Hochhaus der Kunstabteilung. Als dominierendes Wahrzeichen des Campus' ist es ein ebenso klarer und zurückhaltender kubischer Baukörper wie das bekanntere Commercial Union Building in London mit der gleichen wirkungsvollen Ausbildung der Technikgeschosse als zusammenhängende Farbstreifen.

Sevenoaks Hospital, Kent (10)
Exterior detail/Détail extérieur/Detail Außenwand

Upper School, Syston, Leicestershire (21)

Upper School, Syston, Leicestershire (21)
Library- Resource centre/Bibliothèque-Centre de connaissance/
Bibliothek-Aufenthaltsberich

Das Hochhaus der Kunstabteilung, **6**, ist als Mittelpunkt des Campusgeländes vorgesehen und beherrscht es auch aus der Ferne. Dagegen zieht in unmittelbarer Nähe das Biologiegebäude (1971), **22**, die Aufmerksamkeit noch stärker an sich: eine große Scheibe aus leuchtend rotem Klinker, die bei freigehaltener Erdgeschoßzone auf Betonpfeilern ruht. Von Süden erscheint der Bau als gewaltige Backsteinmauer mit 4½ Reihen fast quadratischer Fenster und einem breiteren Klinkerstreifen als oberer Abschluß. Es wirkt unmittelbar als warmer und gefälliger Bau, aber fragt man sich zuerst: „Warum Klinker?" Bei näherer Betrachtung zeigt sich die Intelligenz der Lösung. Das Biologiegebäude ist aus Klinker, weil es an die älteren roten Backsteinbauten aus der Zeit Edwards in mehr oder weniger gotischer Formensprache angrenzt. Die Architekten beschlossen nach langer Gewissensprüfung, daß es weder unehrlich noch falsch wäre, noch etwas mehr Edward-Gotik zu bauen und so eine Verbindung zwischen dem Alten und dem Neuen herzustellen. Die früheren Architekten hatten einen halbfertigen gotischen Turm hinterlassen, GMW vollendeten ihn mit Zacken und allem, was dazugehört.

Das letzte große Gebäude auf dem Campus in Sheffield, das in diesem Buch dargestellt ist, ist das University House (1962), **7**, auf dem gleichen steilen Gelände wie das Mathematik- und Physikgebäude, aber nach einem Programm gebaut, das eine großzügigere Ausstattung ermöglichte. Obgleich mit einem breiten Klinkerstreifen auf Podiumsniveau versehen, hat das University House das gleiche Formenvokabular der großen Glasfenster und des Curtain-Walls wie die Bibliothek und harmoniert mit ihr, dem Kunstgebäude und dem benachbarten Mathematik-/Physikbau.

Der Teil des Gebäudes, der die studentischen Gemeinschaftsräume enthält, hat in den vergangenen zwölf Jahren besondere Belastungen erfahren durch eine sowohl zahlreichere als auch aggressivere Studentenschaft, als die Architekten sie sich vorgestellt hatten. Die obenliegenden Räume für den Lehrkörper haben ihr ursprüngliches Aussehen und den beabsichtigten Eindruck viel besser erhalten. Das Gebäude hat einige heitere, sogar spielerische Merkmale wie den mit orange Mosaik verkleideten Liftschacht, der durch die verglaste Nordwestecke sichtbar ist. Aber es ist, so scheint es, in noch stärkerem Maße als die Bibliothek ein Bau, der seinen Charakter chamäleonhaft von dem übernimmt, was in ihm vorgeht und was ihn umgibt. Die Verbindung mit dem früheren studentischen Gemeinschaftshaus (in schwachem Neoklassizismus der dreißger Jahre) wird durch einen geschickt gekrümmten Curtain-Wall-Bau hergestellt, der die Verwaltungsräume enthält. Zwischen diesem Bau und einer schönen Abschlußmauer aus Backstein liegt ein gepflasterter, mit Efeu bewachsener und mit Bäumen bestandener Hof. Nach Norden öffnet sich der mit rötlichen Klinkern gepflasterte zentrale Bereich zu den anderen Bauten und weiter bis unter Ove Arups geniale Straßenbrücke. Auf fast unerklärliche Weise ist es den Architekten trotz aller Schwierigkeiten, trotz aller Kompromisse infolge des später veränderten Programms und gegen alle Widerstände in beachtlichem Ausmaß gelungen, aus der Vielfalt der Einzelgebäude auf dem Campus ein Ensemble zu bilden.

Die Royal Military Academy in Sandhurst (1970), **18**, stellte völlig andere Probleme. Die Aufgabe lautete, universitätsähnliche Gebäude zu nicht viel mehr als dem Kostenstandard des University Grants Committees zu errichten, jedoch den besonderen militärischen Bedürfnissen sowohl funktional als auch im Hinblick auf die Tradition und die Hierarchie der Armee entsprechend. Die Lösung mußte außerdem eine Situation berücksichtigen, die behutsam zu behandeln war: eine von Nadelwäldern eingefaßte, freie Parklandschaft, deren flache, amphitheatralische Mulde teilweise bereits bebaut war mit einer Kette historischer „großartiger" Bauten – dem „Old College" im Regency-Stil und den „New" und „Victory Colleges" im Stil Edwards.

Das Programm ließ den Architekten praktisch kaum eine andere Wahl, als die Neubauten in der Verlängerung des von den bestehenden Bauten gebildeten Halbkreises anzuordnen. Durch die gewählte Lösung – langgestreckte, verhältnismäßig niedrige Baukörper aus Beton, mit dunkelgrauen Waschbetonplatten verkleidet – gelingt es, die starke Wirkung des „Old College" (eines schönen Bauwerks aus dem Jahre 1812) auszugleichen, ohne seine architektonische Qualität zu beeinträchtigen oder zu verdrängen. Die Wohn- und Unterrichtsgebäude sehen aus der Entfernung an einem grauen Tag aus wie eine Flotte von Kriegsschiffen vor Anker am anderen Ufer des Hafenbeckens. Tatsächlich dehnen sie sich aber hinter diese Silhouette aus und schneiden in den Waldrand ein, der die Royal Military Academy Sandhurst von der anderen, unabhängigen Einrichtung der Generalstabsschule trennt. (Obgleich nur das Minimum der Waldfläche abgeholzt wurde, mußten etwa 2.000 Bäume gefällt werden, um Platz für die Neubauten zu schaffen.) Ein ursprünglich durch das Gelände führender Fluß wurde umgeleitet und verläuft jetzt zwischen den Bauten und dem Parkland. Die Betonfundamente der Gebäude sind zum Wasser abgeschrägt. Das vermittelt den Eindruck abfallender Uferböschungen und reduziert optisch die Baumasse.

Hinter der Hauptreihe der Bauten stehen weitere (im allgemein niedrigere) Blocks im rechten Winkel dazu. Sie wurden so situiert, daß einige schöne, hohe Kiefern und Buschwerk erhalten blieben, welche die entstandenen Gartenvierecke zieren. Parkplätze und Anlieferung sind an die Rückseite der Bauten gelegt, wo sie von einer neuen Umgehungsstraße erschlossen werden. Vom Park sind esi fast durch die vordere Gebäudereihe verdeckt.

Der Halbkreis der Wohn- und Unterrichtsbauten wird mit dem kompakten Gebäude des Hauptquartiers abgeschlossen, das sowohl robust und zweckgerecht militärisch als auch als anmutiges, eigenständiges Bauwerk wirkt. Wie bei der Reihe der Collegebauten kennzeichnen seine großen, dunkelgrauen Waschbetonflächen die dahinterliegenden geschlossenen Unterrichts- und Seminarräume (komischerweise „Studiersäle" genannt, obgleich für Unterrichtsgruppen von nicht mehr als einem Dutzend Studenten vorgesehen). Die Anwendung dieser großen Waschbetonplatten bei den Wohngebäuden führte zu schmalen Fenstern und relativ düsteren Arbeits- und Schlafräumen. Vielleicht hält man das für angemessen für die Lebensweise junger Offiziersanwärter? Jedoch entspricht die Belichtung den geforderten Normen, und von außen ist die Wirkung zweifellos besser als eine behandelte Fassade.

Das äußere Erscheinungsbild der Versammlungshalle mit 1.200 Plätzen leidet etwas durch die dünnen Proportionen der Stützen, welche die Rückseite des schrägen Auditoriums tragen – d.h. der auf den zentralen Bereich des Parks gerichteten Seite, obgleich der Bau von der Linie des Halbkreises zurückgesetzt ist. Diese dünnen Stützen sind vermutlich das Ergebnis der geforderten Sparmaßnahmen. Im Inneren erreicht die Halle jedoch auf erstaunliche Weise jene Kombination aus nüchterner Funktionsgerechtigkeit und Leichtigkeit, die GMW grundsätzlich bei ihren militärischen Bauten anzustreben scheinen. Hier werden Leichtigkeit und Spannung weitgehend erreicht durch das mit Aluminiumleuchten durchsetzte Raumtragwerk des Daches und die Konzentration auf einen riesigen, schwarzen, aufgehängten Zylinder, der den Absaugventilator enthält. Diese Decke ist eine Tour de Force.

Zwei weitere Gruppen militärischer Bauten verdienen besondere Erwähnung. Beim Royal Military College of Science in Shrivenham, **12**, wirkt die Form der drei gedrungenen, burgartigen, runden Bauten des Rutherford Laboratoriums (1968) so absolut folgerichtig, daß man sich nicht vorstellen kann, jemand hätte je eine andere Form für einen Reaktorbau mit dazugehörigen Laboratorien vorgesehen.

Die Ausbildungsstätte des Women's Royal Army Corps in Camberley, **9**, stellte in gewisser Beziehung die gleichen Probleme wie die Militärakademie in Sandhurst: ein schönes, bewaldetes Grundstück, in das sich die neuen Gebäude einfügen mußten, strenge Kostenbeschränkungen und die besonderen Erfordernisse einer militärischen Einrichtung mit immer noch strenger Abgrenzung zwischen Offizieren, Unteroffizieren und Mannschaften. Auf dem etwa 5,25 ha großen Gelände stand früher ein Waisenhaus. Obgleich das Wohngebäude nicht mehr benutzbar war und eine Renovierung nicht lohnte, überzeugten die Architekten ihre Bauherren, die schöne Aula aus den sechziger Jahren des vorigen Jahrhunderts zu erhalten. An diesen Bau fügten sie geschickt eine neue kleine Kapelle an, die außen mit goldfarbigem kolumbianischen Fichtenholz verkleidet ist und durch abgeschrägte Ecken kleiner erscheint, als sie wirklich ist. Sie sitzt auf einer Säulenplatte auf, welche die Proportionen und Formgebung des Erdgeschosses vom viktorianischen Bau aufnimmt.

Die Neubauten in Camberley lassen sich in drei Gruppen einteilen: eingeschossige aus Holz und weißgeschlämmten Ziegeln; zwei- und dreigeschossige aus rötlichem, tragendem Backstein mit sichtbaren Geschoßdecken und die Rahmen- und Pendelstützen-Konstruktion der Offiziersmesse. Die Gestaltung eines tieferliegenden Gartens im früheren Keller des abgerissenen Waisenhauses und die geschickte Erhaltung der natürlichen Landschaft mit Bäumen und Felsen in Gartenhöfen innerhalb und hinter der Offiziermesse sind bemerkenswert. Aber obgleich Offiziere, Offiziersanwärter und Unteroffiziere den schönsten Teil des Grundstücks und bessere Räumlichkeiten erhielten, sind die Mannschaftswohn- und Gemeinschaftsbauten auf ihre Weise ebenso effektiv angeordnet und geplant.

Der britische Terminal auf dem Kennedy Airport in New York (1970), **20**, unterlag sowohl problematischen baulichen und organisatorischen als auch finanziellen Beschränkungen. Als einziger separater Terminal einer ausländischen Fluglinie wurde vom Auftraggeber erwartet, daß er in architektonischer Hinsicht eine nationale Aussage darstellen würde. Gleichzeitig erhielt er das tatsächlich letzte und schwierigste Grundstück, das noch für diesen Zweck verfügbar war. Seine Form wurde entscheidend diktiert durch die Sichtlinien vom Tower und durch die Forderung nach einem genügend starken und ausreichend abgeschirmten Dach für Hubschrauberlandungen. (Es ist ärgerlich und zugleich ironisch, daß Änderungen der Sicherheitsbestimmungen inzwischen die Nutzung für diesen Zweck verhindert haben.)

Trotz all dem und den komplexen technischen Forderungen „spricht" das Gebäude „für England" auf eine Weise, die ihm und seinen Planern zur Ehre gereicht. Es ist einer der wenigen von Briten entworfenen Bauten, die bedeutende Preise in den USA erhalten haben.

Der Terminal der BOAC war jedoch auch als Wendepunkt in der Entwicklung des Büros bedeutend. Er etablierte den Ruf von GMW als Flughafenarchitekten. Weitere Flughafenaufträge folgten: vom gleichen Bauherrn das Boadicea House, das BOAC-Computerzentrum in Heathrow (1967) sowie ein Flughafen-Cateringzentrum (1968); dann, 1970, ebenfalls in Heathrow, ein Servicebau für die Air Canada. Darüber hinaus führte der Terminal zu Planungsaufträgen, in Zusammenarbeit mit den Flughafenberatern Studiengruppe Luftfahrt, für einen zweiten Flughafen in München, **27**, und für den Ausbau des Flughafens Mombassa, **28**, der jetzt im Bau ist.

Das Hallenbad in Woking (1973), **25**, in bescheidenerem Maßstab, zeigt, wie die beste Planung des Architekten durchkreuzt werden kann durch Änderungen der vorgesehenen Flächennutzungsplanung. Als Berater der städtischen Bezirksverwaltung für das neue Bürgerzentrum situierten GMW das Hallenbad in ihrer Ansicht nach funktional und optisch bester Lage in Beziehung zum Stadtzentrum. Ein zentraler Regierungsbeschluß für den Straßenbau setzte ihn auf's Trockene – er geriet in die Mitte eines Rondells, das ursprünglich nicht existierte, und sein Maßstab wurde verändert durch extrem hohe Straßenbeleuchtungen, die zusammen mit dem Rondell errichtet wurden. Doch der Bau – bei dem das große Becken, anstatt wie üblich versenkt, auf Erdgeschoßhöhe gelegt werden mußte – ist trotzdem noch „attraktiv" mit abgeschrägtem Abschluß und sandstrahlbehandelten Betonwänden, wodurch die Fläche gegliedert und die Wirkung der Masse reduziert wird.

Die vermutlich am häufigsten erwähnten Bauten von Gollins Melvin Ward aus den letzten Jahren sind die Commercial Union und Peninsular & Oriental Hochhäuser, **14**, an der Kreuzung Leadenhall Street und St Mary Axe in der City of London. Hier wurden zwei Grundstücke, die separat nicht effektiv zu bebauen waren, d.h. nicht die mögliche optimale Nutzung erreichten, zusammengefaßt und mit einer Komposition aus zwei sich ergänzenden, aber unterschiedlichen Hochhauskörpern bebaut, die sich beide auf einen neugeschaffenen Freibereich öffnen.

Die Commercial Union, mit fast 118 m das höhere von beiden Gebäuden, ist vom Podium aufwärts ein reiner verlängerter Kubus im Stil Mies van der Rohes. Über elf Bürogeschossen mit hohen, rechteckigen Fenstern liegt der doppelgeschossige Lamellenstreifen der in halber Gebäudehöhe angeordneten Haustechnik. Darüber liegen 12 weitere Bürogeschosse mit einem weiteren doppelgeschossigen, lamellenverkleideten Technikraum als Abschluß. Diese Aufteilung ist auch konstruktiv begründet: die Bürogeschosse hängen an Stahl-„Schirmspeichen", die auf Dach- und Mittelebene vom zentralen Kern auskragen.

Unter dem ersten Bürogeschoß ist der „Kubus" aufgebrochen durch ein offenes Podium, das dem unwilligen Architekten und dem Bauherrn aufgezwungen wurde durch das Diktat des ehrgeizigen, aber unbeliebten, auf höherer Ebene gelegenen „Pedway"-(Fußwegsystem-)Projektes der City of London. Optisch ist es nicht von Vorteil für das Gebäude; für den Fußgänger ist es eine Sackgasse; für die Commercial Union ist es lediglich ungenutzter Raum. Unter diesem offenen Deck ist der Bau leicht eingezogen zu einem verglasten Foyer. Die Ansichten darüber, ob dieses kleinere Erdgeschoß ein optischer Erfolg ist oder nicht, differieren. Hätte der Curtain-Wall unmittelbar bis zum Boden reichen sollen? Einige andere bekannte Bauten, bei denen das der Fall ist, wirken in diesem Punkt mangelhaft oder unfertig. Vermutlich ist jedoch dieser Glaskasten die einzige wirkliche Schwäche des Gebäudes.

Von den Fenstern abgesehen (Glas hat einen hohen Anteil an der Verkleidung), ist das Commercial Union-Gebäude mit anodisiertem Aluminium verkleidet. Seine Farbe wechselt erstaunlich mit dem Licht und der Entfernung. Sogar das Herunterlassen der Jalousien hinter dem getönten Glas einiger Fenster erzeugt seltsame Wellen und Glanz über ganze Abschnitte des „Curtains". Aus der Nähe sieht das Metall (wie beabsichtigt) dunkelgrau aus; aus der Entfernung nimmt es jedoch eine dunkelbronzefarbige Tönung an, die meines Erachtens eine der attraktivsten Eigenschaften des Gebäudes darstellt.

Das andere Gebäude auf dem Grundstück, die Hauptverwaltung der Peninsular & Oriental (P & O)-Schiffahrtsgesellschaft, ist in Farbe und Form bewußt anders gehalten. Mit etwa 58 m Höhe im Vergleich zu 118 m bei Commercial Union (14.900 m^2 nutzbare Bürofläche im Vergleich zu 26.000 m^2 bei Commercial Union) hat es auch geringere Geschoßflächen. Aber durch das breitere Podium, die geringere Höhe, die quadratischen Fenster und die auskragenden Geschoßdecken wirkt es gedrungener, massiver als der höhere Nachbarbau. Seine charakteristischen Merkmale sind das Fehlen jeglichen Metallrahmens bei den Eckfenstern, deren Flächen sich im rechten Winkel direkt aneinanderfügen, und das bewußt unterschiedliche Farbsystem. Naturbelassene Aluminiumpaneele (die verhindern sollen, daß die Tauben das Gebäude verunreinigen) liegen noch vor den auskragenden Geschoßdecken. Die Brüstungen sind mit bronzefarbigem Aluminium verkleidet und die Rahmen der Verglasung schwarz.

Beide Gebäude sind auf Podiumsebene durch das höherliegende Fußwegsystem miteinander verbunden, das um den gerippten Beton-Lüftungsschacht der Tiefgarage geführt ist. Die neue Piazza im rechten Winkel zwischen beiden Gebäuden zieren einige halbhohe Linden. In den zum Platz herunterführenden Stufen liegen die Einlaßlamellen zur Belüftung der fünf Untergeschosse des Commercial Union Building: Kantine, Garage, drei Lagergeschosse und Safes. Der Heizungsraum oben im Commercial Union-Hochhaus bedient auch den P & O-Bau. Windkanaltests am Royal Military College of Science in Shrivenham haben ergeben, daß Abgase von beinahe überall aus dem niedrigeren Gebäude sich vermutlich bei bestimmten Windverhältnissen vor einem der beiden Bauten stauen würden.

Wenn Commercial Union jedoch auch bis heute GMWs höchster Bau ist, so ist er – von vielen Seiten durch den wachsenden Wald von Hochhäusern in der City of London verdeckt – doch nicht ihr bedeutendster. Dieser Titel mag dem hohen, weißen Bau des Loughborough College aus vorgefertigten Betonelementen zustehen, **8**; vielleicht auch der großen, weißen Scheibe des Krankenhauses in Hillingdon, **11**, das sich auf den flachen, halb städtischen, halb ländlichen Ebenen des westlichen Middlesex nördlich vom London Airport erhebt. In Hillingdon gibt es ein Krankenhaus seit 1747. Es ist nach dem ersten Weltkrieg, vorwiegend durch die Zunahme der ungeplanten Notwohnungen und anderer Ad-Hoc-Bebauung, gewachsen.

Mit GMWs Bauten aus dem Jahre 1966 erhielt das Krankenhaus auf einen Schlag neue Operationsräume und Laboratorien in einem niedrigen Block im Norden, der auch die ambulanten Abteilungen (und einige schöne Gärten mit Wasserbecken) enthält, ein Hochhaus mit sieben Dreißig-Betten-Stationen nach dem damals modernen Nuffield-Plan, einen eingeschossigen neuen Restaurant- und Küchentrakt und einen Aufzugsturm, der dem Stationsbau angefügt und dafür vorgesehen ist, auch zwei weitere, später zu errichtende Stationstrakte zu bedienen. Es erhielt jedoch noch mehr: der achtgeschossige Stationstrakt mit einem darüberliegenden Technikgeschoß steht als Wahrzeichen in einem flachen Niemandsland, dem bisher vertikale Merkmale fehlten. Was vorher kein „Ort" war in der Monotonie überalterter Schrebergärten und grob verputzter Doppelhäuser, hat jetzt eine starke, klare Identität. Die neuen Stationstrakte werden vermutlich anders organisiert werden, da heute völlig andere Vorstellungen von Größe und Form der Pflegegeschosse bestehen.

Der andere in diesem Buch dargestellte Krankenhausbau von Gollins Melvin Ward, das Hospital in Sevenoaks, **10**, ist, obgleich ebenfalls ein Curtain-Wall-Bau, in Maßstab und Charakter völlig verschieden. Von der Straße zurückgesetzt, gegenüber einem Wirrwarr düsterer Backsteinbauten, aus denen das übrige Krankenhaus besteht, ist es ein bescheidener, weißer, zweigeschossiger Bau, der oben eine sechsundzwanzig-Betten-Entbindungsstation und unten eine neue Ambulanz enthält. Die senkrechten Stützen des graugestrichenen Stahlskeletts stehen vor der Außenhaut des Gebäudes; die matten, weißen Glasplatten und schwarzen Neoprene-Dichtungen verleihen ihm den angemessenen „klinischen", aber keinen unfreundlichen Charakter. Es ist ein bescheidener, zweckentsprechender Bau, der einen freundlichen Eindruck macht und (abgesehen von einigen Klagen über zu viel Verglasung) denen gefällt, die ihn nutzen.

Die Erweiterung der Universitätsbibliothek in Cambridge (1971), **23**, ist einer der zurückhaltenden Bauten des Büros. Er respektiert Giles Gilbert Scotts 1934 erbaute Bibliothek, die, wenn auch als Gebäudegruppe nicht besonders praktisch, beachtliche Ausdruckskraft und Charakter hat. Der Neubau von GMW ist, obgleich richtigerweise ohne jeden Versuch, in falschem Klassizismus zu machen, wie Scotts Bau aus Backstein, mit Betondecken, die häufig die Linien der steinernen Friese des alten Gebäudes aufnehmen. Doch unter den rechtwinkligen Öffnungen erscheint sein starker gestalterischer Ausdruck: braun anodisiertes Aluminium und große Glasflächen. Als funktionales Gebäude erreicht es eine mehrere hundert Prozent größere Effektivität pro Kubikmeter als der alte Bau, mit dem es durch zurückgesetzte, verglaste „Brükken "verbunden ist. Und es hat den großen Vorzug, leicht erweiterbar zu sein, wenn seine 61.000 laufenden Regalmeter gefüllt sind.

Bisher haben wir fertiggestellte und in Benutzung befindliche Bauten besprochen. Andere in diesem Buch dargestellte Projekte sind noch im Bau, bestehen nur auf dem Papier oder sind in manchen Fällen Träume, die möglicherweise nie realisiert werden. Ein Satz von Plänen jedoch – der letzte in einem (bis jetzt) ständig weiterentwickelten Bemühen, die richtige und akzeptable Lösung für ein schwieriges Problem zu finden – verdient einen Kommentar. Es sind die neuesten Entwürfe für die Erweiterung des Covent Garden Royal Opera House in London, **32**.

Seit mindestens drei Jahrzehnten hat die Covent Garden Opera ihren hohen künstlerischen Rang und internationale Bedeutung trotz anstatt dank des Gebäudes gewonnen, in dem sie untergebracht ist. Das Gollins Melvin Ward vom Vorstand der Oper gegebene Programm sah einen zweiten Zuschauersaal vor, Räume für die Opernschule (die gegenwärtig in einem abbruchreifen Gebäude in Hammersmith arbeitet) und für die Ballettschule (die in einem alten Kino in East End untergebracht ist), entsprechende Räume hinter und neben der Bühne des jetzigen Zuschauerraumes (deren Mangel großmaßstäbliche Inszenierungen sehr erschwert), zwei Probenräume, die auch Kulissen aufnehmen können (und daher 10 m hoch sein müssen), weitere Probenräume, neue Umkleideräume als Ersatz für die alten in dem häßlichen, in den dreißiger Jahren westlich an das alte Gebäude angefügten Anbau sowie geräumigere und bessere Einrichtungen für den Opernbesucher einschließlich einem Restaurant. All das sollte erreicht werden mit einem Entwurf, der nicht nur E. M. Barrys alten Opernbau aus dem Jahre 1858 aufwertet, sondern sich in die Pläne des Greater London Councils einfügt, welche die Restaurierung der Markthallen von Charles Fowler aus den dreißiger Jahren des vorigen Jahrhunderts im Süden und der sie umgebenden Piazza bei Verlagerung des Gemüsemarktes südlich der Themse nach Nine Elms im Laufe des Jahres 1974 vorsehen. Die Verlegung des Marktes bedeutete, daß die ursprünglichen Pläne, die Oper nach Norden, Westen und Süden zu erweitern, aufgegeben werden mußten zugunsten der Erweiterung nur nach Süden und Westen auf in öffentlichem Besitz befindlichem Gelände.

Zuerst betrachteten die Architekten die von den Planungsbehörden und Denkmalspflegern auferlegten Beschränkungen zusätzlich zur bereits schwierigen Aufgabe der Erweiterung eines historischen Gebäudes mit dem Ziel funktionaler Effizienz als eine schwere Belastung – als eine ästhetisch kaum lösbare Aufgabe. Die Art, wie ihre Einstellung sich wandelte, ist gleichermaßen charakteristisch für die Bescheidenheit und die Kreativität der Lösung von GMW. Anstatt die Forderung, die neoklassizistischen Arkaden von 1870 auf der Nordseite der Piazza weiterzuführen, entweder zu akzeptieren oder völlig zu verwerfen, quälten sie sich mit der Suche nach einer Lösung, die Fowler und den Charakter der Räume im Süden respektiert, aber in ästhetischer Hinsicht weniger unecht und funktional effektiver wäre als Platz für das Opernhaus sowie als Kulisse für die größeren Räume, derer sie bedarf. Die Lösung, auf die sie sich schließlich, wenn auch keineswegs leichten Herzens, festlegten, ist beinahe als brillant zu bezeichnen. Sie respektiert den Geist der Piazza ohne jede sklavische oder schwache Imitation des Vergangenen. Sie nimmt die Weite und die Proportionen der bestehenden Arkaden auf und fügt neue hin zu, jedoch nicht aus Naturstein oder Ziegel, sondern als modernes Aluminium-Äquivalent zu Joseph Paxtons Kristallpalast aus Gußeisen. Das Erdgeschoß grüßt mit Respekt, doch nicht in unangemessener Unterwürfigkeit die Arkaden von Henry Clutton; das nächste Geschoß ist um ein Modul zurückgesetzt und aufgeteilt, so daß kleinere Abstände zwischen den Pfeilern entstehen. Einige Flächen bestehen aus Arkaden (im Erdgeschoß), andere aus Fenstern, wieder andere aus offenen Galerien. Das System geht durch von der James Street im Osten bis zur Rückseite der Blumenhalle, nach Süden und wieder nach Osten, dann nach Norden und trifft dort auf eine geschickte, obgleich nicht sklavische Restauration der abgerissenen Blumenhalle. PKWs und Taxis fahren unter das Erdgeschoß in eine sehr geräumige und strahlend erleuchtete Art Porte-cochère.

Der östliche Teil der wiederaufgebauten Blumenhalle wird zu einem neuen, großen Foyer, während das gegenwärtige Foyer der Oper als „königlicher oder Galanacht"-Eingang erhalten bleibt. Für das bedeutendste vertikale Merkmal des Entwurfes, den stark vergrößerten, 30 m hohen Kulissenturm, der über dem bestehenden Bau errichtet werden soll, haben die Architekten ohne Skrupel eine historisierende Lösung gewählt. Sie sagen, es gäbe nur eine Möglichkeit, einen großen Kasten auf einem klassizistischen Opernhaus aus den 1850er Jahren zu verkleiden: in Stuck, mit Gesims, Ornament und allem anderen. Verkleidung, und was für eine! Und dennoch haben sie in diesem Fall sicherlich recht. Wird der Entwurf ausgeführt werden? Als dieser Beitrag geschrieben wurde, schien er weniger bedroht durch die Opposition von seiten der Planer oder Denkmalschützer als durch wirtschaftliche Beschränkungen. Ich hoffe, er wird gebaut werden. Der Opernhausverwaltung ist manchmal vorgeworfen worden, daß sie spezielle Wünsche hätte. Aber Covent Garten *ist* ein spezieller Fall.

Genug der Diskussionen und Meinungen. Nun zu den Bauten. Lassen wir die Architektur von Gollins Melvin Ward für sich sprechen.

Buildings and projects/Bâtiments et projets/Bauten und Projekte

1 University of Sheffield

Central Redevelopment 1953–73

University complex: site plan
1. Library 2. Arts and architecture 3. Central boiler house 4. Chemistry north wing 5. Chemistry west wing 6. Chemistry east wing 7. Physics and Mathematics building 8. Lecture theatres 9. University House (Student Union) 10. Biology 11. Bursars department 12. Existing university buildings 13. Public park

Complexe universitaire: plan d'ensemble
1. Bibliothèque 2. Lettres et architecture 3. Chaufferie centrale 4. Chimie aile Nord 5. Chimie aile Ouest 6. Chimie aile Est 7. Physique et Mathématiques 8. Amphithéâtres 9. Maison Universitaire (Union des étudiants) 10. Biologie 11. Economat 12. Bâtiments universitaires existant 13. Jardin public

Komplex der Universitätsneubauten: Lageplan
1. Bibliothek 2. Kunst und Architektur 3. Heizzentrale 4. Chemie Nordflügel 5. Chemie Westflügel 6. Chemie Ostflügel 7. Physik und Mathematik 8. Hörsaalgebäude 9. University House (Studentische Gemeinschaft) 10. Biologie 11. Quästur 12. Vorhandene Universitätsbauten 13. Öffentlicher Park

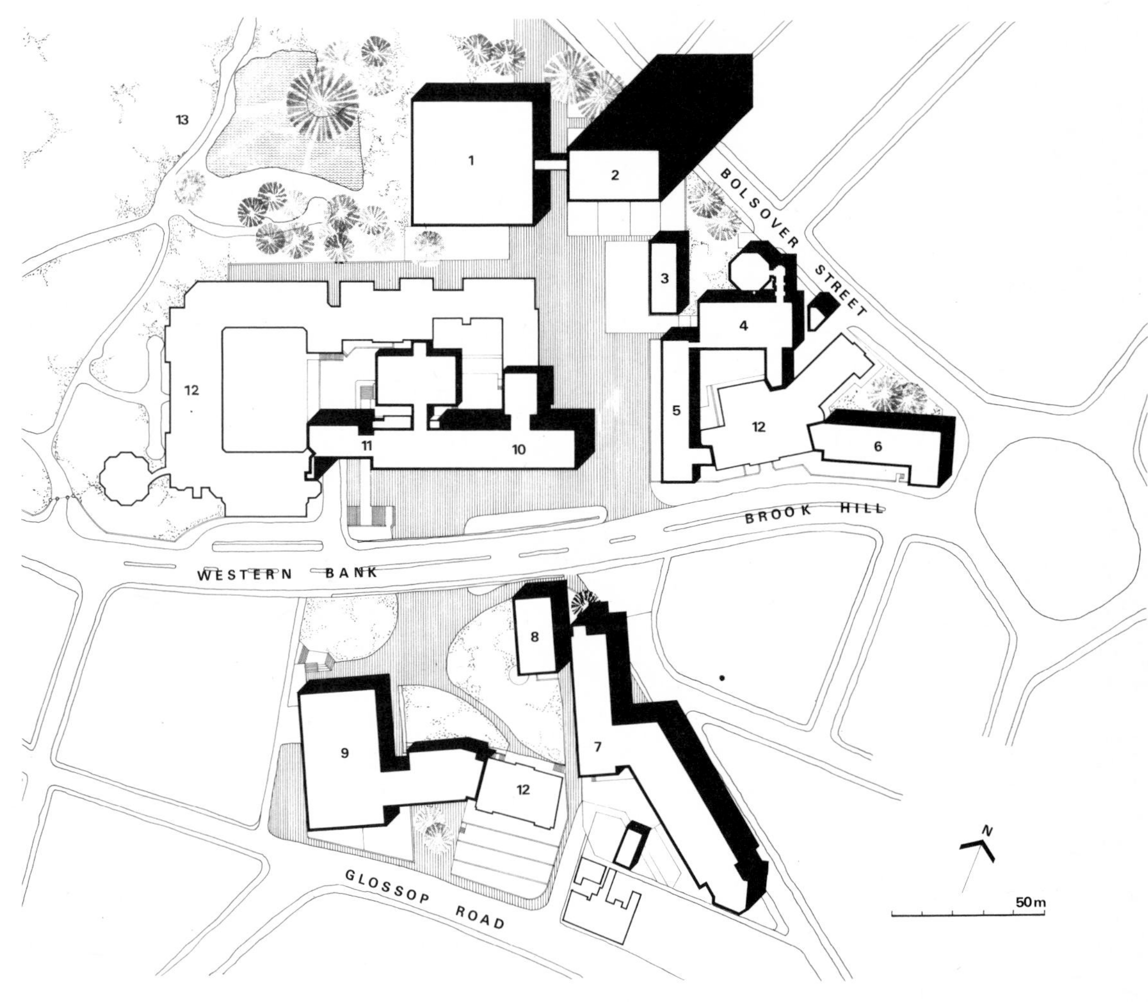

In 1953, the Gollins Melvin Ward Partnership were awarded the first premium in the open competition for the development of the central area of the University of Sheffield. The first building to be completed was the University Library, which was opened by T. S. Eliot in 1959. Since then, the original layout has, throughout the years, been developed to reflect the ever-increasing number of students which the university was asked to take, the ever-changing techniques of undergraduate education, and the differing building priorities.

Gollins Melvin Ward Partnership se virent décerner, en 1953, le premier prix du concours portant sur l'aménagement de la zone centrale de l'Université de Sheffield. Le premier bâtiment terminé fut la Bibliothèque Universitaire, que T.S.Eliot inaugura en 1959. Depuis lors le plan-masse initial a été aménagé, au fil des années, pour tenir compte du nombre toujours croissant d'étudiants qu'on demande aux universités de recevoir, de la perpétuelle évolution dans les techniques d'enseignement, et des variations intervenues dans les priorités de construction.

1953 erhielt die Gollins Melvin Ward Partnership den ersten Preis in einem offenen Wettbewerb für die Planung des zentralen Bereichs der Universität Sheffield. Das erste fertiggestellte Gebäude war die Universitätsbibliothek, die 1959 von T.S.Eliot eröffnet wurde. Seitdem ist der ursprüngliche Bebauungsplan im Laufe der Jahre weiterentwickelt worden entsprechend der wachsenden Zahl von Studenten, den Änderungen des Studiensystems und dem Wandel der Prioritäten der Gebäude.

University of Sheffield

Library 1959

Main Entrance/Entrée principale/Haupteingang

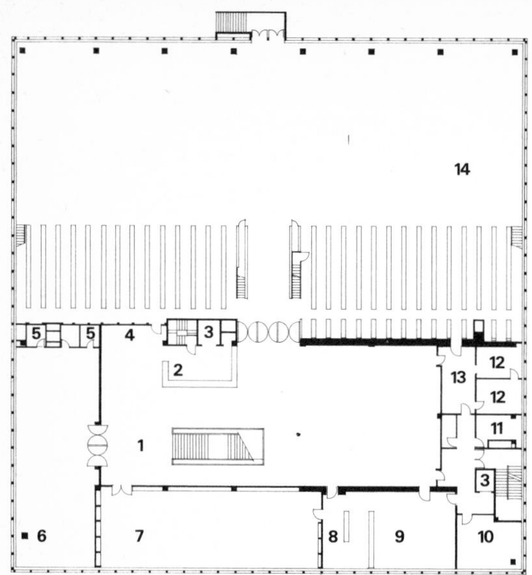

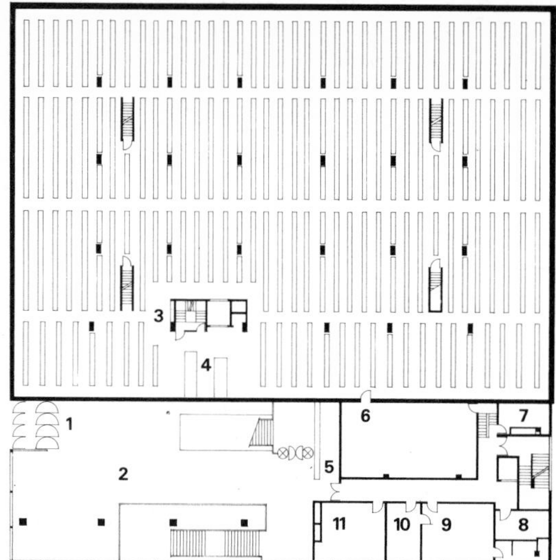

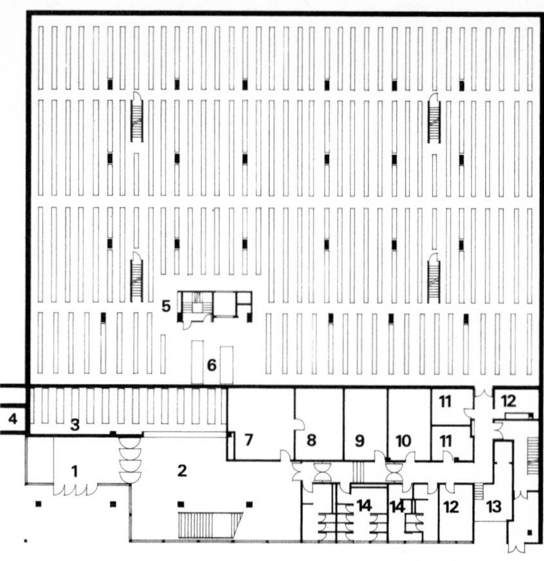

First floor plan
1. Entrance and catalogue hall 2. Stack clerk 3. Lift 4. Trolley store 5. Staff 6. Postgraduate reading room 7. Periodicals reading room 8. Binding and unpacking 9. Catalogue room 10. Labelling 11. Inter library loans 12. Administration 13. Acquisition 14. Reading room

Plan du premier étage
1. Entrée et hall des catalogues 2. Préposé à la réserve fermée 3. Ascenseur 4. Réserve de chariots 5. Bureaux 6. Salle de lecture des chercheurs diplômés 7. Salle de lecture des revues 8. Reliure et dépaquetage 9. Service du catalogue 10. Etiquetage 11. Service des échanges interbibliothèques 12. Administration 13. Service des acquisitions 14. Salle de lecture

Grundriß Obergeschoß
1. Eingang und Kataloghalle 2. Lagerverwalter 3. Aufzug 4. Bücherwagen-Abstellraum 5. Bibliothekspersonal 6. Doktoranden-Lesesaal 7. Zeitschriftenlesesaal 8. Binden und Auspacken 9. Katalograum 10. Beschriftung 11. Auswärtiger Leihverkehr 12. Verwaltung 13. Akzession 14. Lesesaal

Mezzanine
1. Entrance 2. Exhibition space 3. Book stack tier 4. Sorting area 5. Control area 6. Pamphlet room 7. Cleaner 8. Store 9. Librarian 10. Secretary 11. Conference room

Plan de la mezzanine
1. Entrée 2. Emplacement pour expositions 3. Niveau de réserve de livres fermée 4. Zone de tri 5. Poste de surveillance 6. Salle des bulletins 7. Poste de nettoyage 8. Réserve 9. Bibliothécaire 10. Secrétaire 11. Salle de réunions

Grundriß Zwischengeschoß
1. Eingang 2. Ausstellungsraum 3. Freihandbücherei 4. Einordnen 5. Kontrollbereich 6. Broschürensaal 7. Putzraum 8. Abstellraum 9. Bibliotheksleitung 10. Sekretärin 11. Konferenzraum

Ground floor plan
1. Main entrance 2. Foyer 3. Cloakroom 4. Service ducts 5. Book stack tier 6. Sorting area 7. Processing room 8. Dark room 9. Stationery store 10. Strong room 11. Cleaners 12. Dining/rest room 13. Unloading bay 14. Staff and student WC

Plan du rez-de-chaussée
1. Entrée principale 2. Foyer 3. Vestiaire 4. Galerie technique 5. Niveau de réserve de livres fermée 6. Zone de tri 7. Salle de traitement (reproduction, photographie, . . .) 8. Chambre noire 9. Réserve de fournitures 10. Salle des coffres-forts 11. Poste de nettoyage 12. Pièce pour repas et repos du personnel 13. Quai de déchargement 14. WC pour le personnel et les étudiants

Grundriß Erdgeschoß
1. Haupteingang 2. Foyer 3. Garderobe 4. Versorgungsschächte 5. Magazin 6. Einordnen 7. Reproduktion 8. Dunkelkammer 9. Materiallager 10. Safe 11. Putzräume 12. Eß-/Aufenthaltsraum 13. Anlieferung 14. WC Personal und Studenten

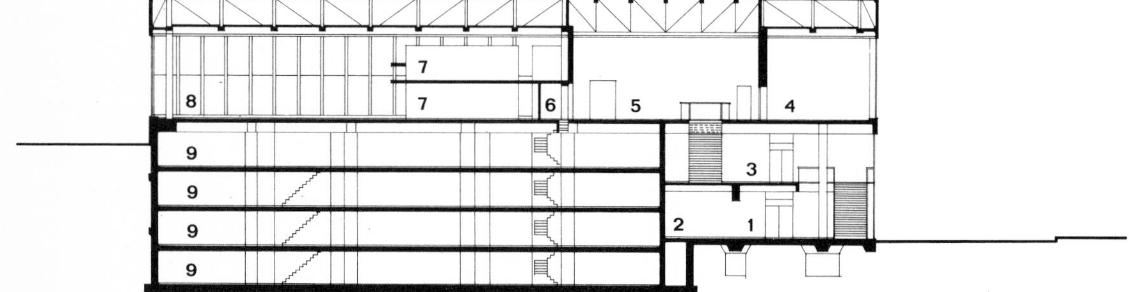

Section
1. Foyer 2. Cloaks 3. Exhibition space 4. Periodicals reading room 5. Catalogue hall 6. Trolley store 7. Book store tier 8. Reading room 9. Book stack tier

Section
1. Foyer 2. Vestiaires 3. Emplacement pour expositions 4. Salle de lecture des revues 5. Hall des catalogues 6. Réserve de chariots 7. Niveau de réserve de livres ouverte 8. Salle de lecture 9. Niveau de réserve de livres fermée

Schnitt
1. Foyer 2. Garderoben 3. Ausstellungsfläche 4. Zeitschriftenlesesaal 5. Kataloghalle 6. Bücherwagen-Abstellraum 7. Freihandbücherei 8. Lesesaal 9. Magazin

10m

Reading Room/Salle de lecture/Lesesaal

The new library is designed to hold one million books. It is therefore one of the largest university library buildings in the country, though this is still small compared with libraries in the United States where more than twelve universities have over one million books each, and both Harvard and Yale have over four million. At Sheffield, some 130,000 books are in the reading room book store, available to all readers, and 870,000 in the closed stack.

There is one main reading room, two small reading rooms for post-graduates, and a periodicals reading room open to all readers, all within the control area; access to all four is from the catalogue hall. At the back of the main reading room which has seventy-six tables for 280 readers, and immediately alongside the entrance and thus approachable without disturbing the readers, is the two-tier open stack book store holding approximately 115,000 octavos and 15,000 quartos. The reading rooms and book stack are air-conditioned and to reduce solar gain and the demand on the refrigeration plant, windows in the reading rooms facing south and west are glazed with anti-sun glass.

La nouvelle bibliothèque a été conçue pour abriter un million de livres. Le bâtiment constitue de ce fait l'une des plus importantes bibliothèques universitaires du pays ce qui est encore modeste si l'on compare aux Etats-Unis où plus de douze universités dépassent le million de livres, et où Harvard et Yale possèdent chacune quelque quatre millions d'ouvrages. A Sheffield il y a 130.000 livres dans les rayons affectés à la salle de lecture, accessibles à tout lecteur, et 870.000 livres dans les bibliothèques fermées.

Il y a une salle de lecture principale, deux petites salles de lecture pour les chercheurs diplômés, et une salle de lecture des revues ouverte à tout lecteur; ces salles sont toutes quatre dans la zone surveillée et on y accède depuis le hall des catalogues. La salle de lecture principale compte soixante-seize tables et peut accueillir 280 lecteurs; placée juste à son entrée et ainsi accessible sans troubler les lecteurs, se trouve la réserve de livres à rayons ouverts, installée sur deux niveaux, qui contient approximativement 115.000 in-octavos et 15.000 in-quartos. Les salles de lecture et réserves de livres sont climatisées, et pour réduire l'influence du soleil sur la consommation d'énergie des installations de climatisation, les fenêtres orientées au Sud et à l'Ouest sont vitrées avec du verre anti-solaire.

Die neue Bibliothek hat eine Kapazität von einer Million Bänden und ist damit eine der größten Universitätsbibliotheken des Landes, obgleich das immer noch wenig ist im Vergleich zu Bibliotheken in den Vereinigten Staaten, wo mehr als zwölf Universitäten je über eine Million Bände besitzen; Harvard und Yale haben beide über vier Millionen. In Sheffield sind etwa 130.000 Bände im Lesesaal als Freihandbücherei allen Lesern zugänglich, 870.000 befinden sich im geschlossenen Magazin.

Die Bibliothek hat einen großen Lesesaal, zwei kleine Lesesäle für Doktoranden und einen allen Lesern zur Verfügung stehenden Zeitschriftenlesesaal, die alle innerhalb des Kontrollbereiches liegen. Der Zugang zu allen vier Sälen erfolgt von der Kataloghalle. An der Rückseite des großen Lesesaals, der 76 Tische für 280 Leser enthält, unmittelbar neben dem Eingang und daher ohne Störung der Leser zugänglich, liegt die zweigeschossige Freihandbücherei, die etwa 115.000 Oktav- und 15.000 Quartbände enthält. Die Lesesäle und das Magazin sind klimatisiert; um Sonneneinstrahlung und die Beanspruchung der Kühlanlage zu reduzieren, sind die nach Süden und Westen orientierten Fenster in den Lesesälen mit Sonnenschutzglas versehen.

Exterior detail/Détail extérieur/Außenwand
Library from the park/Bibliothèque vue du parc/Bibliothek, Blick vom Park

2 The Polytechnic, Sheffield

Education Committee of the City of Sheffield 1954–70

The triangular site, steeply contoured, lies between the main railway station, the civic circle and the link boulevard. The Polytechnic, built in four principal stages, is grouped around a central spine block of twelve floors in which are the schools of building, engineering, science, catering and women's work, and the communal teaching rooms, library, and restaurant. The assembly hall, workshops, school of commerce, and the department of chemistry are each in separate but linked wings.

The site levels are such that the entrance to the central block is on the fifth floor in relation to the subsidiary entrance to the lowest floor from Pond Street, thus allowing students to enter approximately at mid-height level thereby reducing the vertical circulation.

Le terrain, triangulaire et pentu, est situé entre la gare principale et le boulevard de ceinture. L'école professionnelle polytechnique, dont la construction s'est déroulée en quatre phases principales, se rassemble autour d'un bloc central de douze étages abritant les écoles des métiers du bâtiment, d'ingénierie, de sciences, de restauration et d'enseignement ménager, ainsi que les salles de classe communes, la bibliothèque et le restaurant. La salle de réunions, les ateliers, l'école de commerce et le département de chimie sont chacun installés dans des bâtiments séparés mais reliés au bloc central.

Les différences de niveau du terrain sont à ce point accusées que l'entrée du bloc central est au cinquième étage par rapport au niveau de la rue (Pond Street) desservant l'entrée subsidiaire, à la base du bâtiment. Ceci permet aux étudiants de pénétrer dans l'école à peu près à sa mi-hauteur, et réduit d'autant les circulations verticales.

Das dreieckige, stark abfallende Grundstück liegt zwischen Hauptbahnhof, innerstädtischem Ring und verbindendem Boulevard. Das Polytechnikum, in vier Stufen erbaut, ist um ein zentrales, zwölfgeschossiges Hochhaus angeordnet, das die Abteilungen Bauwesen, Ingenieurwesen, Naturwissenschaften, Ernährungslehre und Hauswirtschaft sowie die kommunalen Unterrichtsräume, die Bibliothek und ein Restaurant enthält. Die Aula, Werkstätten, Handelsschule und die Chemieabteilung liegen jeweils in getrennten, aber untereinander verbundenen Trakten.

Die Geländesituation erforderte, den Eingang zum zentralen Gebäude in das fünfte Geschoß zu legen, den Zweiteingang dagegen in das unterste Geschoß an der Pond Street. So können die Studenten etwa auf halber Höhe eintreten, der Vertikalverkehr wird dadurch reduziert.

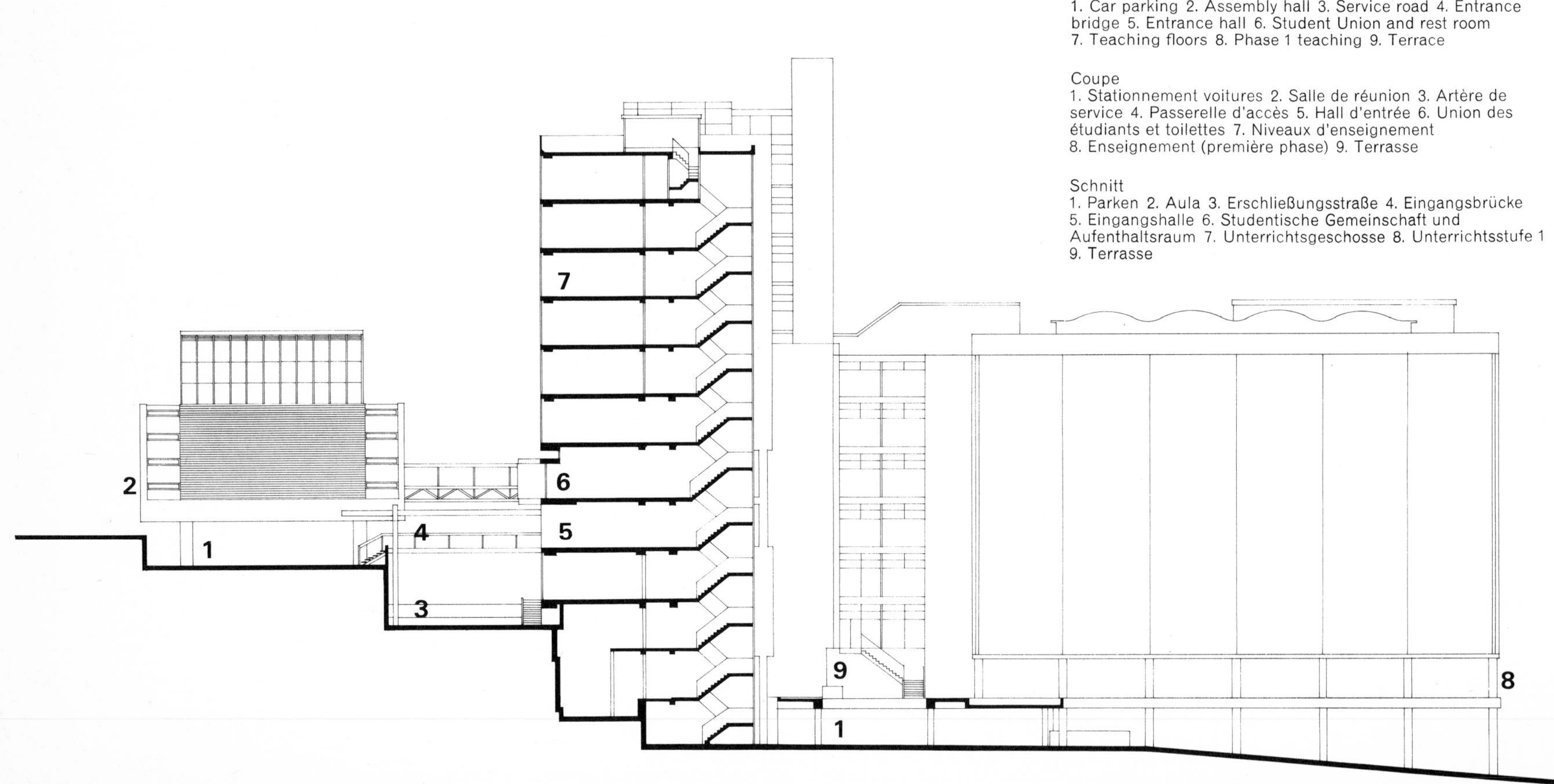

Section
1. Car parking 2. Assembly hall 3. Service road 4. Entrance bridge 5. Entrance hall 6. Student Union and rest room 7. Teaching floors 8. Phase 1 teaching 9. Terrace

Coupe
1. Stationnement voitures 2. Salle de réunion 3. Artère de service 4. Passerelle d'accès 5. Hall d'entrée 6. Union des étudiants et toilettes 7. Niveaux d'enseignement 8. Enseignement (première phase) 9. Terrasse

Schnitt
1. Parken 2. Aula 3. Erschließungsstraße 4. Eingangsbrücke 5. Eingangshalle 6. Studentische Gemeinschaft und Aufenthaltsraum 7. Unterrichtsgeschosse 8. Unterrichtsstufe 1 9. Terrasse

3 New Cavendish Street, London W1

Great Portland Estates 1955 and 1957

Left/A gauche/Links: Nos 118–26

Right/A droite/Rechts: Nos 93–7, Nos 118–26

93–7 New Cavendish Street
Electrin House, on the north side of New Cavendish Street between Bolsover Street and Great Titchfield Street, provides the maximum area of divisible office space on the upper floors and showroom space on the ground floor. The basement area was designed for storage only.

The curtain wall, one of the earliest if not the first in London, is constructed of extruded aluminium sections with steel opening lights painted black. The infill panels are in opaque blue green glass.

93–7 New Cavendish Street
L'Electrin House, sur le versant Nord de la New Cavendish Street, entre la Bolsover Street et la Great Titchfield Street, comprend des étages offrant le volume maximum d'espace divisible à usage de bureaux, et un rez-de-chaussée destiné à des vitrines et éventaires. Le sous-sol a été exclusivement destiné à l'entreposage.

Le mur-rideau, qui a été l'un des tout premiers sinon même le premier qu'on ait construit à Londres, est constitué de sections d'aluminium extrudé avec les chassis des fenêtres en acier peint en noir. Les panneaux de remplissage sont en verre bleu-vert opaque.

93–7 New Cavendish Street
Das Electrin House an der Nordseite der New Cavendish Street zwischen Bolsover Street und Great Titchfield Street enthält ein Maximum an variabel nutzbarer Bürofläche in den Obergeschossen und Ausstellungsfläche im Erdgeschoß. Das Untergeschoß ist Lagerzwecken vorbehalten.

Der Curtain-Wall, einer der frühesten, wenn nicht der erste in London, besteht aus stranggepreßten Aluminiumelementen mit Fenstereinfassungen aus schwarzgestrichenem Stahl. Die Ausfüllelemente sind aus blaugrünem Glas.

118–26 New Cavendish Street
The principal front is to New Cavendish Street with short return fronts to Gosfield Street and Great Titchfield Street. The office accommodation is on four upper floors and the ground floor was designed as showrooms. The street elevations are clad with continuous rows of steel windows with opaque white spandrel panels framed with aluminium channels painted black.

118–26 New Cavendish Street
Cet immeuble a sa façade principale donnant sur la New Cavendish Street et de courts retours d'angle sur la Gosfield Street et la Great Titchfield Street. Il est aménagé pour contenir des bureaux dans ses quatre étages, et des vitrines et éventaires au rez-de-chaussée. Les façades sont garnies de rangées continues de fenêtres aux chassis en acier et de panneaux de soubassement en verre blanc opaque enserrés dans une armature de bandeaux d'aluminium peints en noir.

118–26 New Cavendish Street
Die Hauptfront des Gebäudes liegt an der New Cavendish Street mit Schmalseiten zur Gosfield Street und Great Titchfield Street. Die Büroräume sind in vier Obergeschossen untergebracht, das Erdgeschoß ist für Ausstellung vorgesehen. Die zur Straße gerichteten Fassaden sind mit durchgehenden Fensterbändern aus Stahl und weißen Plattenelementen, die mit schwarzgestrichenem Aluminium ausgerüstet sind, verkleidet.

4 Radley College, Berkshire

Classrooms and Assembly Hall 1960

The eight additional classrooms, each for twenty boys and with their own store, are single storey, thus presenting less obstruction to the view from the playing fields and acting as a foil to the speech hall to which they are related in a single architectural composition. They face south-east and as the site slopes fairly steeply, are in two groups of four to minimize the cost of foundations and site works; they are linked by an open-sided corridor.

Ces huit classes supplémentaires, conçues pour vingt élèves chacune et ayant leur propre réserve, ont été bâties sur un seul niveau, de façon à offrir ainsi moins d'obstacle à la vue depuis les terrains de jeu et à mettre en valeur la salle de réunion à laquelle elles sont reliées dans une composition architecturale unie. Les classes regardent le Sud-Est et comme le terrain a une pente assez prononcée, elles ont été rassemblées en deux groupes de quatre pour minimiser le coût des fondations et travaux de chantier. Les deux groupes sont reliés par une allée couverte.

Die acht neuen Klassentrakte für je 20 Jungen mit jeweils einem eigenen Abstellraum sind eingeschossig. Dadurch behindern sie die Aussicht von den Sportplätzen weniger und bilden den Hintergrund für den Hörsaalbau, mit dem sie eine architektonische Einheit bilden. Die Klassen sind nach Südosten orientiert und, da das Gelände steil abfällt, in zwei Vierergruppen angeordnet, um die Kosten der Gründung und der Erdbewegung zu reduzieren. Sie sind durch einen überdachten Gang miteinander verbunden.

Though finances, in the event, did not allow its construction, it was originally intended that the hall should be adjacent to the new classrooms and as the school already possesses halls with flat floors it was possible to plan a conventional auditorium with stepped seating for 500, and a proscenium stage which could be modified for choral and orchestral works and for classical plays requiring a large apron. The external walls, largely of clear glass, allow advantage to be taken of the natural surroundings, an awareness of which is an essential factor of the architectural character of the interior.

Quoiqu'en fait des raisons financières n'aient pas permis sa construction, il avait été prévu à l'origine qu'une grande salle de réunion jouxterait les nouvelles salles de classe et comme l'école possède déjà différentes salles de réunion au plancher horizontal, on avait élaboré le projet d'un auditorium classique en gradins, de 500 places, avec une scène pourvue d'une avant-scène – c'est-à-dire un dispositif pouvant s'adapter pour accueillir chorales et orchestres, et permettre des représentations théâtrales exigeant un vaste tablier. Un large emploi du verre transparent dans les façades permet de tirer parti de l'environnement naturel extérieur, dont la perception constitue un facteur essentiel du caractère architectural donné à l'intérieur.

Obgleich der geplante Aulabau aus finanziellen Gründen nicht ausgeführt werden konnte, war ursprünglich beabsichtigt, die Halle neben den neuen Klassentrakten zu errichten. Da in der Schule bereits Säle mit ebenem Boden vorhanden sind, war es möglich, eine konventionelle Aula mit ansteigenden Sitzen für 500 Zuschauer und einer Proszeniumsbühne zu planen, die auch für Chor- und Orchesteraufführungen nutzbar ist sowie für Klassikeraufführungen, die eine große Plattform benötigen. Die durchsichtig verglasten Außenwände bieten den Vorteil, daß die Landschaft als wesentliches Element der Architektur des Innenraumes dienen kann.

5 174-204 Marylebone Road, London W1 - Castrol House

Hammerson Group of Companies 1960

The restrictions imposed by the town planning authorities and the ground landlord largely dictated the form of this building inasmuch as they required that the Marylebone Road frontage should be continuous and not less than two storeys high, that no part of the building was to be higher than the tower of the Marylebone Town Hall opposite, and that the whole area of the site be built on, thus precluding ground-level courts. The floor to site area was not to exceed 3·5 to 1. In 1955 when design work started there was considerable uncertainty as to whether offices in this area would attract adequate rents, and it was therefore essential to plan as economically as possible and to ensure that the offices could be let either to one or to several tenants; in the event, but subsequent to the commencement of construction, the building was let entirely to Castrol Limited, for whom special requirements, including a canteen, boardroom suite, cinema, and conference rooms had to be introduced. The importance of Marylebone Road as a main thoroughfare and of the local government building opposite required that the building should have a distinctive and outstanding appearance.

The thirteen-storey tower rises from the part two- and part three-storey podium. The main entrance from Marylebone Road immediately under the tower leads directly to a large double-height entrance hall from which a free-standing staircase rises to the first-floor upper hall, designed for exhibitions and displays. To avoid machinery and plantrooms obtruding above the roof level, the lifts stop one floor below the roof, to which access is gained by staircase and which is occupied by the executive and managerial lounge, the caretaker's flat, and visitors' bedrooms. A spiral staircase leads to the roof from the lounge. The basement car park to which entry is from Balcombe Street, has space for 100 cars.

The building is enclosed with an aluminium curtain wall and consists of black anodized mullions connected by deep transoms and cills in an anodized natural finish. The spandrel panels on the three main elevations are of white Sicilian marble. The curtain walling of the tower is formed by a deep anodized aluminium grid, the mullions and cills having a black anodized finish with the spandrel panels in green glass. On the wall of the two-storey main hall facing the entrance is a cast aluminium relief sculpture by Geoffrey Clarke 15 m long and 7 m high rising to the ceiling of the upper hall depicting the history of the oil industry.

Sir Hugh Casson and Neville Conder were in association.

Les contraintes imposées par les services de l'urbanisme et le propriétaire du terrain ont largement influé sur la forme donnée au bâtiment, dans la mesure où il était exigé que la façade donnant sur l'artère de Marylebone Road fût continue et haute d'au moins deux étages, qu'aucun élément du bâtiment ne dépassât la hauteur de la tour d'en face (l'hôtel de ville de Marylebone), et que toute la surface au sol fût construite, ce qui excluait les cours au rez-de-chaussée. Enfin le rapport surface utile totale/surface au sol ne devait pas dépasser 3,5. Lorsque commença le travail de conception, en 1955, il n'était absolument pas assuré qu'une offre de bureaux dans ce quartier rencontrât une demande disposée à acquitter des loyers suffisants; il était donc essentiel que la conception visât au plus économique et permît aussi bien une location des bureaux à un seul locataire que leur répartition entre plusieurs. En fait – mais postérieurement au commencement de la construction – l'immeuble fut loué en entier à la société Castrol, pour les besoins de laquelle il fallut introduire dans le programme divers aménagements particuliers, tels que: cantine, pièces du Conseil d'Administration, cinéma et salles de conférence. L'importance de Marylebone Road en tant qu'artère principale, et de l'immeuble de l'administration locale situé en vis à vis exigeait que le bâtiment ait un aspect distinctif et marquant.

La tour de treize niveaux s'élève au dessus d'un podium dont une partie a deux niveaux et une partie trois niveaux. L'entrée principale débouche de Marylebone Road directement sous la tour dans un vaste hall d'entrée occupant en hauteur deux niveaux, où un escalier indépendant conduit au niveau supérieur du hall, destiné à des affichages, expositions, etc. Pour éviter que la machinerie et les locaux techniques ne déparent l'esthétique de l'ensemble en formant une masse inopportune sur le toit, les ascenseurs s'arrêtent un niveau en dessous de celui-ci, et l'on gagne par un escalier le dernier niveau qui, outre la machinerie, est occupé par le salon des directeurs et cadres supérieurs, l'appartement du concierge et des chambres pour visiteurs. Du salon un escalier en spirale mène à la terrasse du toit. Le garage en sous-sol, auquel on accède par Balcombe Street, a de la place pour 100 voitures.

Le bâtiment est contenu dans un mur-rideau d'aluminium et constitué de meneaux noir anodisés reliés par des linteaux et traverses épais d'une teinte naturelle anodisée. Les panneaux de remplissage sur les trois niveaux du podium sont en marbre blanc de Sicile. Le mur-rideau de la tour est formé par un treillis d'aluminium anodisé en profondeur, les meneaux et linteaux ayant un fini noir anodisé et les panneaux de remplissage étant en verre vert. Sur le grand mur du hall d'entrée et face à celle-ci, une sculpture en relief en aluminium coulé, due à Geoffrey Clarke, monte jusqu'au plafond du hall supérieur; elle représente l'histoire de l'industrie du pétrole.

Sir Hugh Casson et Neville Conder étaient associés, pour ce projet, à la Gollins Melvin Ward Partnership.

Die von den städtischen Planungsbehörden auferlegten Beschränkungen und die Wünsche des Bauherrn bestimmten weitgehend die Form dieses Gebäudes. Sie forderten, daß die Fassade zur Marylebone Road geschlossen und nicht höher als zwei Stockwerke sei, daß kein Teil des Gebäudes die Höhe des gegenüberliegenden Rathausturmes von Marylebone überschreiten durfte und daß das gesamte Grundstück zu überbauen und damit die Anordnung erdgeschossiger Freiflächen auszuschließen sei. Die Geschoßflächenzahl sollte 3,5 nicht überschreiten. Zu Beginn der Planungsarbeiten 1955 war noch nicht abzusehen, ob Büros in diesem Gebiet entsprechende Mieten erreichen würden. Daher mußte so wirtschaftlich wie möglich geplant und sichergestellt werden, daß die Büros sowohl an nur einen als auch an mehrere Mieter abgegeben werden konnten. Schließlich wurde aber noch während der Bauzeit das Gebäude ganz an die Firma Castrol vermietet, für die besondere Einrichtungen – eine Kantine, eine Gästesuite, ein Kino und Konferenzräume – vorgesehen werden mußten. Die Bedeutung der Marylebone Road als Hauptverkehrsstraße und die gegenüberliegende Bezirksverwaltung forderten einen qualitätvollen Bau.

Das dreizehngeschossige Hochhaus erhebt sich von einem teils zwei-, teils dreigeschossigen Podium. Der Haupteingang von Marylebone Road unmittelbar unter dem Hochhaus führt direkt zu einer Eingangshalle in doppelter Geschoßhöhe, von der eine freistehende Treppe zu der Halle im Obergeschoß führt, die für Ausstellungen bestimmt ist. Um zu vermeiden, daß Technik und Maschinenräume über die Dachebene hinausragen, hält der Aufzug ein Stockwerk unter dem Dachgeschoß, zu dem der Zugang über eine Treppe erfolgt. Es enthält Aufenthaltsräume für leitende Angestellte und die Geschäftsführung, die Wohnung des Hausmeisters und Gästeappartements. Eine Wendeltreppe führt vom Aufenthaltsraum auf das Dach. Die Tiefgarage im Untergeschoß, mit Zugang von der Balcombe Street, hat Abstellplätze für 100 Wagen.

Der Curtain-Wall des Podiums ist eine Aluminiumkonstruktion. Die Stützen sind schwarz anodisiert, die horizontalen Elemente naturbelassen, die Füllelemente der drei Hauptfassaden aus weißem sizilianischen Marmor. Der Curtain-Wall des Hochhauses besteht aus einem stark anodisierten Aluminiumraster, Stützen und Horizontalelemente sind schwarz mit Ausfüllung aus grünem Glas. Die Wand in der zweigeschossigen Halle gegenüber dem Eingang nimmt ein ca. 15× 7 m großes, gegossenes Aluminiumrelief von Geoffrey Clarke ein, das sich bis zur Decke der oberen Halle erstreckt und die Geschichte der Ölindustrie darstellt.

Mitarbeiter waren Sir Hugh Casson und Neville Conder.

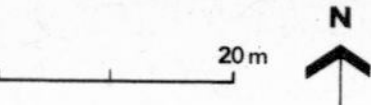

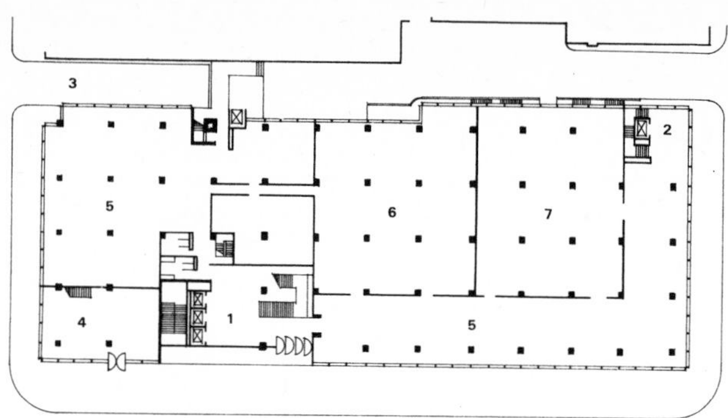

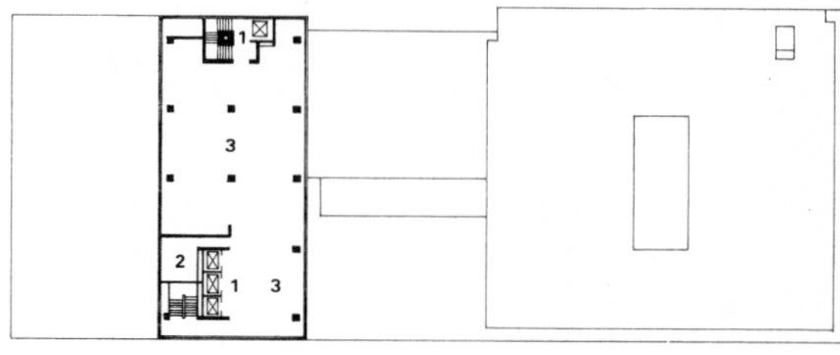

Ground floor plan
1. Entrance hall 2. Service entrance 3. Ramp to garage 4. Bank
5. Office 6. Restaurant 7. Kitchen

Plan du rez-de-chaussée
1. Hall d'entrée 2. Entrée de déchargement 3. Rampe d'accès au garage 4. Banque 5. Bureaux 6. Restaurant 7. Cuisine

Grundriß Erdgeschoß
1. Haupteingang 2. Anlieferung 3. Rampe zur Tiefgarage
4. Bank 5. Bürofläche 6. Restaurant 7. Küche

Typical floor plan
1. Lift lobby and stairs 2. WC 3. Office space

Plan type d'étage
1. Vestibule des ascenseurs et escalier 2. WC 3. Bureaux

Grundriß Normalgeschoß
1. Aufzugshalle und Treppen 2. WC 3. Bürofläche

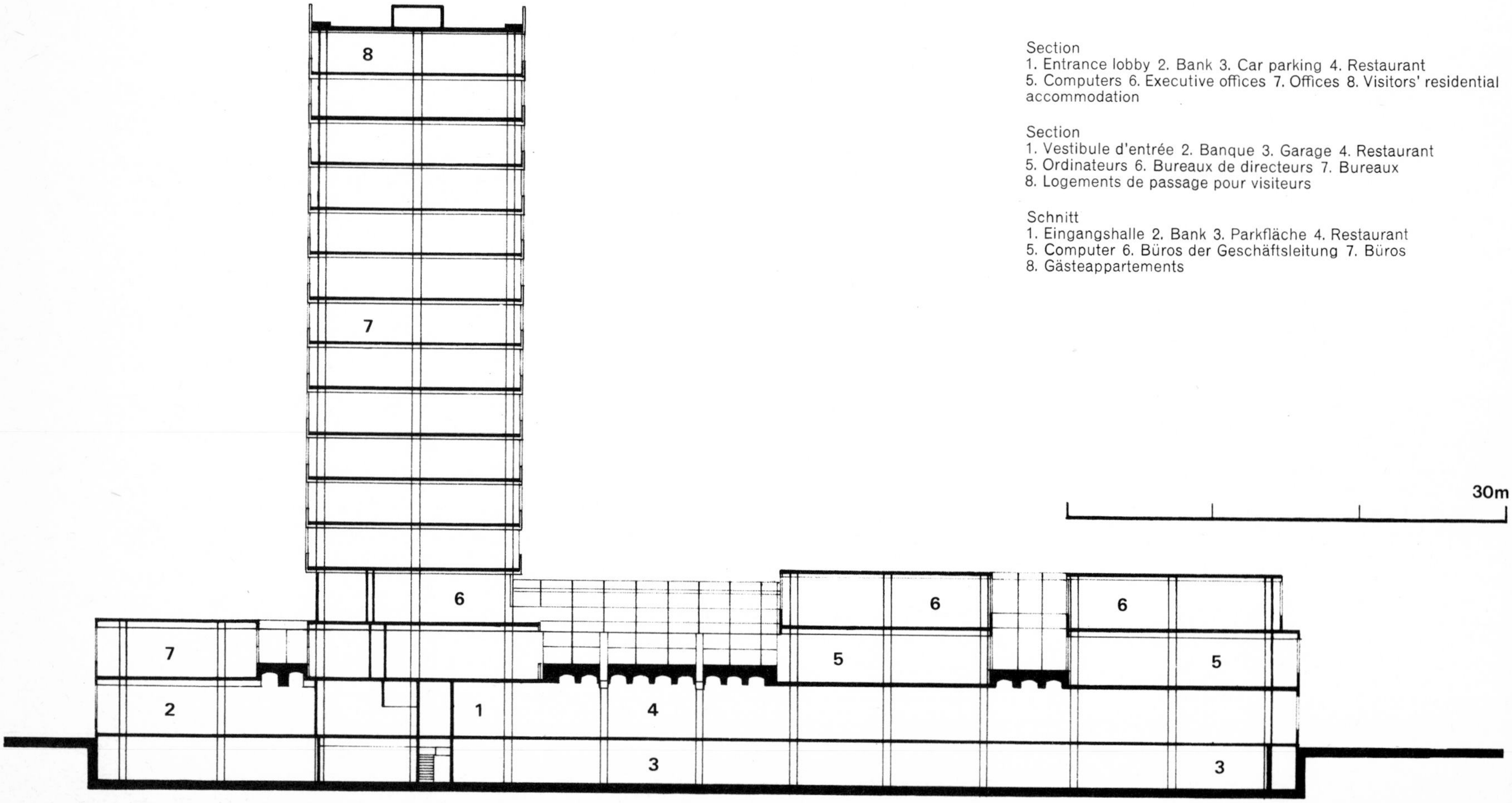

Section
1. Entrance lobby 2. Bank 3. Car parking 4. Restaurant
5. Computers 6. Executive offices 7. Offices 8. Visitors' residential accommodation

Section
1. Vestibule d'entrée 2. Banque 3. Garage 4. Restaurant
5. Ordinateurs 6. Bureaux de directeurs 7. Bureaux
8. Logements de passage pour visiteurs

Schnitt
1. Eingangshalle 2. Bank 3. Parkfläche 4. Restaurant
5. Computer 6. Büros der Geschäftsleitung 7. Büros
8. Gästeappartements

Entrance lobby stairs/Escalier, vestibule d'entrée/Treppe, Eingangshalle

6 University of Sheffield

Faculties of Arts, Economics and Social Studies 1965

One of the chief factors affecting the proposals for the central redevelopment was that there should be one dominant feature in the layout, a role which is filled by the tower housing the faculties of arts, economics, and social studies. The accommodation required for these departments subdivides into two categories, the lecture theatres common to all departments and the departments themselves. These requirements, when considered in relationship to the site and its relationship to the other buildings in the immediate vicinity, suggested that the lecture theatres should be below ground level and the departments planned above in a rectangular tower block. This disposition ensured that there would be a minimum area of site built on at courtyard level and allowed the tower block to become the climax of the central university precinct, with the square planned library and the long low west chemistry building completing the architectural composition proposed in the competition scheme.

The pooled lecture theatres are all planned below ground level, six on the lower ground floor and three on the floor immediately below with easy and direct access from the main entrance on the ground floor.

The ground floor is the entrance floor, and as such has been left free of accommodation. At mezzanine level there is a covered link to the library and on the first floor the administration. On the top four floors is the department of architecture and on the floors below are planned the faculty departments. As far as possible, departments are planned on one floor and cognate departments are either alongside or immediately above or below each other. Each department also generally follows a similar floor pattern, with staff rooms on the narrow south side and the seminar, lecture rooms, and libraries on the wider north side. On all floors the centre of the building is occupied by the circulation and service core; two seventeen-passenger lifts serve all floors, a smaller passenger lift serves from the thirteenth to the eighteenth floor, and a paternoster runs from the lower ground floor to floor thirteen.

L'un des éléments importants du programme qu'avaient à prendre en compte les propositions pour l'aménagement de la zone centrale de l'Université, était que le plan-masse devait comprendre une particularité dominante, un point focal. C'est le rôle que joue la tour abritant la Faculté des Lettres et des Sciences économiques et sociales. Les installations propres à ces départements se répartissent en deux catégories: les amphithéâtres communs à tous les départements d'une part, ces départements eux-mêmes d'autre part. Ces besoins, rapportés aux caractéristiques du terrain et aux relations de la Faculté avec les autres bâtiments implantés dans son voisinage immédiat, ont conduit à préconiser des amphithéâtres enterrés, et des départements d'études situés au dessus dans un immeuble-tour rectangulaire. Cette disposition permet qu'il n'y ait qu'un minimum de terrain construit au niveau du sol et fait de l'immeuble-tour le point culminant de l'enceinte universitaire, l'immeuble carré de la bibliothèque et le long corps bas du bâtiment Ouest des départements de chimie complétant la composition architecturale qui avait été présentée au concours.

Les amphithéâtres ont donc été groupés en dessous du niveau du sol, six au premier sous-sol et trois au deuxième sous-sol, avec un accès direct aisé depuis l'entrée principale au rez-de-chaussée de la Faculté.

Le rez-de-chaussée est le niveau d'accès, et à ce titre il est pratiquement dépourvu d'installations et d'équipements. Au niveau de la mezzanine une galerie couverte conduit à la bibliothèque; le premier étage est réservé à l'administration. Les quatre étages supérieurs contiennent le département d'architecture, et les étages intermédiaires les autres départements. On a autant que possible cherché à ce qu'un département donné soit distribué sur un même étage, et que des départements apparentés soient installés côte à côte ou juste en dessus ou en dessous les uns des autres. Les départements ont aussi, généralement, une distribution analogue, les salles de travail étant au Sud sur le côté étroit, et les pièces destinées aux groupes de travail, conférences et bibliothèques étant sur le côté plus large orienté au Nord. Le centre de chaque étage est occupé par le noyau de circulation et de services; deux ascenseurs d'une capacité de dix-sept personnes desservent tous les étages; un ascenseur plus petit s'y ajoute entre le treizième et le dixhuitième étage et un monte-charge circule du dernier sous-sol au treizième étage.

Zu den wichtigsten Faktoren, welch die Planung der zentralen Neubauten bestimmten, gehörte die Absicht, einen Schwerpunkt zu setzen. Diese Rolle erfüllt das Hochhaus für die Fakultäten Kunst, Wirtschafts- und Sozialwissenschaften. Die für diese Abteilungen benötigten Räume lassen sich in zwei Kategorien aufteilen: Vorlesungsräume, die allen Abteilungen dienen, und die Institutsräume selbst. Diese Anforderungen legten – unter Berücksichtigung der Grundstückssituation und der anderen, unmittelbar benachbarten Bauten – nahe, die Vorlesungssäle unter Eingangsniveau zu legen und die Abteilungen in einem quaderförmigen Hochhaus darüber unterzubringen. Diese Anordnung ermöglichte, nur einen minimalen Bereich des Geländes auf Eingangsniveau zu überbauen. Das Hochhaus ist Höhepunkt des zentralen Universitätsbereiches, der zusammen mit dem geplanten quadratischen Bibliotheksbau und dem langen, niedrigen Chemiegebäude im Westen die architektonische Komposition des Wettbewerbsentwurfes vervollständigt.

Die Vorlesungssäle sind alle unter Geländeniveau zusammengefaßt, sechs im unteren Erdgeschoß und drei im Geschoß unmittelbar darunter mit direktem Zugang vom Eingangsgeschoß.

Das Erdgeschoß dient nur als Eingangsgeschoß. Vom Zwischengeschoß führt ein überdachter Verbindungsgang zur Bibliothek. Im ersten Obergeschoß befindet sich die Verwaltung. Die obersten vier Geschosse nimmt die Architekturabteilung ein, in den darunterliegenden Stockwerken sind die anderen Fakultäten untergebracht. Soweit möglich, wurden die Abteilungen jeweils auf einem Stock zusammengefaßt, die Abteilungen verwandter Disziplinen nebeneinander oder unmittelbar über- oder untereinander angeordnet. Jede Abteilung hat etwa das gleiche Grundrißsystem mit Arbeitsräumen auf der schmalen Südseite und Seminar-, Vorlesungsräumen und Bibliothek auf der breiteren Nordseite. In allen Geschossen liegt der Verkehrs- und Servicekern im Mittelpunkt des Gebäudes; zwei Aufzüge für je 17 Personen bedienen alle Stockwerke, ein kleinerer Personenaufzug führt vom 13. zum 18. Geschoß und ein Paternoster vom Untergeschoß bis zum 13. Stock.

Typical floor plan
1. Entrance and lift lobby 2. WC 3. Library 4. Administration 5. Laboratories and workrooms 6. Seminar 7. Conference room

Plan-type d'étage
1. Entrée et vestibule des ascenseurs 2. WC 3. Bibliothèque 4. Administration 5. Laboratoires et salles de travail 6. Groupes de travail 7. Salle de conférence

Grundriß Normalgeschoß
1. Eingangs- und Aufzugshalle 2. WC 3. Bibliothek 4. Verwaltung 5. Institute und Arbeitsräume 6 Seminarräume 7. Konferenzraum

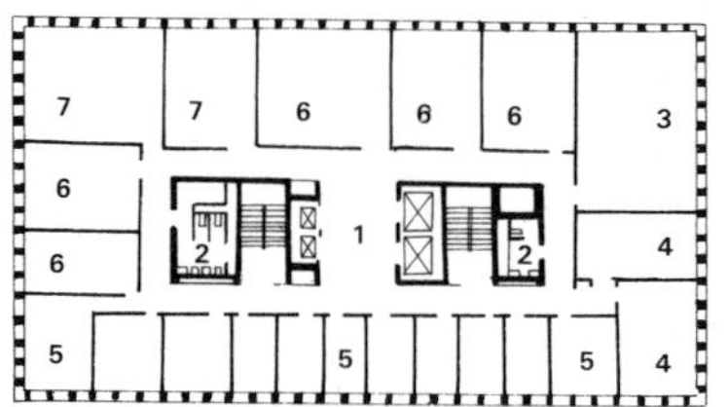

Lower ground floor plan
1. Entrance and lift lobby 2. Cloakroom 3. WC 4. Service ducts 5. Lecture theatres 6. Projection room 7. Stage 8. Terrace

Plan du premier sous-sol
1. Entrée et vestibule des ascenseurs 2. Vestiaire 3. WC 4. Galerie technique 5. Amphithéâtres 6. Salle de projection 7. Scène 8. Terrasse

Grundriß Untergeschoß
1. Eingangs- und Aufzugshalle 2. Garderobe 3. WC 4. Versorgungsschächte 5. Vorlesungssäle 6. Projektionsraum 7. Bühne 8. Terrasse

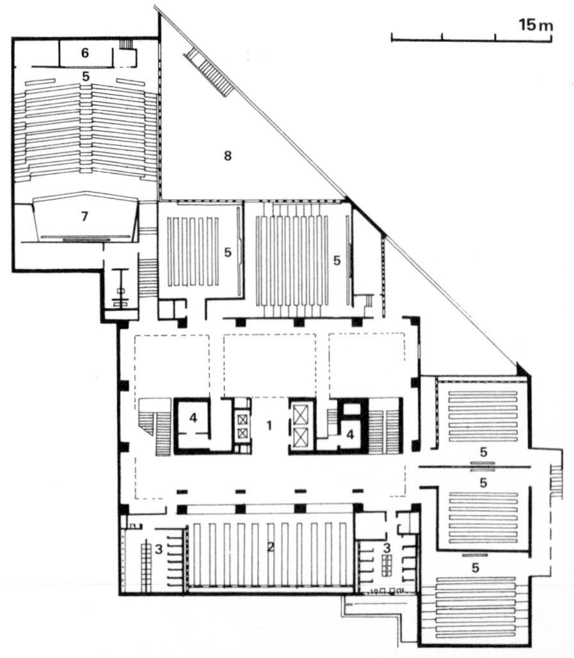

7 University of Sheffield

University House 1962

Unlike so many of the other buildings in the central area, most of the rooms in University House have an individual character which can be expressed elevationally inasmuch as they vary greatly in both area and height. The two large dining halls are above each other, each with double floor heights, and the planning alongside these rooms of four floors of normal height accommodation required that a bold external treatment be adopted. The top floor of this five-storey block is occupied by the senior common room club; provision has been made for the addition in the future of a sixth floor for the technical and clerical staff club.

A la différence de tant d'autres bâtiments de la zone centrale de l'Université, la plupart des pièces de la Maison Universitaire présentent un caractère d'individualité qui peut s'exprimer en élévation, dans la mesure où les dimensions de ces pièces varient autant en surface qu'en hauteur. Les deux grands réfectoires sont installés l'un au dessus de l'autre, chacun occupant en hauteur deux niveaux, et le long de ce bloc on a prévu quatre étages de pièces de hauteur normale, ce qui exigeait qu'un parti hardi soit adopté pour le traitement des façades. Le cinquième et dernier étage est occupé par l'association des professeurs; on a ménagé la possibilité d'ajouter ultérieurement un sixième étage, destiné aux employés de l'Université.

Im Gegensatz zu zahlreichen anderen Gebäuden im zentralen Bereich haben die meisten Räume im University House individuellen Charakter, der sich in der Fassade ausdrückt, da sie in Fläche und Höhe stark variieren. Die beiden großen, zweigeschossigen Eßsäle liegen übereinander. Die Planung neben diesen Räumen auf vier Geschossen forderte eine unkonventionelle äußere Gestaltung. Das oberste Stockwerk des fünfgeschossigen Baues nimmt der Dozenten-Klubraum ein; für später vorgesehen ist ein zusätzliches sechstes Geschoß für die Klubs der Techniker und der Theologen.

8 College of Education, Loughborough, Leicestershire

Leicestershire Education Committee 1965

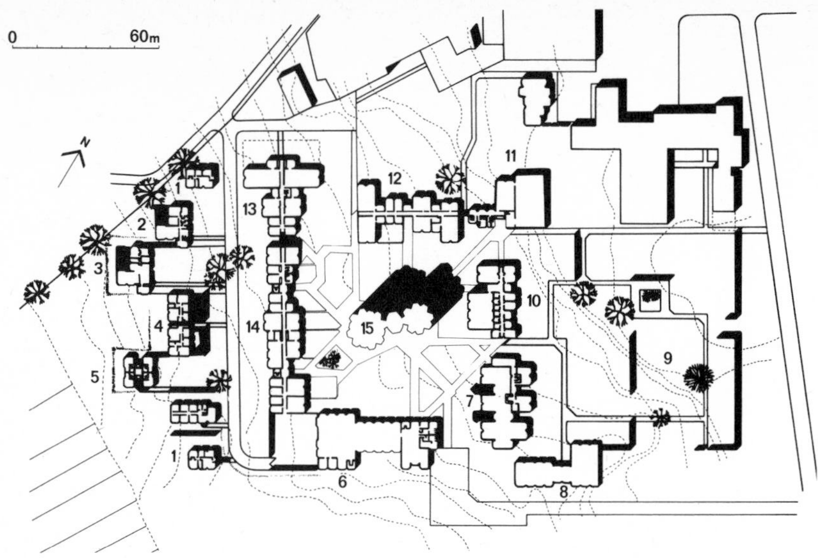

Site plan
1. Caretaker 2. Vice-principal 3. Principal 4. Tutors' flats 5. Domestic flats 6. Refectory and common rooms 7. Library 8. Study locker block 9. Walled garden 10. Music 11. Women's gymnasium 12. Arts and crafts 13. Workshops 14. Teaching 15. Study-bedroom tower

Plan d'ensemble
1. Concierge 2. Sous-directeur 3. Directeur 4. Appartements des professeurs directeurs d'études 5. Appartements des employés 6. Réfectoire et salles communes 7. Bibliothèque 8. Permanence et cabinets de travail individuels 9. Jardin clos 10. Bâtiment de musique 11. Gymnase des étudiantes 12. Travaux artistiques et manuels 13. Ateliers 14. Locaux d'enseignement 15. Tour-résidence des étudiants

Lageplan
1. Hausmeister 2. Stellvertretender Direktor 3. Direktor 4. Tutorenwohnungen 5. Personalwohnungen 6. Mensa und Gemeinschaftsräume 7. Bibliothek 8. Arbeitsräume mit Schließfächern 9. Garten 10. Musikraum 11. Turnhalle Studentinnen 12. Kunst und Kunsthandwerk 13. Werkstätten 14. Unterrichtsräume 15. Arbeits-/Schlafraum-Hochhaus

Study-bedroom tower/Tour résidence des étudiants/Arbeits-Schlafraum-Hochhaus

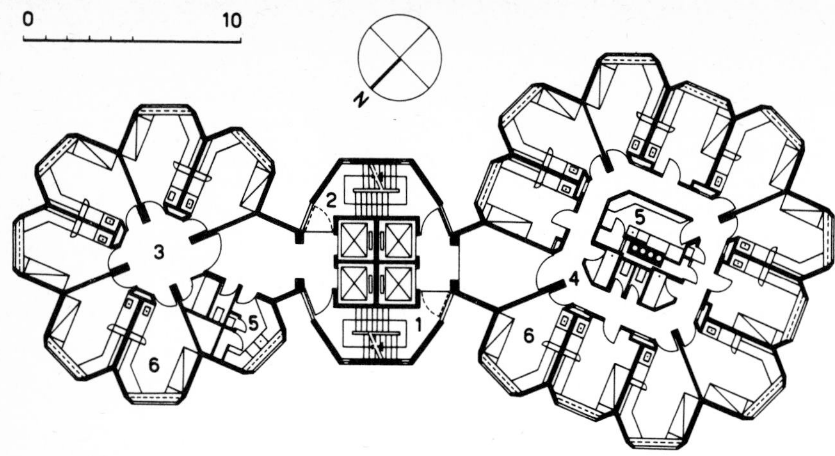

Typical floor plan
1. Men's stairs 2. Women's stairs 3. Hostel men 4. Hostel women 5. Utility room 6. Study bedroom

Plan-type d'étage
1. Escalier des hommes 2. Escalier des femmes 3. Résidence étudiants 4. Résidence étudiantes 5. Lingerie-office
6. Chambres d'étudiant

Grundriß Normalgeschoß
1. Treppe weiblicher Trakt 2. Treppe männlicher Trakt
3. Studentenwohnheim 4. Studentinnenwohnheim
5. Wirtschaftsraum 6. Arbeits-/Schlafraum

The extensions to the teachers' training college at Loughborough form part of the educational complex planned on a site on the south-west outskirts of the town, and which includes a college of advanced technology, and a college of further education. The college is primarily for the training of teachers for general classroom subjects with either handicraft or physical education as a specialist subject. The new buildings house 600 men and 300 women students and the new residential accommodation has study-bedrooms for 100 men and 200 women. Besides general classrooms there are workshops, art, craft, and music rooms, a gymnasium, library, and refectory and also residential accommodation for teaching and domestic staff.

To preserve as much land as possible for playing fields and to assure the college a more distinctive place in the educational complex, the student residential accommodation comprising a series of similar recurring units was planned in a tower block with the teaching accommodation planned around it in single- or double-storey buildings forming an informal court with the tower rising up from the centre, an arrangement which allows easy access for the students to all parts of the college. The bed-sitting rooms, arranged in two 'petal' plans and constructed of large storey-high precast concrete units, one twenty-two and the other eighteen floors high, are linked by a vertical circulation core with four lifts, two for each of the towers, and two staircases, each serving one tower but both accessible from either tower in case of emergency.

Les extensions de l'école normale de Loughborough constituent une partie du complexe pédagogique implanté dans les faubourgs Sud-Ouest de la ville, qui comprend d'autre part une école technique supérieure et une école d'enseignement supérieur. L'école normale assure essentiellement la formation de professeurs d'enseignement général, dont la formation est complétée par une spécialisation soit dans les travaux manuels soit en éducation physique. Les nouveaux bâtiments hébergent 600 hommes et 300 femmes et les nouveaux locaux résidentiels offrent des chambres d'étudiants à 100 étudiants et 200 étudiantes. Outre les salles de classe, il y a des ateliers, des salles pour les travaux artistiques ou manuels, des salles de musique, un gymnase, une bibliothèque et un réfectoire ainsi que des logements pour les professeurs et les employés.

Afin de préserver le maximum de surface pour les terrains de sports, et de conférer à l'école normale une position marquante au sein du complexe pédagogique, les logements des étudiants ont été conçus comme une série d'éléments répétitifs rassemblés dans un immeuble-tour, et les locaux d'enseignement ont été disposés à leur base dans des bâtiments à un ou deux niveaux, formant une trame assez lâche au centre de laquelle s'élève la tour – ce qui assure aux étudiants un accès commode à toutes les parties de l'école. Les chambres des étudiants s'insèrent dans un « plan en pétales », et constituent de grandes « unités de préfabrication » en béton, l'une haute de vingt-deux et l'autre de dix-huit étages, reliées par un noyau vertical de circulation comprenant quatre ascenseurs, deux pour chacune des unités, et deux escaliers, chacun desservant une unité mais étant accessible de l'autre en cas d'urgence.

Die Erweiterung der Pädagogischen Hochschule in Loughborough ist Teil eines auf einem Gelände im südwestlichen Außenbezirk der Stadt geplanten Ausbildungskomplexes, zu dem außerdem ein Technikum sowie eine Schule für berufliche Weiterbildung gehören. Das College dient vorwiegend der Ausbildung von Lehrern für allgemeine Fächer mit Handarbeit oder Sport als Spezialfach. Die neuen Gebäude können 600 männliche und 300 weibliche Studenten aufnehmen; Unterbringungsmöglichkeiten in Arbeits-/Schlafräumen für 100 Studenten und 200 Studentinnen sind vorhanden. Neben allgemeinen Unterrichtsbereichen sind Werkstätten, Kunsterziehungs-, Werk- und Musikräume, eine Turnhalle, Bibliothek, Mensa und Wohnräume für Lehr- und Hauspersonal eingeplant.

Um soviel Flächen wie möglich für Sportplätze freizuhalten und dem College einen bevorzugten Platz im Gesamtkomplex zu sichern, wurden die Studentenwohnungen als sich wiederholende Einheiten in einem Hochhauskörper angeordnet und die Unterrichtsräume in ein- oder zweigeschossigen Trakten in lockerer Bebauung mit dem Hochhaus im Zentrum – eine Gruppierung, die den Studenten leichten Zugang zu allen Teilen des Colleges ermöglicht. Die Schlaf-/Wohnräume aus großen, geschoßhohen, vorgefertigten Betonelementen sind in zwei Körpern mit sternförmigen Grundrissen von 22 und 18 Geschossen angeordnet und durch vertikale Verkehrskerne mit je zwei Aufzügen und zwei Treppenhäusern, die im Notfall von beiden Trakten zugänglich sind, miteinander verbunden.

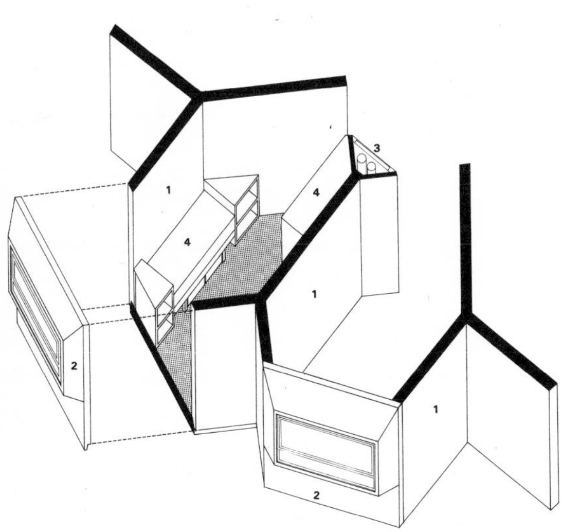

Detail of typical study bedroom
1. Precast concrete structural wall 2. Precast concrete window panel 3. Vertical service duct 4. Built-in bed and fittings

Détail de la chambre d'étudiant
1. Mur porteur en béton préfabriqué 2. Panneau de fenêtre en béton préfabriqué 3. Gaine technique verticale 4. Literie et garniture encastrées

Detail eines Standard-Arbeits-/Schlafraums
1. Vorgefertigte tragende Betonwand 2. Vorgefertigtes Beton-Fensterelement 3. Vertikaler Versorgungsschacht
4. Eingebautes Bett und Einrichtungsgegenstände

9 Women's Royal Army Corps College, Camberley, Surrey

Department of the Environment 1965

The site of approximately 5 hectares was previously occupied by the Royal Albert Orphanage for Boys, which has been demolished with the exception of the assembly hall now incorporated in the new development in an identical capacity. The accommodation falls into four main categories, which have been disposed around the centrally sited parade ground and playing fields: the administrative section is as near the entrance of the camp as possible, the training wings are reasonably central and are accessible to the various groups of personnel, but entirely separate from recreational and sleeping areas, the officers' living accommodation is separate from the main circulation, the other ranks' accommodation is similarly separate from the working areas and has its own environment with easy access from the entrance without passing through the main part of the camp.

There is accommodation for thirty student officers, fifty officer cadets, and sixty other ranks students, also for 150 training and camp maintenance staff.

Le terrain de l'école d'instruction des Auxiliaires féminines de l'armée, d'une superficie d'environ 5,2 hectares, était initialement occupé par un orphelinat de garçons (Royal Albert Orphanage for Boys); celui-ci a été démoli à l'exception de la salle de réunion qu'on a incorporée dans le nouveau projet en lui conservant une capacité inchangée. Les installations peuvent être classées dans quatre catégories principales distribuées autour du terrain de parade et des aires de jeux situés au centre: la section administrative est placée au plus près de l'entrée du camp; les bâtiments d'instruction sont – logiquement – centraux et accessibles aux diverses catégories de personnel mais entièrement séparés des zones de détente et des chambres; les résidences des officiers sont à l'écart de la circulation principale, et de même les installations résidentielles pour les autres grades sont séparées des zones de travail et ont leur environnement propre, avec un accès facile depuis l'entrée qui évite de traverser la majeure partie du camp.

Les installations peuvent recevoir trente aspirants, cinquante élèves-officiers et soixante élèves des autres grades, ainsi qu'un personnel d'instruction et de maintenance de 150 personnes.

Auf dem etwa 5 ha großen Grundstück stand früher das Royal Albert-Waisenhaus für Knaben, das – mit Ausnahme der Aula, die jetzt mit gleicher Nutzung in die neue Bebauung integriert ist – abgerissen wurde. Die Anlage besteht aus vier Baugruppen, die um den zentral gelegenen Paradeplatz und die Sportplätze angeordnet sind. Der Verwaltungstrakt wurde so nahe wie möglich an den Eingang zum Camp gelegt, die Unterrichtstrakte liegen verhältnismäßig zentral und für alle Gruppen zugänglich, aber völlig getrennt von den Freizeit- und Schlafbereichen. Die Wohnräume der Offiziere liegen abseits vom Verkehrsbereich, die Wohnräume der anderen Dienstgrade sind ebenfalls getrennt von den Arbeitsbereichen mit eigenem Freiraum und leichten Zugang vom Eingang, ohne daß der Hauptteil des Camps zu passieren ist.

Insgesamt können 30 junge Offiziere, 50 Offizierskadetten und 60 Anwärter für andere Ränge sowie 150 Ausbilder und Unterhaltspersonal aufgenommen werden.

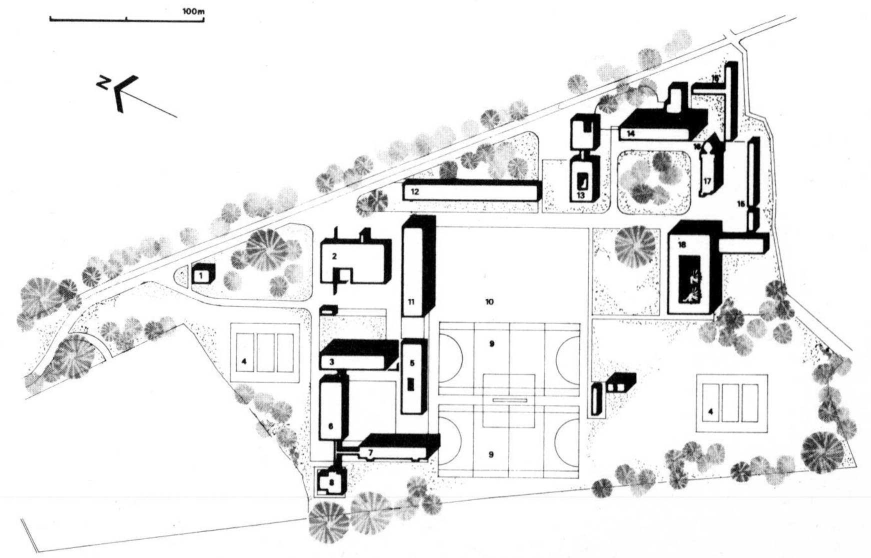

Site plan
1. Guard house 2. Headquarters 3. Rank and file barracks 4. Tennis courts 5. Junior ranks club 6. Rank and file mess 7. Students' barracks 8. Medical wing 9. Playing fields and squash courts 10. Parade ground 11. Gymnasium and instruction area 12. Training wing 13. Warrant officers and sergeants 14. Officer cadets 15. Garages 16. Chapel 17. Assembly hall 18. Officers' mess

Plan d'ensemble
1. Salle de garde 2. Quartier-général 3. Baraquements de la troupe 4. Courts de tennis 5. Club des jeunes gradés 6. Mess de la troupe 7. Baraquements des aspirants 8. Service médical 9. Terrains de jeux et courts de squash 10. Terrain de parade 11. Gymnase et zone d'instruction 12. Bâtiments d'instruction 13. Logements adjudants et sergents 14. Logements élèves-officiers 15. Garages 16. Chapelle 17. Salle de réunion 18. Mess des officiers

Lageplan
1. Wache 2. Hauptquartier 3. Mannschaftskasernen 4. Tennisplätze 5. Klub für die unteren Ränge 6. Mannschaftsmesse 7. Kadettenkasernen 8. Sanitätstrakt 9. Sport- und Spielplätze 10. Paradeplatz 11. Turnhalle und Trainingsbereich 12. Unterrichtstrakt 13. Feldwebel und Unteroffiziere 14. Offizierskadetten 15. Garagen 16. Kapelle 17. Versammlungshalle 18. Offiziersmesse

Officers' mess/Mess des officiers/Offiziersmesse

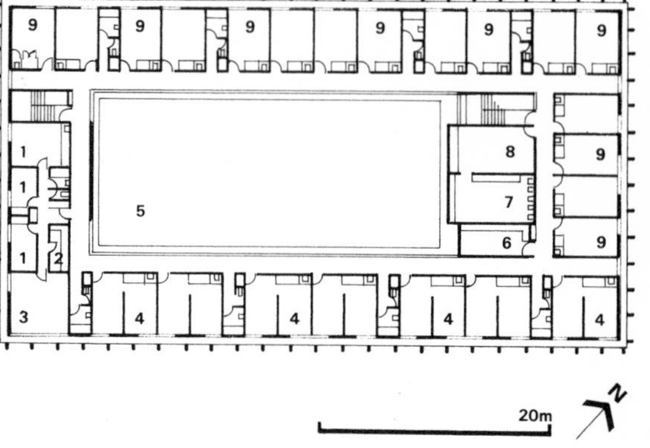

Officers' mess: second floor plan
1. Bedroom 2. Kitchen 3. Lounge 4. Typical field officer's flat 5. Courtyard 6. Baggage 7. Drying 8. Ironing 9. Junior officers room

Mess des officiers: plan du second étage
1. Chambre 2. Cuisine 3. Foyer 4. Appartement d'officier supérieur 5. Cour intérieure 6. Resserre à bagages 7. Séchoirs 8. Buanderie (repassage) 9. Chambre d'officier subalterne

Offiziersmesse: Grundriß zweites Obergeschoß
1. Schlafraum 2. Küche 3. Aufenthaltsraum 4. Standard-Offizierswohnung 5. Innenhof 6. Gepäck 7. Trockenraum 8. Bügelraum 9. Offiziersanwärter

Courtyard, officers' mess/Cour intérieure, mess des officiers/ Innenhof, Offiziersmesse

Warrant officers and sergeants, officer cadets, residential accommodation/Logements adjudants et sergents, logements élèves-officiers/Wohnquartiere, Feldwebel und Unteroffiziere, Offizierskadetten

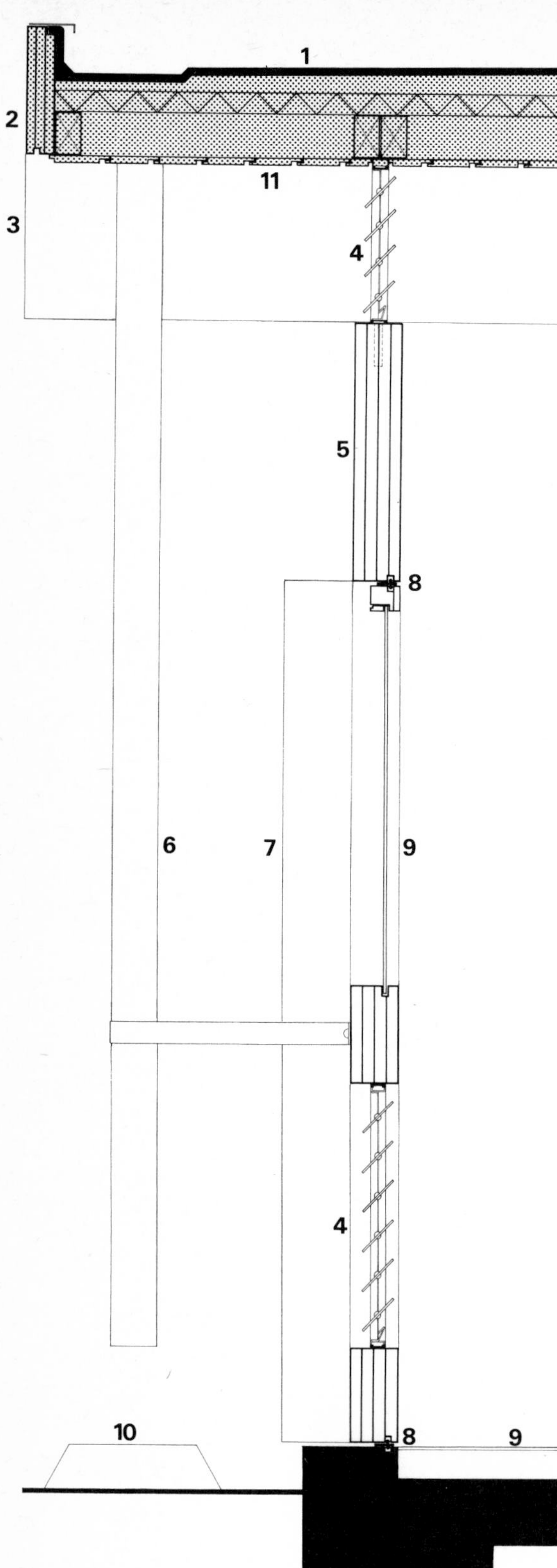

External wall detail
1. Asphalt roof and perimeter gutter 2. 300 × 75 Laminated fascia in Columbian pine 3. 350 × 75 Laminated cross beams 4. Adjustable glass louvres 5. 600 × 75 Laminated transfer beam 6. Free standing extruded aluminium RWP 7. 275 × 75 Laminated columns 8. Neoprene gasket 9. Timber window unit in Columbian pine 10. Precast concrete gulley unit 11. Boarded soffittes in Columbian pine

Détail du mur extérieur
1. Toiture asphaltée et cheneau périphérique 2. Bandeau de 300 × 75 habillage en pin de Colombie 3. Poutres transversales de 350 sur 75 habillées bois 4. Persiennes en verre mobiles 5. Poutres de reprise de 600 × 75 habillées bois 6. Ouvertures extérieures autoporteuses en aluminium extrudé 7. Poteaux de 275 × 75 habillés bois 8. Joints de néoprène 9. Fenêtre bois en pin de Colombie 10. Retombées revêtues de pin de Colombie

Außenwanddetail
1. Asphaltdach und umlaufende Dachrinne 2. 300×75 verleimte Brüstung aus kolumbianischer Fichte 3. 350×75 verleimter Unterzug 4. Verstellbare Glaslamellen 5. 600×75 verleimtes Verbindungselement 6. Aufgehängtes, stranggepreßtes Aluminiumelement 7. 275×75 verleimte Stützen 8. Neoprenedichtung 9. Fensterelement aus kolumbianischer Fichte 10. Vorgefertigter Ablauf aus Beton 11. Unterseite aus kolumbianischer Fichte

External wall detail
1. Asphalt roof and perimeter gutter 2. 300 × 75 Laminated fascia in Columbian pine 3. 300 × 75 Laminated cross beams 4. Adjustable glass louvres 5. 225 cavity brickwork 6. Finished floor level

Détail du mur extérieur
1. Toiture asphaltée et cheneau périphérique 2. Bandeau de 300 × 75 habillage en pin de Colombie 3. Poutres transversales de 300 × 75 habillées bois 4. Persiennes en verre mobiles 5. Mur double de 225 avec vide d'air ventilé 6. Niveau fini

Außenwanddetail
1. Asphaltdach und umlaufende Dachrinne 2. 300 × 75 verleimte Brüstung aus kolumbianischer Fichte 3. 300 × 75 verleimter Unterzug 4. Verstellbare Glaslamellen 5. 225 Hohlziegelmauerwerk 6. Oberkante Fußboden

10 Sevenoaks Hospital, Kent

Outpatients' and Maternity Departments

South-East Metropolitan Regional Hospital Board 1965

This project is the first stage in the development of the present Sevenoaks Hospital into a small district general hospital, and comprises an out-patients department with consultants' suites and treatment rooms on the ground floor and a maternity unit with twenty-six beds on the first. Both floors are planned on the race-track principle with services and sanitary accommodation in an artificially lit and ventilated core and all the main rooms on the perimeter.

The structural frame, cladding frame, and external cladding are fully integrated and present an original method of construction. The smaller cladding steel members were welded to the structural steel frame, and the whole of the external curtain-wall treatment, whether clear or opaque white glass panels, glazed direct to the structure by means of neoprene gaskets.

Ce projet représente le premier stade de la transformation de l'actuel hôpital de Sevenoaks en un petit hôpital général de district. Il comprend un service de consultations externes avec l'ensemble des pièces affectées aux médecins consultants et des salles de soins au rez-de-chaussée, et une maternité de trente-six lits au premier étage. Les deux étages ont été conçus sur le principe de la double circulation: les services et les installations sanitaires à l'intérieur dans un noyau climatisé et éclairé à la lumière artificielle, et toutes les pièces principales sur le périmètre.

La structure, le support de bardage et le bardage sont entièrement intégrés et présentent une méthode de construction originale. Les plus petits éléments métalliques du bardage ont été soudés à la structure principale, et l'ensemble du mur-rideau de revêtement extérieur (panneaux de verre clair ou blanc opaque) est encastré directement dans la structure au moyen de joints de néoprène.

Dieses Projekt ist der erste Abschnitt der Erweiterung des gegenwärtigen Hospitals von Sevenoaks in ein kleines allgemeines Distriktskrankenhaus. Er umfaßt eine Ambulanz mit Untersuchungs- und Behandlungsräumen im Erdgeschoß sowie eine Entbindungsstation mit 26 Betten im Obergeschoß. Beide Geschosse sind dreibündig angelegt mit Versorgung und sanitären Einrichtungen im künstlich belichteten und belüfteten Kern, alle übrigen Räume sind außenliegend.

Die tragende Außenwandkonstruktion und die ausfüllenden Elemente sind voll integriert und stellen ein besonderes Konstruktionsprinzip dar. Die kleineren Stahlelemente der Außenwand sind an den tragenden Stahlrahmen angeschweißt, und der gesamte Curtain-Wall aus durchsichtigen oder weissen, undurchsichtigen Glasplatten ist mit Neoprene-Dichtungen unmittelbar an die Konstruktion angeschlossen.

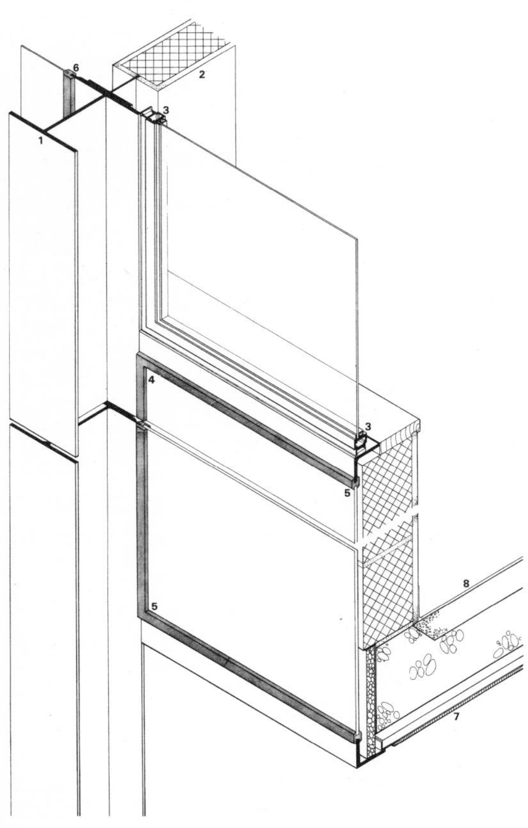

Detail of integrated structural window wall
1. Structural R.S.J. column 2. Partition 3. Opening window subframe 4. White glass spandril panel 5. Neoprene gasket 6. Fixed glazing neoprene to structural steel 7. Asbestos soffitte 8. Finished floor level

Détail du mur-rideau intégré
1. Poteau de structure (R.S.J.) 2. Cloison 3. Dormant de fenêtre 4. Panneau de remplissage en verre blanc 5. Joint de néoprène 6. Joint de néoprène entre la structure acier et les vitrages fixes 7. Coffrage de retombée en amiante-ciment 8. Niveau fini

Detail der tragenden Fensterwand
1. Doppel-T-Stütze 2. Trennwandelement 3. Fensterrahmen 4. Vorgehängte Milchglasplatte 5. Neoprenedichtung 6. Neopreneanschluß 7. Asbestunterseite 8. Oberkante Fußboden

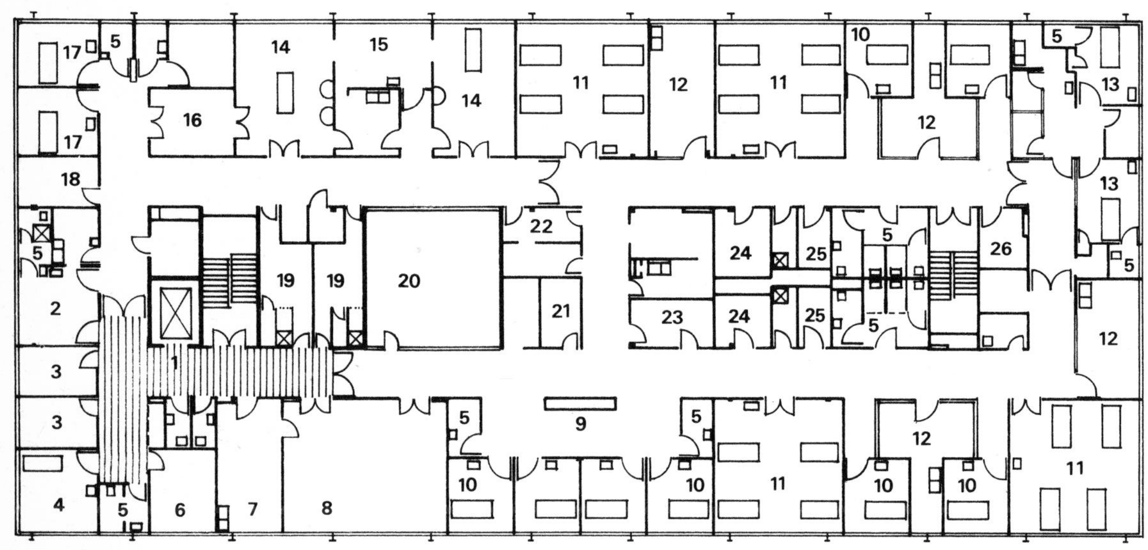

First floor plan
1. Entrance and lift 2. Reception 3. Sister 4. Consulting 5. WC 6. Nurses' cloaks 7. Kitchen 8. Day dining room 9. Nurses' station 10. Single room 11. Four-bed ward 12. Nursery 13. Isolation 14. Delivery room 15. Sterilizing and wash up area 16. Anaesthetic 17. First stage rooms 18. Office 19. Changing rooms 20. Light well 21. Milk preparation 22. Laundry 23. Utility area 24. Bathrooms 25. Linen 26. Stores

Plan du premier étage
1. Entrée et ascenseur 2. Réception 3. Infirmière-chef 4. Consultation 5. WC 6. Vestiaires des infirmières 7. Cuisine 8. Salle à manger 9. Poste d'infirmières 10. Chambre individuelle 11. Chambre à 4 lits 12. Nursery 13. Pièce d'isolation 14. Salle d'accouchement 15. Stérilisation et nettoyage 16. Anesthésie 17. Salles de travail 18. Bureau 19. Cabines d'habillage 20. Patio 21. Biberonnerie 22. Blanchisserie 23. Dépôt sale 24. Salles de bain 25. Lingerie 26. Réserves/magasins

Grundriß Obergeschoß
1. Eingang und Aufzug 2. Aufnahme 3. Oberin 4. Sprechzimmer 5. WC 6. Schwesternzimmer 7. Küche 8. Eßsaal 9. Stationszimmer 10. Einzelzimmer 11. Vier-Betten-Station 12. Kinderzimmer 13. Isolation 14. Kreißsaal 15. Sterilisationsraum 16. Anästhesie 17. Wehenzimmer 18. Büro 19. Umkleideräume 20. Lichthof 21. Milchküche 22. Wäscherei 23. Abstellraum 24. Badezimmer 25. Wäsche 26. Lager

20 m

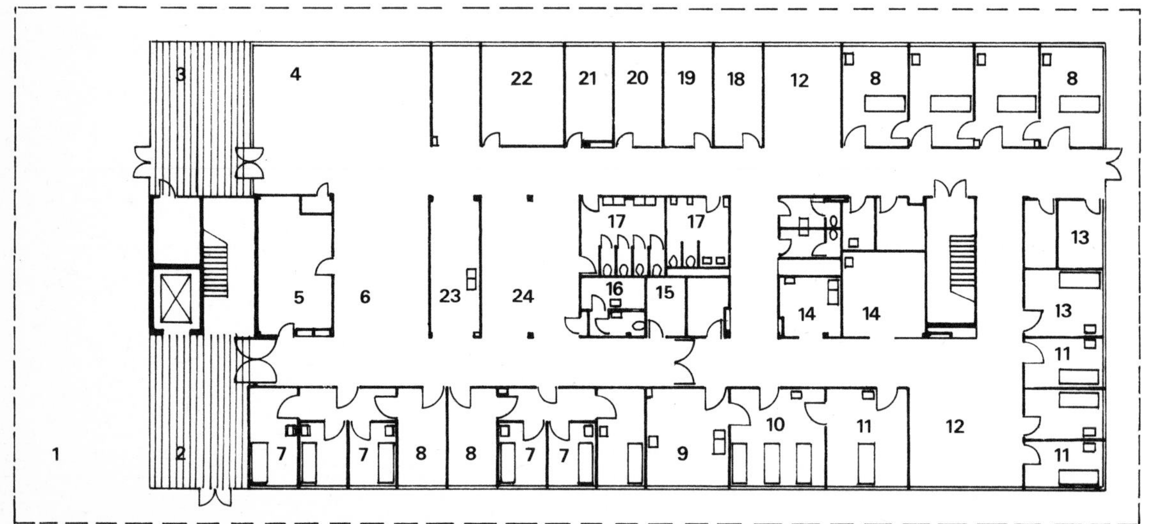

Ground floor plan
1. Pram park 2. Maternity entrance and lift 3. Outpatients entrance lobby 4. Waiting area 5. Records 6. Reception 7. Examination rooms 8. Consulting rooms 9. Plaster room 10. Recovery room 11. Treatment area 12. Sub-waiting area 13. Surgical fittings 14. Utility area 15. Weighing room 16. Test room 17. WC 18. Health visitor 19. Almoner 20. Sister 21. Medical staff 22. Typists 23. Buffet 24. Sub-waiting and demonstration

Plan du rez-de-chaussée
1. Emplacement pour les landaux 2. Entrée de la maternité et ascenseur 3. Vestibule d'entrée des consultants externes 4. Hall d'attente 5. Archives 6. Réception 7. Salles d'examen 8. Salles de consultation 9. Salle des plâtres 10. Salle de repos 11. Salle de soins 12. Salle d'attente 13. Appareillage chirurgical 14. Dépôt sale 15. Salle de pesée 16. Salle de tests 17. WC 18. Assistante sociale 19. Aumônier 20. Infirmière-chef 21. Personnel médical 22. Secrétariat 23. Buffet 24. Salle d'attente et de démonstration

Grundriß Erdgeschoß
1. Kinderwagen-Abstellraum 2. Eingang und Aufzug Entbindungsstation 3. Eingangshalle Ambulanz 4. Wartebereich 5. Akten 6. Aufnahme 7. Untersuchungsräume 8. Sprechzimmer 9. Gipsraum 10. Ruheraum 11. Behandlungsbereich 12. Warteraum 13. Chirurgische Instrumente 14. Abstellraum 15. Wiegezimmer 16. Testlabor 17. WC 18. Sozialfürsorgerin 19. Sozialpfleger 20. Oberin 21. Medizinisches Personal 22. Sekretariat 23. Büffet 24. Warteraum

11 District General Hospital, Hillingdon, Middlesex

North-West Metropolitan Regional Hospital Board 1966

The earliest hospital buildings date back to 1747, and with many additions built since, are now due for replacement. The hospital will eventually have 700 beds; Stage 1, which includes the majority of the ancillary departments planned in a three-storey podium around three internal courtyards, will have 210 beds in seven wards.

As the nearest hospital, it serves London Heathrow Airport and the casualty department has been planned to deal with exceptional emergencies. This proximity also restricted the height of the building to 45m.

Les plus anciens bâtiments de cet hôpital datent de 1747; ils sont à remplacer, de même que les nombreux ajouts qui ont été construits depuis. Le nouvel hôpital aura probablement 700 lits. La première phase, qui rassemble la majorité des services auxiliaires dans un podium de trois niveaux entourant trois cours intérieures, comprendra 210 lits répartis dans sept unités de soins.

Etant l'hôpital le plus proche de l'Aéroport Londres-Heathrow, il le dessert et le service des urgences a été conçu de manière à pouvoir faire face à une ampleur exceptionnelle de celles-ci. Cette proximité a également limité la hauteur du bâtiment à 45 m.

Die ersten Bauten dieses Krankenhauses stammen aus dem Jahre 1747 und sind, mit den zahlreichen, seither entstandenen Erweiterungen, jetzt zum Neubau fällig. Das Krankenhaus wird im Endstadium 700 Betten haben. Die erste Baustufe, welche die Mehrzahl der dienstleistenden Abteilungen umfaßt, ist als dreigeschossiges Podium um drei Innenhöfe geplant und wird 210 Betten in sieben Stationen aufnehmen.

Als nächstgelegenes Krankenhaus dient es dem Flugplatz London-Heathrow; die Unfallabteilung soll in Notfällen zur Verfügung stehen. Die Nähe des Flughafens beschränkte die Höhe der Bauten auf 45 m.

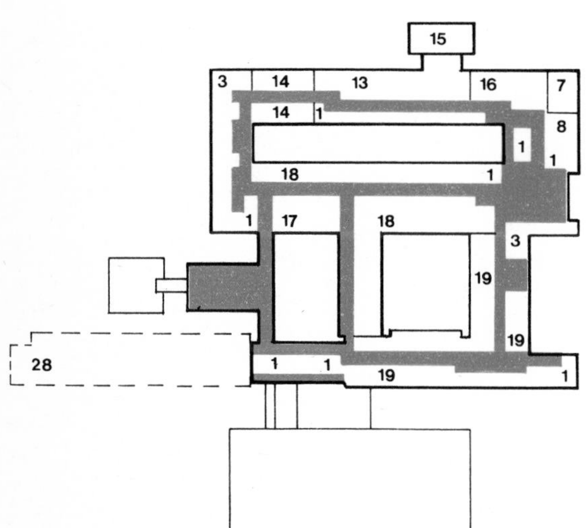

Ground floor plan/Rez-de-chaussée/Grundriß Erdgeschoß

Second to eighth floors plan/Du deuxième au huitième étage/ Grundriß zweites bis achtes Obergeschoß

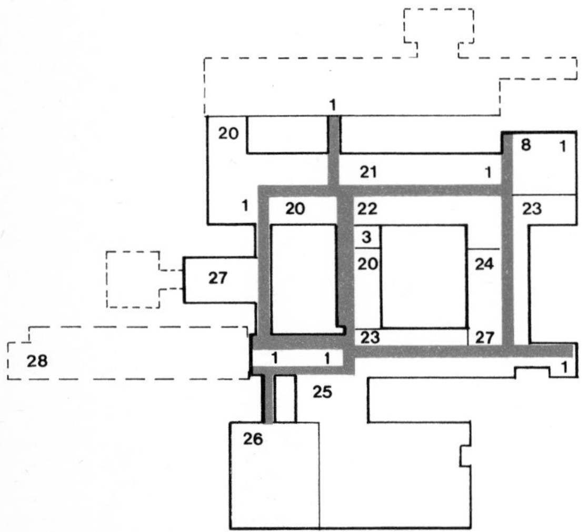

Lower ground floor plan/Premier sous-sol/ Grundriß Untergeschoß

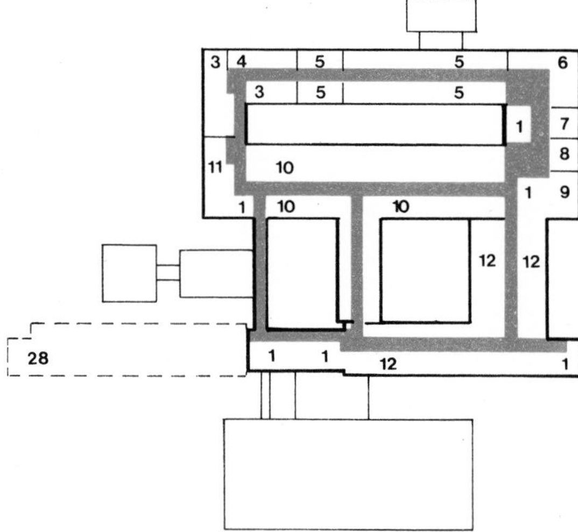

First floor plan/Premier étage/Grundriß Obergeschoß

1. Lift and stairs 2. Wards 3. Administration 4. ECG and clinical photography 5. Surgical medical clinics 6. ENT and ophthalmic clinic 7. Medical social workers 8. Records 9. Dental department 10. Operating theatre suite 11. Consultants' offices and library 12. Laboratories 13. Physiotherapy 14. Occupational therapy 15. Gymnasium 16. Fracture clinic 17. Doctors' changing room 18. X ray 19. Accidents and emergencies 20. Staff changing and dining room 21. Pharmacy 22. Central sterile supply 23. Stores 24. Mortuary 25. Kitchen 26. Dining room 27. Chapel 28. Future extension

1. Ascenseur ou escalier 2. Unités de soins 3. Administration 4. Electrocardiographie et exploration photo 5. Consultations médecine et chirurgie 6. Oto-rhino-laryngologie et ophtalmologie 7. Assistantes sociales médicales 8. Archives 9. Département dentaire 10. Ensemble des blocs opératoires 11. Bureau des médecins consultants et bibliothèque 12. Laboratoires 13. Physiothérapie 14. Rééducation fonctionnelle 15. Gymnase 16. Traitement des fractures 17. Vestiaires des médecins 18. Rayons X 19. Accidents et urgences 20. Vestiaires et salle à manger du personnel 21. Pharmacie 22. Stérilisation centrale 23. Réserves/magasins 24. Morgue 25. Cuisine 26. Salle à manger 27. Chapelle 28. Zone d'extension future

1. Aufzüge, Treppen 2. Stationsräume 3. Verwaltung 4. EKG und klinische Fotografie 5. Chirurgische und medizinische Klinik 6. Otorhino-Laryngologie und Augenklinik 7. Sozialpfleger 8. Akten 9. Zahnklinik 10. Operationsräume 11. Büros und Bibliothek 12. Laboratorien 13. Physiotherapie 14. Beschäftigungstherapie 15. Turnhalle 16. Bruchklinik 17. Umkleideraum Ärzte 18. Röntgen 19. Unfall- und Notaufnahme 20. Personalumkleide- und Eßraum 21. Apotheke 22. Zentrale Sterilisationsabteilung 23. Lager 24. Leichenhalle 25. Küche 26. Eßsaal 27. Kapelle 28. Geplante Erweiterung

Primary circulation

50m N

Site plan
1. Residential accommodation 2. Gymnasium 3. Physio and occupational therapy out-patient clinics 4. Operating theatres and X ray 5. Wards 6. Main entrance 7. Accident and emergency entrance 8. Maternity unit 9. Kitchen dining block 10. Nurses training unit 11. Car parking 12. Service yard

Plan d'ensemble
1. Blocs résidentiels 2. Gymnase 3. Cliniques de consultations externes de physiothérapie et de rééducation 4. Blocs opératoires et rayons X 5. Unités de soins 6. Entrée principale 7. Entrée des urgences et des accidents 8. Maternité 9. Bloc cuisine et repas 10. Ecole d'infirmières 11. Stationnement voitures 12. Cour de service

Lageplan
1. Wohngebäude 2. Gymnastikhalle 3. Physio- und Beschäftigungstherapie für ambulante Behandlung 4. Operationssäle und Röntgen 5. Stationen 6. Haupteingang 7. Unfall- und Notaufnahme 8. Entbindungsstation 9. Küche, Eßsaal 10. Schwesternausbildung 11. Parkplatz 12. Anlieferung

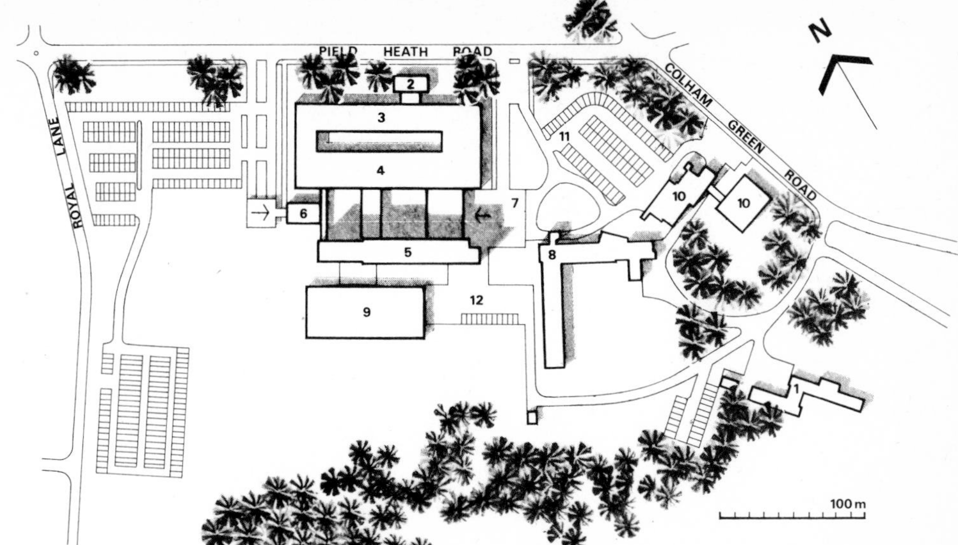

12 Royal Military College of Science, Shrivenham, Wiltshire

Department of the Environment 1968

The Rutherford Laboratory comprises three circular and linked buildings. The largest and central building is the nuclear science laboratory, of which three-quarters of the accommodation is 'active' and one-quarter 'non-active'. Access is by means of an underground tunnel which terminates in the centre core, from which a circular staircase rises to the ground and principal floor. The 'active' area can only be reached via two monitoring rooms and the 'non-active' area by two radial corridors. In the second circular building is the high-intensity radiation laboratory, which is approached by an enclosed corridor link from the central building about 20 m away. In the third and smallest of the circular buildings are the lecture theatre and demonstration hall.

Le Laboratoire de Rutherford comprend trois bâtiments circulaires reliés entre eux. Le plus vaste des trois, le bâtiment central, est le laboratoire des sciences nucléaires, dont les trois quarts des installations sont dans une zone « active », et le quart restant en zone « non-active ». On y accède par un tunnel souterrain qui aboutit dans le noyau central, d'où un escalier circulaire conduit au rez-de-chaussée qui est l'étage principal. On ne peut accéder à la zone active que par deux salles de contrôle et à la zone non-active que par deux corridors radiaux. Le second bâtiment circulaire abrite le laboratoire des radiations de haute intensité, auquel on accède depuis le bâtiment central, distant d'une vingtaine de mètres, par un corridor fermé. Le troisième bâtiment, le plus petit, abrite l'amphithéâtre et la salle de démonstration.

Das Rutherford Laboratorium besteht aus drei kreisförmigen, miteinander verbundenen Gebäuden. Der größte, zentrale Bau ist das Kernforschungslaboratorium, in dem drei Viertel der Räume „aktiv" und ein Viertel „nicht aktiv" sind. Der Zugang erfolgt durch einen unterirdischen Tunnel, der im zentralen Kern endet. Von dort aus führt ein kreisförmiges Treppenhaus zum Erdgeschoß, das zugleich Hauptgeschoß ist. Der „aktive" Bereich ist nur über zwei Monitorräume zu erreichen, der „nicht aktive" Bereich über zwei radiale Korridore. Im zweiten kreisförmigen Bau befindet sich das hochintensive Strahlenlaboratorium, das durch einen geschlossenen Korridor vom etwa 20 m entfernten Zentralgebäude zugänglich ist. Im dritten und kleinsten der Kreisbauten sind der Vorlesungssaal und die Demonstrationshalle untergebracht.

Nuclear science laboratory: ground floor
1. Tunnel to main entrance 2. Main lobby 3. Scientific back-up 4. Research 5. WC 6. Basic physics teaching laboratory 7. High level chemistry laboratory 8. Low level chemistry laboratory 9. Open court 10. Scientific demonstration 11. Reading and reference 12. Office and staff room 13. Dark rooms 14. Service entrance

Lecture and demonstration wing
15. Lobby 16. Demonstration hall 17. Store 18. Calorifier 19. Preparation room 20. Lecture room 21. WC

High intensity radiation wing
22. Special projects 23. Van de Graaf linear accelerator neutron generator 24. Radiation effects laboratory 25. Control laboratory 26. Equipment section

Rez-de-chaussée du laboratoire de sciences nucléaires
1. Tunnel de l'entrée principale 2. Vestibule principal (noyau central) 3. Logistique scientifique 4. Salles de recherche 5. WC 6. Laboratoire d'enseignement de physique générale 7. Laboratoire de chimie avancée 8. Laboratoire de chimie courante 9. Cour à ciel ouvert 10. Salle de démonstrations scientifiques 11. Salle de lecture et de répertoires scientifiques 12. Bureaux et administration du laboratoire 13. Chambres noires 14. Entrée de service

Aile de cours et de démonstration
15 Vestibule 16. Salle de démonstration 17. Magasin 18. Chaudière 19. Salle de préparation 20. Amphithéâtre 21. WC

Aile des radiations de haute intensité
22. Projets spéciaux 23. Générateur de neutrons à accélérateur linéaire de Van de Graaf 24. Laboratoire d'étude des effets des radiations 25. Laboratoire de contrôle 26. Matériel

Kernforschungslaboratorium: Erdgeschoß
1. Tunnel zum Haupteingang 2. Haupteingangshalle 3. Wissenschaftliche Mitarbeiter 4. Forschung 5. WC 6. Physiklaboratorium, Grundstufe 7. Chemie-Laboratorium, Unterstufe 8. Chemie-Laboratorium, Oberstufe 9. Hof 10. Wissenschaftliche Demonstrationen 11. Bibliothek 12. Büro und Personalraum 13. Dunkelkammer 14. Anlieferung

Vorlesungs- und Demonstrationstrakt
15. Eingangshalle 16. Demonstrationssaal 17. Abstellraum 18. Heizung 19. Präparationsraum 20. Vorlesungssaal 21. WC

Hochintensive Strahlenabteilung
22. Besondere Projekte 23. Van de Graaf-Akzelerations-Neutronen-Generator 24. Labor für Strahlenwirkung 25. Kontrollabor 26. Zubehör

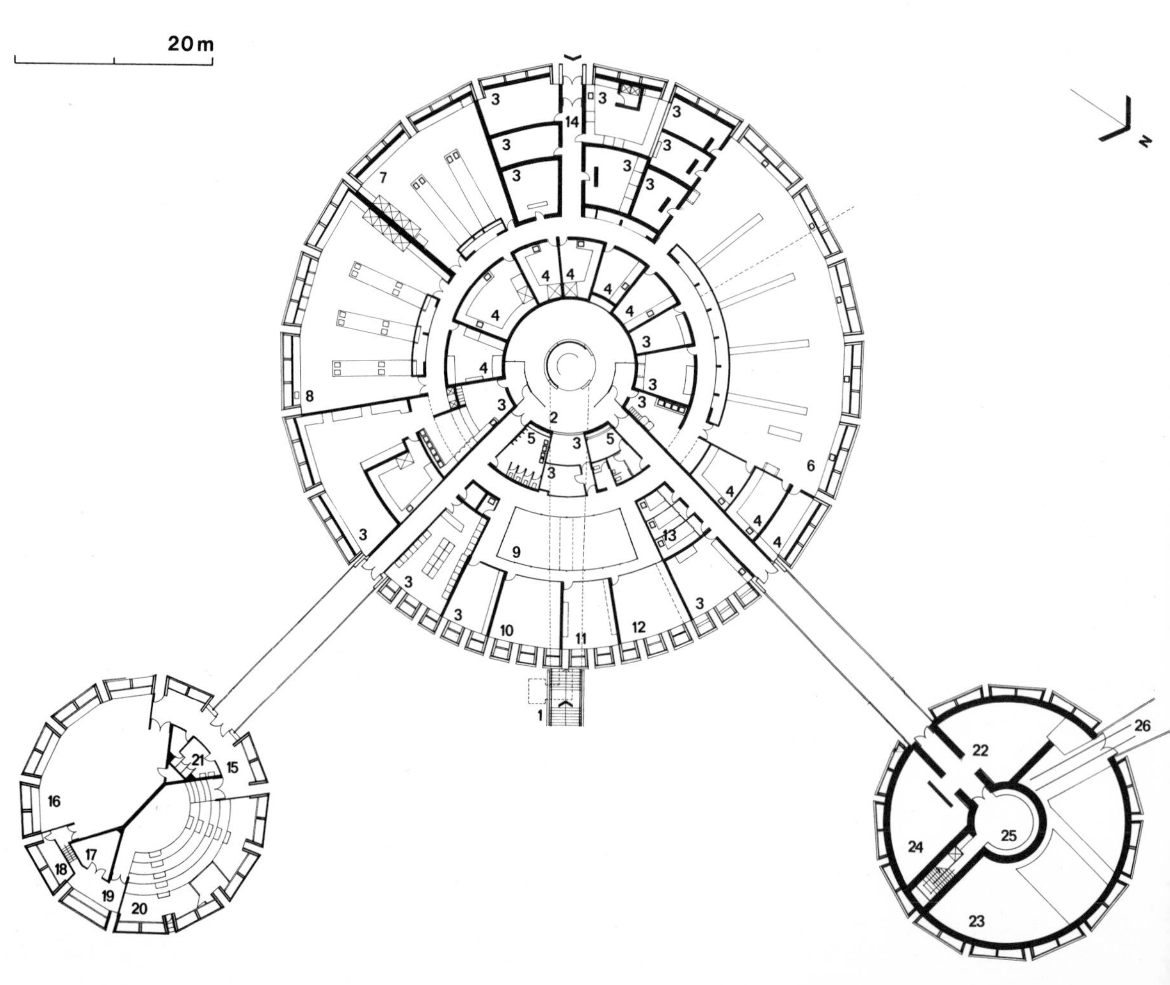

13 Headquarter Offices, St. Mellons, Monmouthshire

South Wales Electricity Board 1968

Courtyard/Cour intérieure/Innenhof

Due to the impracticability of finding temporary accommodation and the inconvenience of making two moves, we were required to plan the new offices on the site already in the Board's possession in such a manner that their existing offices, which were in a series of uncoordinated single- and two-storey buildings added throughout the years as the need had arisen, did not have to be disturbed until the new building could be occupied. The existing car park, on the higher part of the site which slopes gently southwards to the Cardiff/Newport Road and has magnificent views over the Severn Estuary, was, however, large enough for the new offices which were planned in a rectangular building of three storeys around an enclosed courtyard.

Il paraissait impossible de trouver des locaux temporaires et de plus effectuer deux déménagements successifs aurait entraîné de graves difficultés pratiques. Il nous fut donc demandé de concevoir l'implantation des nouveaux bureaux sur le terrain dont la Direction de l'Electricité était déjà propriétaire, de telle manière que le chantier ne perturbât en rien le fonctionnement des bureaux existants (une série de bâtiments à un ou deux niveaux, érigés d'année en année sans souci de coordination à mesure que le besoin de nouveaux locaux se faisait sentir), jusqu'à ce que le nouvel immeuble pût être occupé. Il s'est trouvé que le parc de stationnement existant, situé dans la partie supérieure du terrain qui descend doucement vers le Sud et la route Cardiff–Newport en ménageant des vues magnifiques sur l'estuaire de la Severn, était assez grand pour loger les nouveaux locaux, constitués par un bâtiment rectangulaire de trois niveaux entourant une cour intérieure.

Wegen der Schwierigkeit, provisorische Räume zu finden, und um zwei Umzüge zu vermeiden, bestand die Forderung, die neuen Bürogebäude auf dem bereits von der Gesellschaft erworbenen Gelände so zu planen, daß die bestehenden Büros – die in einer Reihe unkoordinierter, ein- und zweigeschossiger Bauten im Laufe der Jahre je nach Bedarf entstanden waren – bis zum Bezug der Neubauten weiterarbeiten konnten. Der vorhandene Parkplatz auf dem höhergelegenen Teil des Grundstücks, das zur Straße Cardiff – Newport leicht abfällt und wunderbare Aussicht auf die Mündung des Flusses Severn bietet, genügte jedoch auch für das neue Bürogebäude, das als rechteckiger, dreigeschossiger Bau um einen Innenhof angelegt wurde.

The ground floor is largely open with views from the entrance approach directly into the inner courtyard and beyond to the boiler and plant room, which the Board required should be all electric and be easily appreciated by visitors. Also at ground level is the printing department and near the main entrance a conference hall which can also be used as a small theatre or recreation room. The offices on the first and second floors are some 11,000 m² in area; they are designed to provide the maximum floor space in open-plan areas with a minimum of private offices. The building, which is fully air-conditioned, is faced externally with white mosaic. The windows have aluminium frames and are glazed with green-tinted glass. The ceilings are overall luminous and the floors carpeted.

Le rez-de-chaussée est largement ouvert à la vue, permettant ainsi lorsqu'on s'approche de l'entrée d'apercevoir la cour intérieure, et au-delà la chaufferie et la salle des machines, dont le client avait demandé que l'équipement, intégralement électrique, puisse être aisément distingué par les visiteurs. A ce même rez-de-chaussée sont installés le service de reprographie et, près de l'entrée principale, une salle de conférences qui peut aussi servir de petit théâtre ou de salle de détente. Les bureaux installés aux premier et second étages occupent environ 11.000 m²; ils sont conçus pour offrir le maximum d'espace en plateaux traités en bureaux paysagers, les bureaux individuels fermés étant réduits au nombre minimum. L'immeuble, qui est entièrement climatisé, est revêtu extérieurement d'une mosaïque blanche. Les fenêtres ont des encadrements d'aluminium et des vitres de verre teinté en vert. L'éclairage est partout incorporé dans les plafonds et les planchers sont recouverts de moquette.

Das Erdgeschoß ist weitgehend offen mit Durchblicken vom Eingangsbereich über den Innenhof zum Kessel- und Maschinenraum, der – entsprechend der Forderung der Firma – vollelektrisch und für Besucher leicht erfaßbar sein sollte. Ebenfalls im Erdgeschoß befinden sich die Druckerei und neben dem Haupteingang ein Konferenzsaal, der auch als kleines Theater oder Freizeitraum dienen kann. Die Büroflächen im ersten und zweiten Obergeschoß betragen insgesamt etwa 11.000 m², sie sind überwiegend als Großraumbüros mit einem Minimum an Individualräumen vorgesehen. Das vollklimatisierte Gebäude ist außen mit weißem Mosaik verkleidet. Die Fenster haben Aluminiumrahmen und grüngetöntes Glas. Das ganze Gebäude ist mit Leuchtdecken und Teppichböden ausgestattet.

Entrance lobby/Vestibule d'entrée/Eingangshalle

First floor plan
1. Entrance lobby 2. Courtyard 3. Cloakrooms 4. Office areas

Plan du premier étage
1. Vestibule d'entrée 2. Cour intérieure 3. Vestiaires 4. Bureaux

Grundriß erstes Obergeschoß
1. Eingangshalle 2. Innenhof 3. Garderoben 4. Büroflächen

Ground floor plan
1. Entrance hall 2. Courtyard 3. Covered area 4. Conference room 5. Plant 6. Storage and printing 7. Service entrance

Plan du rez-de-chaussée
1. Hall d'entrée 2. Cour intérieure 3. Zone couverte 4. Salle de conférence 5. Salle des machines 6. Magasins et service de reprographie 7. Entrée de service

Grundriß Erdgeschoß
1. Eingangshalle 2. Innenhof 3. Überdachter Bereich 4. Konferenzsaal 5. Maschinenraum 6. Lager und Druckerei 7. Liefereingang

N

20m

14 Headquarter Offices, Leadenhall Street, London EC3

CU 1969, P&O 1968

In 1961 the Commercial Union Assurance Company acquired the old Shell building in Great St Helens intending to adapt it and to build an extension on the adjacent site which they had also bought in St Mary Axe. At the same time the Peninsular and Oriental Steam Navigation Company was also considering rebuilding their long established but obsolescent offices immediately adjoining in Leadenhall Street. Due to the backland character of the Commercial Union site and its poor access and the restricted width of the Peninsular and Oriental site, it was impossible to obtain the permitted maximum floor areas without infringing the light angles. By developing comprehensively, however, and re-allocating the site boundaries it was possible to meet the floor area requirements and at the same time by forming an open space at the junction of Leadenhall Street and St Mary Axe, allow both companies to have frontages to the main thoroughfare, while still retaining site areas equivalent to their previous freeholds. The floor-to-site-area ratio in Commercial Union is 5·5:1 and in P & O is 5:1. To conform to the City of London Development plan it was necessary to plan subsidiary entrances from the upper level pedestrian walkway network which will eventually link to the adjoining sites when these are redeveloped.

The Commercial Union Tower is 38 m square and has 26,000 m² of usable office space on twenty-four floors. The staff restaurant, seating 800, is underneath the new open space in front of the building and on the twenty-second and twenty-third floors are the managerial, executive, and boardroom suites.

En 1961 la compagnie d'assurances Commercial Union acheta le vieil immeuble Shell dans le quartier de Great St Helens avec l'intention de l'aménager et de construire une extension sur le terrain adjacent donnant sur la St Mary Axe, qu'elle avait également acheté. A la même époque la compagnie de navigation Peninsular and Oriental (P & O) envisageait de reconstruire ses bureaux, installés de longue date sur l'emplacement contigu donnant sur la Leadenhall Street, et devenus désuets. Du fait de la situation en retrait du terrain de la Commercial Union et de l'étroitesse de son accès, ainsi que de la largeur restreinte de du terrain de la P & O, il était impossible d'atteindre les maxima de surface constructible permis sans enfreindre les dispositions réglementaires portant sur les angles d'éclairement à préserver entre bâtiments. Un remaniement à l'amiable des limites respectives des terrains a permis aux deux compagnies d'une part de parvenir aux surfaces constructibles qui leur étaient nécessaires et d'autre part, en constituant un espace libre à la jonction de Leadenhall Street et de St Mary Axe, d'avoir chacune une façade donnant sur l'artère principale, tout en restant propriétaires de surfaces de terrain équivalentes à celles des propriétés d'origine. Le rapport surface construite/surface au sol est de 5,5 pour la Commercial Union et de 5 pour la P & O. Le plan d'aménagement de la Cité de Londres a imposé de prévoir dans les bâtiments des entrées subsidiaires à un niveau correspondant au niveau supérieur du futur réseau de circulation piétonnière qui pourrait relier ces immeubles à ceux du voisinage, lorsque ceux-ci auront été reconstruits.

La tour de la Commercial Union a une section carrée de près de 38 m de côté et une surface utile de bureaux de 26.000 m² répartis sur vingt-quatre étages. Le restaurant du personnel, qui compte 800 places, est situé sous l'espace libre ouvert devant l'immeuble, et les vingt-deuxième et vingt-troisième étages sont occupés par les pièces et les bureaux de la direction et du Conseil.

1961 erwarb die Versicherungsgesellschaft Commercial Union das alte Shell-Gebäude in Great St Helens mit der Absicht, es umzubauen und auf dem ebenfalls erworbenen Nachbargrundstück in St Mary Axe einen Neubau zu errichten. Zur gleichen Zeit erwog die Schiffahrtsgesellschaft Peninsular and Oriental Steam Navigation Company den Neubau ihrer unmittelbar benachbarten Büros in der Leadenhall Street, die überaltert waren. Wegen der Hinterhofsituation des Grundstücks der Commercial Union und seiner schlechten Erschließung sowie der geringen Breite des Peninsular and Oriental-Geländes war es unmöglich, die zugelassene maximale Geschoßflächenzahl zu erzielen, ohne gegen die Abstandsregeln zu verstoßen. Durch Gesamtüberbauung und Umlegung der Grundstücksgrenzen war es jedoch möglich, den Flächenbedarf zu erfüllen und gleichzeitig – durch Bildung eines Freiraumes an der Kreuzung der Leadenhall Street und St Mary Axe – die Hauptfassaden beider Firmen an die Hauptstraße zu legen bei Einhaltung der früheren Grundbesitzrelationen. Die Geschoßflächenzahl der Commercial Union ist 5,5, die der Peninsular and Oriental 5,0. Der Bebauungsplan der City of London forderte Nebeneingänge vom höherliegenden Niveau des Fußgängernetzes, das später die anliegenden Grundstücke nach der Sanierung verbinden wird.

Das Hochhaus der Commercial Union ist etwa 38 m im Quadrat und enthält ca. 26.000 m² Büronutzfläche in 24 Geschossen. Die Kantine mit 800 Plätzen liegt unter dem neuen Freiraum vor dem Gebäude. Im 22. und 23. Geschoß befinden sich die Räume für die Direktion, die Geschäftsführung und den Aufsichtsrat.

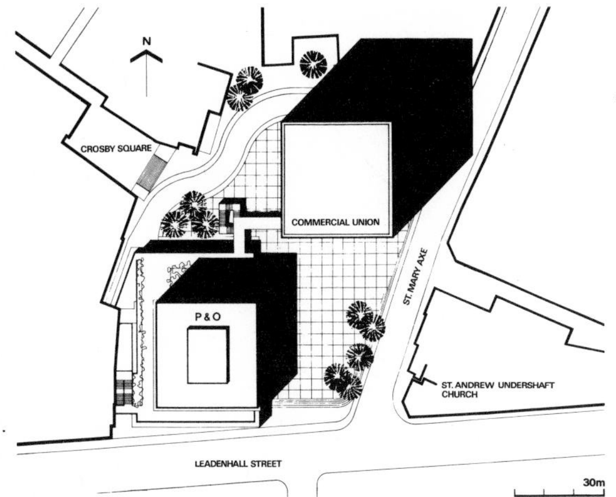

Commercial Union

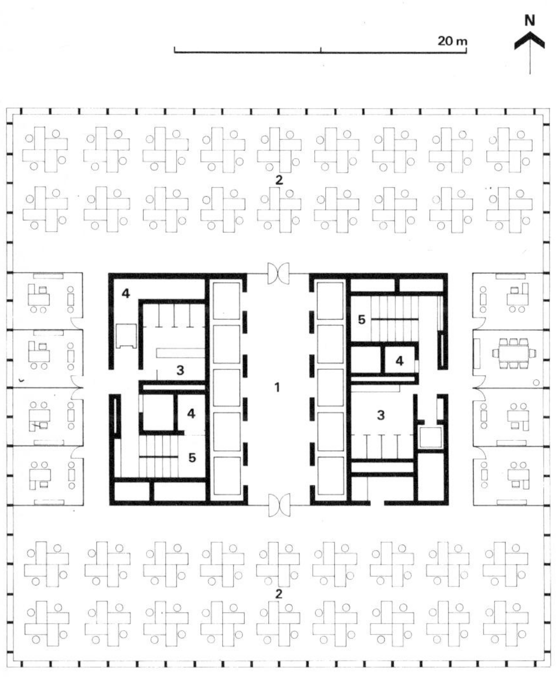

CU: typical floor plan
1. Lift lobby 2. Office space 3. WC 4. Service ducts 5. Stairs

CU: plan-type d'étage
1. Vestibule des ascenseurs 2. Bureaux 3. WC 4. Galeries techniques 5. Escalier

CU: Grundriß Normalgeschoß
1. Aufzugshalle 2. Bürofläche 3. Toiletten
4. Versorgungsschächte 5. Treppen

This building has a suspended type structure, which was the logical outcome of economic studies aimed at providing the maximum floor area and a minimum number of columns through the ground and basement floors.

The building consists initially of a concrete services core surrounded by a steel structure suspended from two cantilevered steel truss sections at mid and roof level plant floors. The upper plant room structure, containing the boilers, supports twelve floors while the lower plant room containing air-conditioning equipment supports thirteen floors. The two systems are quite independent of each other. The hangers, which are loaded purely in tension, vary in size from 0·23 m × 0·02 m to 0·23 m × 0·05 m and are contained entirely within alternate window mullions.

Ce bâtiment possède une structure de type suspendu – le choix de cette solution étant le résultat logique des études économiques menées pour combiner une surface de plancher maximum avec un nombre minimum de poteaux porteurs traversant les sous-sols.

Le bâtiment consiste initialement en un noyau de services en béton armé entouré, à mi-hauteur et au niveau du toit, par deux sections de poutres-caissons en porte-à-faux. La structure du niveau technique supérieur, qui contient la chaufferie, supporte douze étages, tandis que le niveau technique intermédiaire, qui contient les équipements de climatisation, supporte treize étages. Les deux systèmes sont tout à fait indépendants l'un de l'autre. Les suspentes, qui sont uniquement chargées en tension, ont des dimensions variant de 23×2 cm à 23×5 cm et sont entièrement logées dans les meneaux d'une fenêtre sur deux.

Dieser Bau hat eine Hängekonstruktion, die das Ergebnis von Wirtschaftlichkeitsuntersuchungen für maximale Flächengewinnung bei einem Minimun an Stützen im Erdgeschoß und den Untergeschossen darstellt.

Zuerst entstand der Beton-Versorgungskern, der von einer an zwei aus den Technikgeschossen vorkragenden Stahlträgern auf halber Höhe und auf Dachebene aufgehängten Stahlkonstruktion umgeben wurde. Das obere Technikgeschoß enthält die Kessel und trägt 12 Geschosse, während der in der Mitte liegende Maschinenraum, der die Klimaanlage enthält, 13 Geschosse trägt. Beide Systeme sind völlig unabhängig voneinander. Die Aufhängung, die nur unter Zug steht, variiert von ca. 23 x 2 cm bis 23 x 5 cm und liegt in jedem zweiten senkrechten Fassadendetail.

Commercial Union

The Peninsular and Oriental Tower is 33·50 m square and 58·20 m high, with ten floors rising from a three-storey podium and has in all 14,900 m^2 of office area. The two upper floors, which have been designed to show with advantage the fine Peninsular and Oriental collection of portraits and drawings, are occupied by the managerial and boardroom suites.

La tour de la Peninsular and Oriental a une section carrée de 33,5 m et une hauteur de plus de 58 m; elle comporte dix étages surmontant un podium de trois niveaux offrant au total une surface utile de bureaux de 14.900 m^2. Les deux étages supérieurs, dont la disposition intérieure a été conçue pour mettre en valeur la belle collection de portraits et de dessins de la collection de la P & O, sont occupés par les pièces et bureaux de la direction et du Conseil d'Administration.

Das Hochhaus der Peninsular and Oriental ist etwa 33,50 m im Quadrat und etwa 58 m hoch mit zehn Geschossen über einer dreigeschossigen Plattform und umfaßt insgesamt etwa 15.000 m^2 Bürofläche. Die beiden obersten Geschosse, die zugleich als Ausstellungsraum für die wertvolle Kunstsammlung der Firma von Portraits und Zeichnungen dienen, enthalten die Räume für die Geschäftsführung und den Aufsichtsrat.

In 1970 the two buildings received the Civic Trust Award for townscape and design co-ordination, and the Commercial Union building the Structural Steel Design Special Award sponsored by the British Steel Corporation and the British Constructional Steelwork Association.

En 1970 les deux immeubles on reçu le prix de la « Civic Trust for townscape and design co-ordination » (exaltant la qualité du paysage urbain et la cohérence de la conception) et la tour de la Commercial Union a reçu pour la conception de sa structure métallique le « Structural Steel Design Special Award », décerné par la Corporation britannique de l'Acier et l'Association britannique pour l'utilisation des structures métalliques dans la construction.

Im Jahre 1970 erhielten beide Gebäude den Civic Trust-Preis für Stadtgestaltung und städtebauliche Koordination und der Commercial Union-Bau den von der British Steel Corporation und der British Constructional Steelwork Association gestifteten Structural Steel Design Special Award.

P & O: tenth floor plan
1. Lift lobby 2. Reception area 3. Waiting area 4. Managing directors 5. Chairman 6. Deputy chairman 7. Secretaries 8. Board room 9. Ante room 10. Senior management dining room 11. Kitchen 12. Chairman's dining room 13. Conference room 14. WC 15. Stairways

P & O: plan du dixième étage
1. Vestibule des ascenseurs 2. Réception 3. Salon d'attente 4. Directeurs 5. Président 6. Vice-Président 7. Secrétaires 8. Salle du Conseil d'administration 9. Salle d'attente 10. Salle manger des Directeurs 11. Cuisine 12. Salle à manger du Président 13. Salle de conférence 14. WC 15. Escalier

P & O:Grundriß 10. Obergeschoß
1. Aufzugshalle 2. Rezeption 3. Warteraum 4. Direktoren 5. Geschäftsführer 6. Stellvertretender Geschäftsführer 7. Sekretärinnen 8. Aufsichtsrat 9. Vorzimmer 10. Eßraum der Direktion 11. Küche 12. Eßraum des Geschäftsführers 13. Konferenzsaal 14. WC 15. Treppenhaus

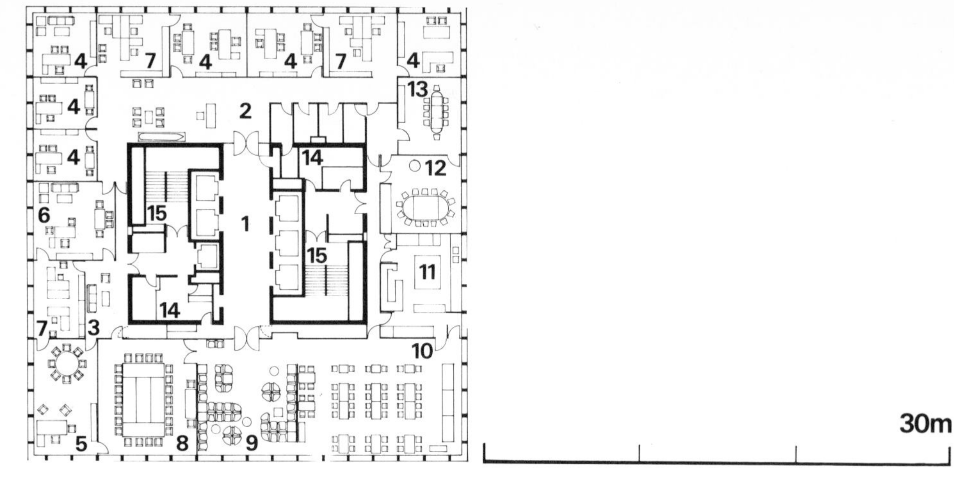

P & O: section
1. Offices 2. Shops 3. First floor 4. Ground floor 5. Lower ground floor 6. Car park 7. Strong room 8. Plant room 9. Street level

P & O: section
1. Bureaux 2. Boutiques 3. Deuxième niveau du podium 4. Rez-de-chaussée 5. Premier sous-sol 6. Garage 7. Chambre forte 8. Locaux techniques/machinerie 9. Niveau de la rue

P & O: Querschnitt
1. Büros 2. Läden 3. Erstes Obergeschoß 4. Erdgeschoß 5. Untergeschoß 6. Tiefgarage 7. Safe 8. Technik 9. Straßenniveau

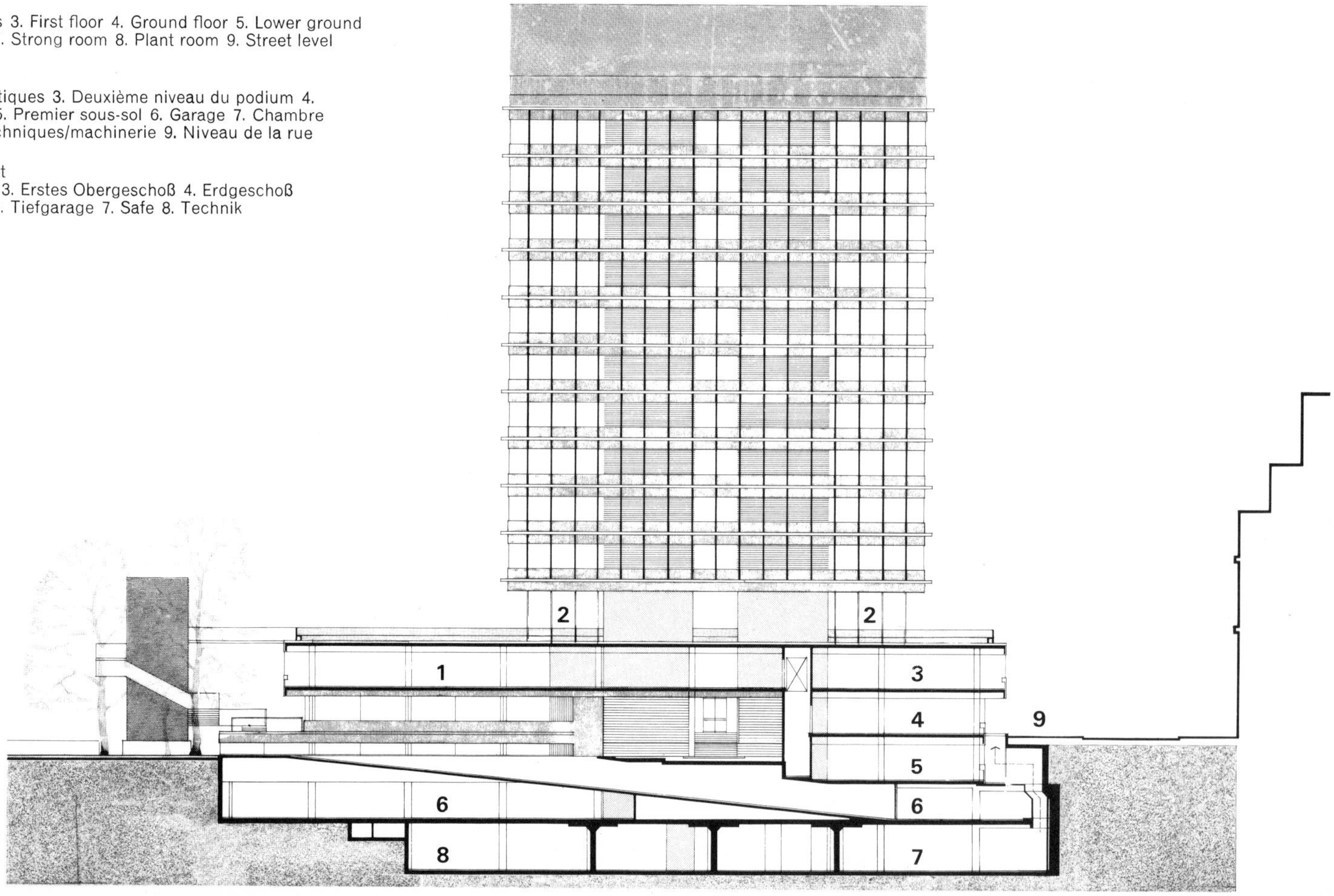

Ante room/Salle d'attente/Vorzimmer

Lift lobby/Vestibule des ascenseurs/Aufzugshalle

15 House on Campden Hill, London W8

Private client 1969

The site, square in shape, is on the corner of Pitt Street and Hornton Street on the southern slope of Campden Hill. Beyond the confines of the site the level drops steeply to the south – about 2·5 m allowing good views from the first floor.

The three-storey almost square in plan building has a car port for two cars, the front entrance and a swimming pool at ground level; a large 'L' -shaped living, dining, and library area and a small kitchen on the first floor; the main bedroom and a self-contained two-bedroom flat with bathroom and kitchenette on the second floor. The rooms are planned around a central core, which both supports the structure and houses a two-passenger lift.

Le terrain, de forme carrée, se trouve à l'angle de Pitt Street et de Hornton Street, sur le versant Sud de Campden Hill. Au delà des limites du terrain, vers le Sud, le niveau s'abaisse brutalement de 2,5 m, ce qui permet d'avoir une belle vue du premier étage.

La maison, de plan presque carré, a trois niveaux. Au rez-de-chaussée un garage à ciel ouvert pour deux voitures, l'entrée principale et une piscine. Au premier étage une vaste salle de séjour en forme de L, la salle à manger, un emplacement de bibliothèque et la cuisine; au deuxième étage la chambre principale et un petit appartement indépendant avec deux chambres, salle de bains et kitchenette. Les pièces sont disposées autour d'un noyau central qui supporte la structure et qui contient un ascenseur pour deux personnes.

Das quadratische Grundstück liegt an der Ecke der Pitt Street und Hornton Street am südlichen Abhang des Campden Hill. An der Begrenzung fällt das Gelände etwa 2,5 m steil nach Süden ab und bietet einen schönen Ausblick vom ersten Obergeschoß.

Das dreigeschossige, im Grundriß fast quadratische Wohnhaus hat Abstellplätze für zwei Wagen, den Haupteingang und einen Swimmingpool auf Erdgeschoßniveau; einen großen, L-förmigen Wohn-, Eß- und Bibliotheksbereich sowie eine kleine Küche im ersten Obergeschoß und eine abgeschlossene Wohnung mit zwei Schlafräumen, Badezimmer und Kleinküche im zweiten Obergeschoß. Die Räume sind um einen zentralen Kern angeordnet, der sowohl die Konstruktion trägt als auch einen Zweipersonenaufzug enthält.

Second floor
Second étage
Zweites Obergeschoß

First floor
Premier étage
Erstes Obergeschoß

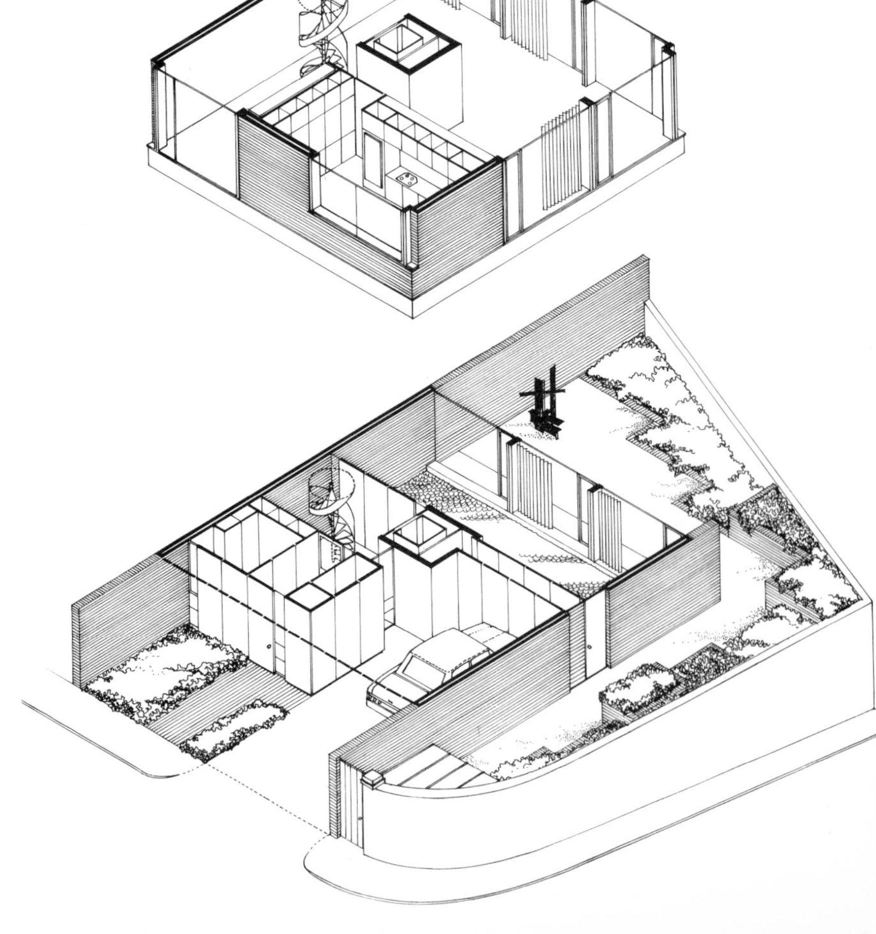

Ground floor
Rez-de-chaussée
Erdgeschoß

16 HMS Caledonia Naval Barracks, Rosyth, Scotland

Department of the Environment Stage 1 1970

The first part of the five-stage rebuilding plan for HMS *Caledonia* consists of six three-storey residential buildings, having altogether accommodation for 600 apprentices, 120 mechanicians, and twenty-four petty officers. They are situated at the western end of the site in a staggered formation stepped one below the other following the natural contours.

Each block is entered on the ground floor from two sides through an open area, each entrance having identical facilities, and is planned around an artificially lit and ventilated central core containing ancillary and toilet accommodation. The four-man dormitories in sets of three are approached from the two staircases.

La première des cinq phases du plan de reconstruction du dépôt des équipages de la flotte « Le Caledonia » comprend six bâtiments résidentiels de trois étages, correspondant à un effectif total de 600 apprentis, 120 mécaniciens et vingt-quatre officiers mariniers. Ces bâtiments sont situés dans la partie Ouest du terrain, en décrochement les uns par rapport aux autres suivant la pente naturelle de ce terrain. Chaque bloc est accessible de la cour extérieure par deux entrées symétriquement opposées et ayant la même disposition; le plan s'organise autour d'un noyau central éclairé artificiellement et ventilé, qui contient les installations domestiques et de toilette. Les dortoirs prévus chacun pour quatre hommes sont disposés par groupe de trois, et accessibles des deux escaliers.

Der erste Abschnitt der geplanten fünfstufigen Neubauten der Caledonia-Marinekasernen besteht aus sechs dreigeschossigen Wohngebäuden mit Unterbringungsmöglichkeit für insgesamt 600 Lehrlinge, 120 Mechaniker und 24 Unteroffiziere. Sie liegen im Westen des Geländes in terrassierter Anordnung, der natürlichen Geländeformation folgend.

Jeder Block ist im Erdgeschoß von zwei Seiten über einen Freibereich erschlossen, beide Eingangshallen sind gleich angelegt um einen künstlich belichteten und belüfteten zentralen Kern, der Nebenräume und Toiletten enthält. Die Vierpersonen-Schlafräume in Dreiergruppen sind über zwei Treppenhäuser erschlossen.

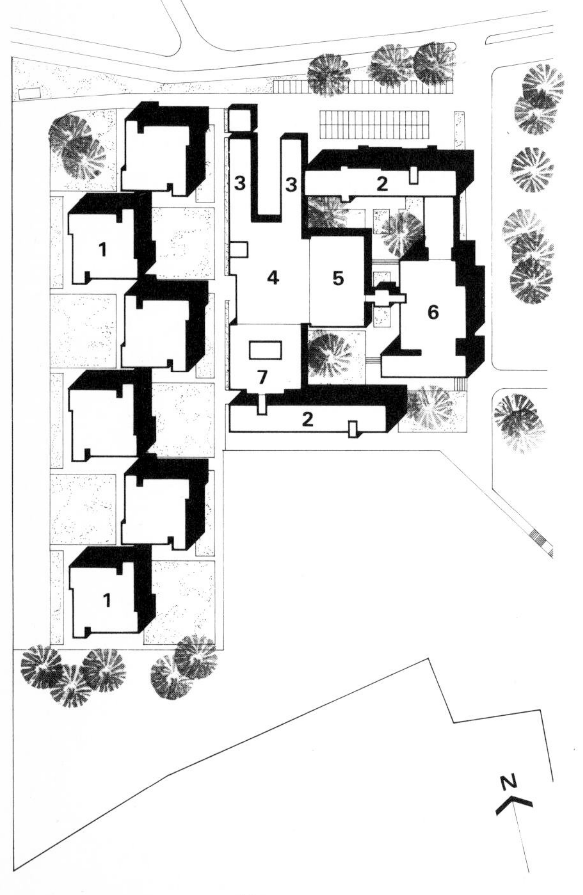

Site plan
1. Ratings residential accommodation 2. Officers' residential accommodation 3. Stores 4. Galley 5. Dining 6. Recreation 7. Mess building

Plan d'ensemble
1. Logements des matelots et gradés 2. Logements des officiers 3. Magasins 4. Coquerie 5. Réfectoire 6. Jeux et loisirs 7. Mess

Lageplan
1. Mannschaftswohnungen 2. Offizierswohnungen 3. Magazin 4. Küche 5. Essen 6. Aufenthaltsbereich 7. Messe

Dormitory block: typical floor plan
1. Entrance 2. Petty officer 3. Bathroom 4. WC 5. Dormitories

Dortoirs: plan-type d'étage
1. Entrée 2. Officier marinier 3. Salle de bains 4. WC 5. Dortoirs

Schlafraumtrakt: Normalgeschoß
1. Eingang 2. Unteroffizier 3. Bad 4. WC 5. Schlafräume

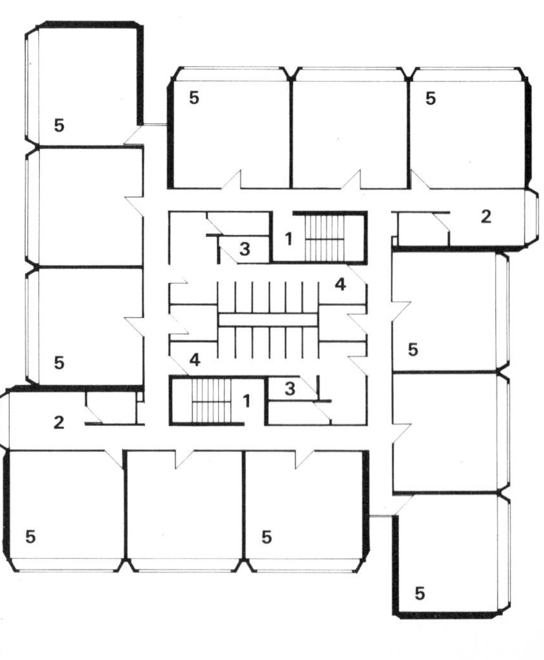

Ratings residential accommodation/Logements de matelots et gradés/Mannschaftswohnungen

17 Royal Air Force, West Drayton, Middlesex

Residential Accommodation

Department of the Environment 1970

The new domestic development is in unpromising surroundings – part industrial, part suburban – and is on the whole a low-rise complex mainly in single-storey buildings and with nothing higher than six storeys. Accommodation for officers, senior non-commissioned officers, airmen, and airwomen, includes mess buildings, sleeping quarters, medical, educational, and administrative buildings, car parks, garages, and recreation grounds. Realizing that the surroundings of the site were unattractive, the buildings – with the exception of the officers' mess which is on a separate but nearby site of its own – look predominantly inwards onto specially landscaped grounds which have an intimate and domestic environment secluded from the industrial atmosphere of the technical work areas, and entered only at particular points from the perimeter access road, to which vehicular traffic is restricted.

The basis of planning of the majority of the buildings is a spine corridor, from which rooms, irrespective of size, are directly accessible. To unify the various building types and the widely varying sized rooms, white concrete blocks have been used as the chief building material. These were considered to have a scale particularly suitable to the suburban industrial setting and the blockwork has been used to form sculptural groups of buildings – a quality accentuated by eliminating horizontal fascias at roof level and by setting the high-level windows at an angle – a detail which allows better views from the inside and more daylight at the backs of deep rooms, while increasing the areas of glazing as little as possible. Both the single and multi-storey buildings are designed on the cross wall principle and constructed with dense limestone aggregate blocks of the same dimensions, but with crushing strengths graded to the differing building heights. External walls are of cavity construction with both leaves supporting the floor slabs.

Le programme d'aménagement de ces nouveaux quartiers s'insère dans un environnement peu prometteur – une zone mi-industrielle mi-suburbaine – et représente dans l'ensemble un complexe économique composé de bâtiments le plus souvent d'un seul niveau et dont aucun ne dépasse six niveaux. Les installations destinées aux officiers, sous-officiers supérieurs, aviateurs et aviatrices comprennent: des mess, des dortoirs et des chambres-studios, des bâtiments médicaux, administratifs et d'enseignement, des parcs de stationnement automobile, des garages et des terrains de jeux. Du fait que les alentours du terrain étaient peu attrayants, les bâtiments – à l'exception du mess des officiers, installé sur un terrain voisin mais bien individualisé – sont principalement orientés vers l'intérieur où l'on a façonné un paysage ayant un caractère intime et familier nettement distinct de l'atmosphère industrielle des zones techniques, et où l'on n'accède que par quelques entrées greffées sur la route de desserte périphérique, sur laquelle le trafic des véhicules est contrôlé et limité.

Le principe de base de la conception de la majorité des bâtiments est l'existence d'un corridor formant épine dorsale, à partir duquel toute les pièces, quelles qu'en soient les dimensions, sont directement accessibles. Pour donner une unité à des bâtiments de forme très variée comprenant des pièces de dimensions également très variées, on a partout utilisé comme principal matériau de construction des blocs de béton blanc. On a considéré que l'échelle de ce matériau convenait particulièrement au cadre suburbain industriel, et qu'il permettait de constituer des groupes de bâtiments aux silhouettes sculpturales; on a accentué cette qualité en éliminant les rebords horizontaux des toits par l'installation de fenêtres hautes ayant leur plan supérieur incliné: ce détail améliore la vue que l'on a de l'intérieur des pièces, et assure plus de lumière dans le fond des pièces profondes, tout en accroissant aussi peu que possible la surface totale des vitrages. Les plans des bâtiments sans étage comme de ceux à étages relèvent d'une architecture de l'angle droit; les uns et les autres sont construits de blocs d'agrégat de calcaire dense ayant les mêmes dimensions, mais des résistances à la pression graduées selon les différentes hauteurs des bâtiments. Les murs extérieurs sont montés en creux, leurs deux tranches supportant les dalles de plancher.

Die Neubauten liegen in einer wenig ansprechenden Umgebung – teils Industriegebiet, teils vorstädtisches Wohngebiet – und bilden eine relativ niedrige Bebauung überwiegend in eingeschossigen und nicht höher als sechsgeschossigen Bauten. Zu den Wohnungen für Offiziere, Unteroffiziere sowie weibliches und männliches Flugpersonal gehören auch Kasinos, Schlafquartiere, medizinische Einrichtungen, Unterrichts- und Verwaltungsgebäude, Parkplätze, Garagen sowie Freizeitanlagen. Da die nähere Umgebung des Geländes unattraktiv ist, sind die Bauten – mit Ausnahme der Offiziersmesse, die auf einem anderen, aber nahegelegenen Grundstück liegt – überwiegend nach innen orientiert auf speziell angelegte Grünflächen, die eine intime und heimelige Atmosphäre schaffen, abseits vom Industriecharakter der technischen Arbeitsbereiche, nur an bestimmten Stellen von der umlaufenden Straße erschlossen, auf die der Fahrverkehr beschränkt ist.

Der Grundriß der Mehrzahl der Gebäude beruht auf dem gleichen Prinzip: ein mittig durchlaufender Korridor, von dem aus die Räume ohne Rücksicht auf ihre Größe direkt erschlossen sind. Um die verschiedenen Bautypen und die in der Größe stark variierenden Räume zu vereinheitlichen, wurden weiße Betonsteine als bevorzugtes Baumaterial gewählt. Man meinte, damit den Maßstab der vorstädtischen Industrielandschaft aufzunehmen. Die Betonsteine wurden benutzt, um stark plastische Bauten zu bilden – ein Merkmal, das betont wird durch Weglassen des horizontalen Abschlusses auf Dachebene und durch schräge Anordnung der Fenster im obersten Geschoß. Dieses Detail ermöglicht bessere Aussicht von innen und bessere Belichtung tiefer Räume an der Innenseite, während die Fläche der Verglasung nur wenig vergrößert wird. Sowohl die ein- als auch die mehrgeschossigen Bauten sind nach dem Kreuzwandprinzip geplant mit tragenden Wänden aus Betonsteinen mit starkem Kalksandstein-Zuschlag in gleichen Abmessungen, aber unterschiedlicher Tragfähigkeit je nach Gebäudehöhe. Die Außenwände sind zweischalig ausgebildet, beide Wandflächen tragen die Deckenplatten.

Airmen's accommodation/Quartier des aviateurs/Wohnungen Flugpersonal

Sergeants' quarters/Quartier des sergents/Unteroffiziersquartiere

Site plan
1. Officers' mess 2. Officers' quarters 3. Officers' car park
4. Guardhouse 5. Station headquarters 6. Medical centre
7. Education centre 8. WRAF accommodation block 9. Bedding store 10. Airmen's accommodation 11. Sergeants' quarters
12. Sergeants' mess 13. Sergeants' garages 14. Airmen's club
15. Airmen's mess 16. Landscaped gardens

Plan d'ensemble
1. Mess des officiers 2. Quartier des officiers 3. Parc de stationnement automobile des officiers 4. Corps de garde
5. Quartier-général 6. Centre médical 7. Locaux d'enseignement
8. Quartier du personnel féminin (WRAF) 9. Magasin de literie
10. Quartier des aviateurs 11. Quartier des sergents 12. Mess des sergents 13. Garages des sergents 14. Club des aviateurs
15. Mess des aviateurs 16. Jardins paysagers

Lageplan
1. Offiziersmesse 2. Offiziersquartiere 3. Parken Offiziere
4. Wache 5. Hauptquartier 6. Sanitätszentrum
7. Unterrichtszentrum 8. Wohntrakt für weibliches Personal
9. Bettzeuglager 10. Wohnungen Flugpersonal
11. Unteroffiziersquartiere 12. Unteroffiziersmesse 13. Parken Unteroffiziere 14. Klub Flugpersonal 15. Messe Flugpersonal
16. Garten

100m

N

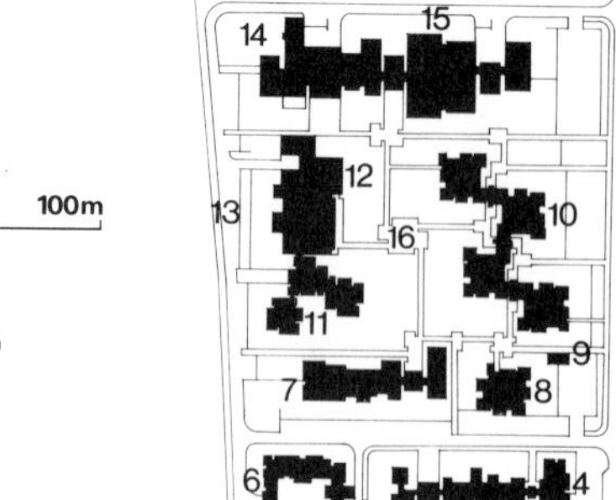

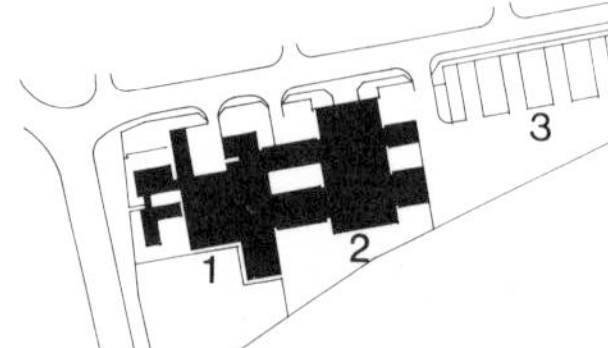

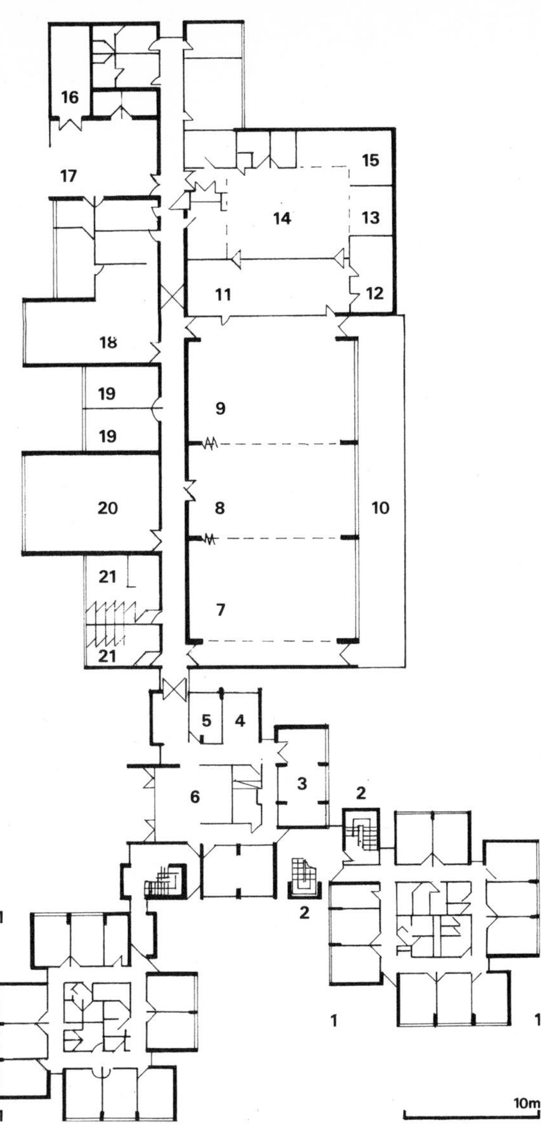

Senior NCOs' mess and quarters: ground floor plan
1. Bedroom block (three storeys) 2. Staircase 3. Visitors' room 4. Cloakroom 5. Office 6. Entrance hall 7. Ante room 8. Recreation room 9. Mess room 10. Terrace 11. Servery 12. Wash up 13. Pan wash 14. Kitchen 15. Larder 16. Substation 17. Yard 18. Bar 19. TV room 20. Billiard room 21. WC

Mess et quartiers des sous-officiers supérieurs: plan du rez-de-chaussée
1. Bloc des chambres (3 étages) 2. Escalier 3. Parloirs 4. Vestiaire 5. Bureau 6. Hall d'entrée 7. Salle d'attente 8. Salle de loisirs 9. Mess 10. Terrasse 11. Office 12. Salle de plonge 13. Lave-vaisselle 14. Cuisine 15. Garde-manger 16. Réserve 17. Petite cour 18. Bar 19. Salle TV 20. Salle de billard 21. WC

Unteroffiziersmesse und -quartiere: Grundriß Erdgeschoß
1. Schlafraumtrakt (dreigeschossig) 2. Treppenhaus 3. Besucherzimmer 4. Garderobe 5. Büro 6. Eingangshalle 7. Vorraum 8. Aufenthaltsraum 9. Messe 10. Terrasse 11. Anrichte 12+13. Spülküche 14. Küche 15. Speisekammer 16. Trafo 17. Hof 18. Bar 19. Fernsehraum 20. Billardzimmer 21. WC

18 Royal Military Academy, Sandhurst, Camberley, Surrey

Department of the Environment 1970

The Royal Military Academy, Sandhurst, centred on Old College which was built in the early nineteenth century, has developed this century in an *ad hoc* manner without the benefit of an overall plan. The design problem, therefore, consisted of rationalizing the traffic circulation and providing the new buildings to meet the present and future needs of the R M A so that they would form, with the existing buildings that remain, a functional and orderly arrangement which would preserve and complement the distinguished architectural character of the principal buildings in their fine landscaped setting.

The first and most important group of buildings to be constructed was recently completed. This consisted of a new college for 333 cadets, a new HQ office building to serve the whole Academy, and a new assembly hall seating 1,200. These buildings are sited in wooded surroundings alongside the playing fields and form, with James Wyatt's masterpiece, Old College, and the Edwardian New and Victory colleges, the major architectural composition in the Academy grounds.

The problems presented by the domestic character of the accommodation in relation to the scale of the elevations of the existing colleges, arising from the generously proportioned rooms and architectural language of a past age, were solved by the adoption of two-storey high pre-cast concrete cladding units with exposed aggregate finish and two-storey high windows in bronze-coloured aluminium. The use of this industrialized system of construction, appropriate to the present day, imposed a unifying rhythmic discipline throughout the scheme and imparted to the buildings a suitably distinguished contemporary architectural character.

The headquarters and college buildings won the 1970 Concrete Society Award.

L'Académie Militaire Royale de Sandhurst, centrée sur « l'Old College » qui a été construit au début du dix-neuvième siècle, s'est développée au vingtième au coup par coup hors de tout plan d'ensemble. Le problème de conception consistait donc d'une part à rationaliser les circulations, d'autre part à prévoir de nouveaux bâtiments adaptés aux besoins actuels et futurs de l'académie militaire et qui puissent former, avec les bâtiments actuels conservés, un ensemble fonctionnel et ordonné préservant et même rehaussant l'esthétique architecturale incontestable que présentent, dans le cadre du beau paysage où ils s'inscrivent, les principaux bâtiments.

Le premier et le plus important des groupes de bâtiments à construire a été récemment achevé. Il s'agit d'un nouveau collège pour 333 élèves-officiers, d'un nouveau quartier-général coiffant l'ensemble de l'Académie, et d'une nouvelle salle de réunion comprenant 1.200 places assises.

Ces bâtiments sont situés dans un secteur boisé en bordure des terrains de jeux et forment avec le chef d'œuvre de James Wyatt: l'Old College, et les New College et Victory College édouardiens, la composition architecturale majeure de toute l'Académie.

Il y avait une certaine opposition entre le caractère fonctionnel et pratique des installations de quartiers et l'échelle d'élévation des collèges existants – héritée du langage architectural du passé avec ses pièces aux proportions généreuses: on a résolu cette opposition en adoptant pour les nouveaux bâtiments des unités de façade en béton préfabriqué avec une finition en agrégat visible, haute de deux niveaux et des fenêtres également hautes de deux niveaux aux encadrements d'aluminium coloré en bronze. L'utilisation de ce système de construction industrialisée approprié à notre époque, a imposé à tout le programme une discipline et un « rythme » unificateur, et conféré aux bâtiments un aspect esthétique exprimant une architecture contemporaine de qualité.

Le quartier-général et le collège ont gagné le prix de la Concrete Society de 1970.

Die Königliche Militärakademie in Sandhurst, mit dem Old College als Mittelpunkt, wurde Anfang des 19. Jahrhunderts erbaut und in unserem Jahrhundert in Ad-hoc-Manier ohne einen Gesamtplan erweitert. Das Planungsproblem bestand daher darin, den Verkehr zu rationalisieren und die Neubauten so anzulegen, daß sie gegenwärtigen und zukünftigen Erfordernissen gerecht werden. Darüber hinaus sollten sie zusammen mit den vorhandenen Altbauten eine funktionale und geordnete Anlage darstellen, ohne den außergewöhnlichen architektonischen Charakter der wichtigen Bauten und ihre gelungene Einordnung in die Landschaft zu beeinträchtigen.

Die erste und wichtigste Gruppe von Neubauten wurde kürzlich fertiggestellt. Sie besteht aus einem neuen College für 333 Offiziersanwärter, einem neuen Hauptquartier für die gesamte Akademie und einer neuen Versammlungshalle mit 1200 Plätzen. Diese Bauten wurden in das Waldgebiet neben den Sportplätzen situiert und bilden, zusammen mit James Wyatts Meisterstück, dem Old College, und den New und Victory Colleges aus der Zeit König Edwards, den architektonischen Schwerpunkt der Bebauung.

Das Problem bestand darin, den intimen Charakter der Wohnbauten in ein Verhältnis zum Maßstab der Fassaden der bestehenden Colleges – bedingt durch die großzügig proportionierten Räume und die Architekturformen der Vergangenheit – zu setzen. Es wurde gelöst durch Anwendung von doppelgeschoßhohen, vorgefertigten Verkleidungselementen aus Beton und doppelgeschoßhohen Fenstern aus bronzegetöntem Aluminium. Dieses zeitgemäße, industriell gefertigte Konstruktionssystem verleiht der gesamten Bebauung eine einheitliche, rhythmische Disziplin und den Bauten den angemessenen Charakter guter moderner Architektur.

Das Hauptquartier und die Collegebauten erhielten 1970 den Preis des britischen Betonverbandes.

Site plan
1. Old College 2. New College 3. Victory College 4. Officers' mess 5. Fresh College 6. Library 7. Gymnasium 8. Chapel 9. Parade ground 10. Lake 11. Playing fields

Plan d'ensemble
1. Old College 2. New College 3. Victory College 4. Mess des officiers 5. Fresh College 6. Bibliothèque 7. Gymnase 8. Chapelle 9. Place d'armes 10. Lac 11. Terrains de jeux

Lageplan
1. Old College 2. New College 3. Victory College 4. Offiziersmesse 5. Fresh College 6. Bibliothek 7. Sporthalle 8. Kapelle 9. Exerzierplatz 10. See 11. Sportfelder

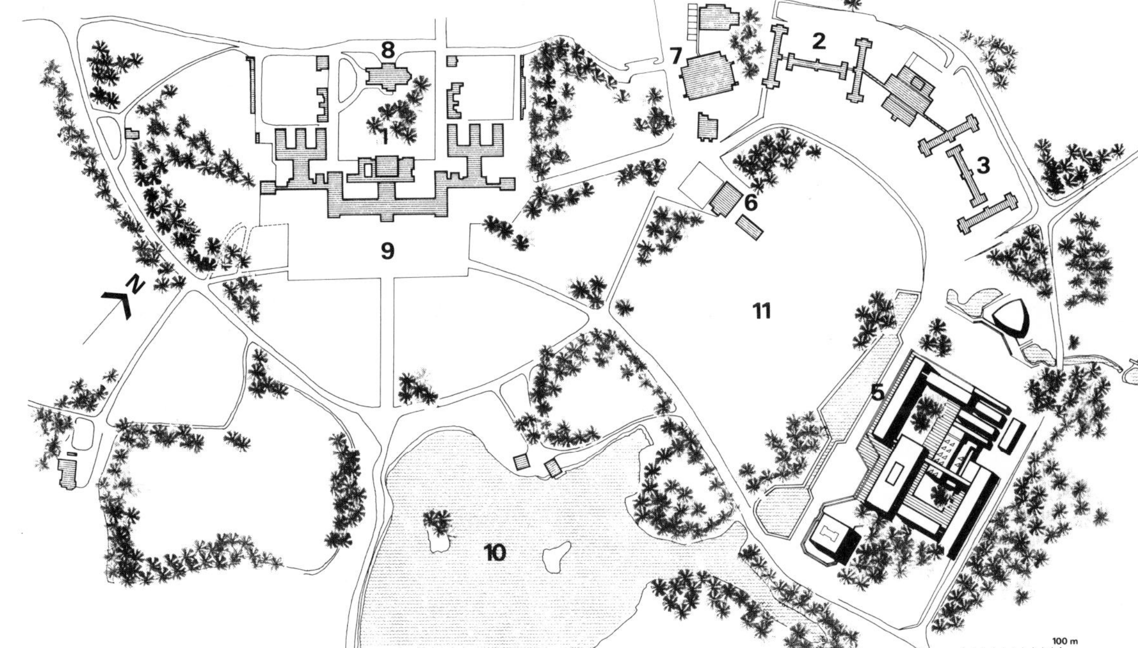

Cadets' accommodation: typical plan
1. Study bedroom 2. Staircase 3. Servant 4. Ironing 5. Drying 6. Baggage 7. WC 8. Shower and drying area 9. Cleaning 10. Hoist

Plan-type de casernement d'élèves-officiers
1. Chambre d'élève 2. Escalier 3. Ordonnance 4. Repassage 5. Séchoirs 6. Dépôt de bagages 7. WC 8. Douches et vestiaires 9. Nettoiement 10. Mât des couleurs

Kadettenquartiere: Grundriß Normalgeschoß
1. Arbeits-/Schlafraum 2. Treppenhaus 3. Hausdiener 4. Bügelzimmer 5. Trockenraum 6. Gepäck 7. WC 8. Dusch- und Trockenräume 9. Reinigung 10. Aufzug

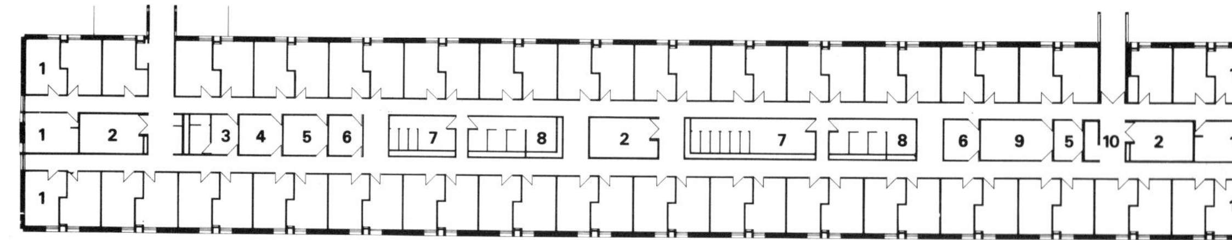

Headquarter building/Quartier-général/Hauptquartier

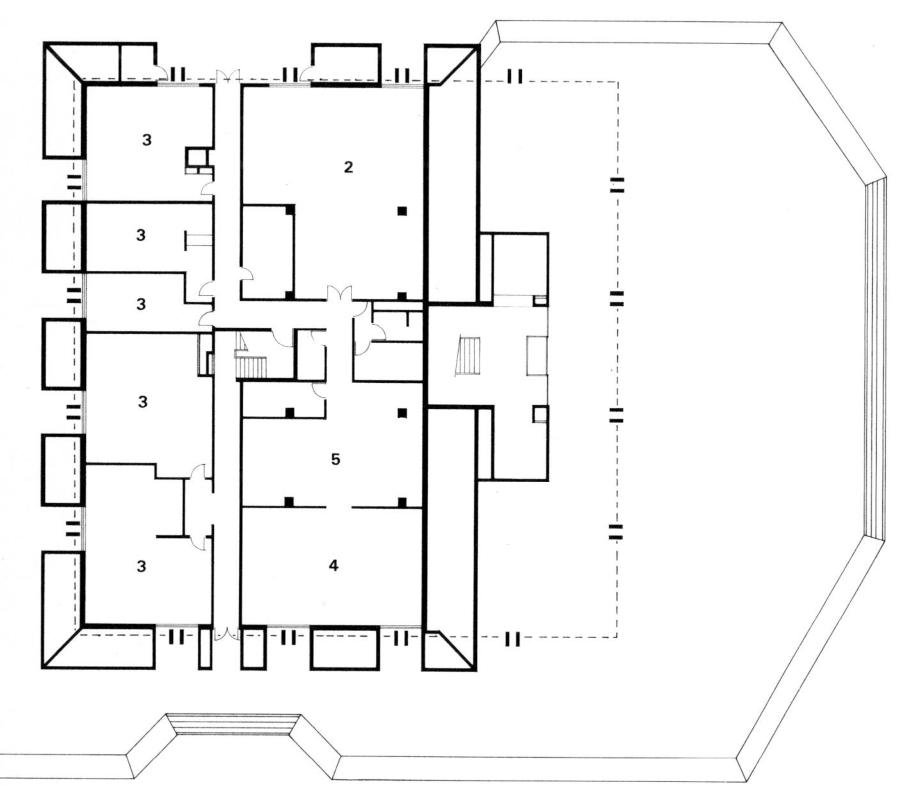

HQ: ground floor plan
1. Staircase 2. Stores 3. Office 4. Printing 5. Library

Quartier-général: plan du rez-de-chaussée
1. Escalier 2. Magasins 3. Bureaux 4. Reprographie
5. Bibliothèque

Hauptquartier: Grundriß Erdgeschoß
1. Treppenhaus 2. Magazine 3. Büro 4. Druckerei
5. Bibliothek

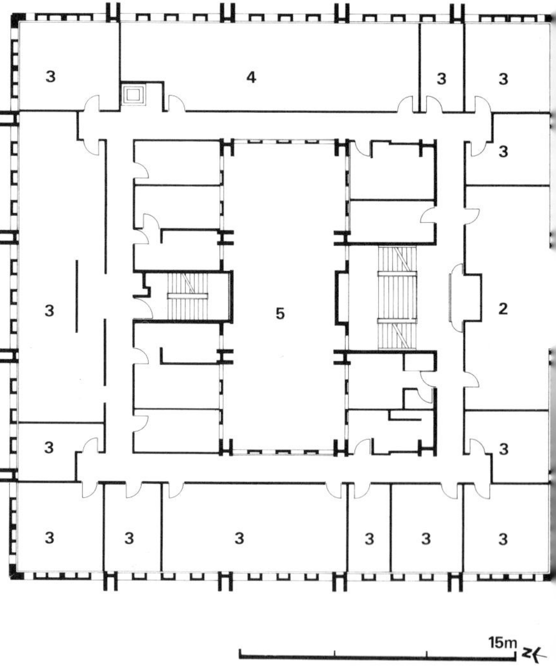

HQ: first floor plan
1. Staircase 2. Information room 3. Office 4. General registry
5. Courtyard

Quartier-général: plan du premier étage
1. Escalier 2. Salle d'information 3. Bureaux 4. Registre général 5. Patio

Hauptquartier: Grundriß erstes Obergeschoß
1. Treppenhaus 2. Informationsraum 3. Büro 4. Zentralkartei
5. Innenhof

The assembly hall has 1,200 seats and is three sided with walls set at a curve of approximately 56 m radius with sides 39 m long. The framework of the superstructure is in structural steel and the roof framework consists of thirty circular and rectangular hollow section lattice girders. To achieve repetition of members, the setting out of the roof is based on an equilateral triangle and circular curves in the plane of the sloping roof.

La salle de réunion comprend 1.200 sièges et est enclose dans trois murs courbes d'un rayon d'environ 56 m et de 39 m de long. La charpente de la superstructure est en acier et la structure du toit comprend trente poutres à croisillons bombées de section rectangulaire creuse. Pour permettre la répétition des éléments de construction, le dessin du toit est basé sur un triangle équilatéral et des courbes de niveau circulaires épousant la pente du toit.

Die dreieckige Versammlungshalle mit 1200 Plätzen hat etwa 39 lange, in einem Radius von etwa 56 m gekrümmte Außenwände. Die Primärkonstruktion ist aus Stahl. Die Decke ist ein Raumtragwerk mit 30 Gitterbalkenträgern aus runden und rechteckigen Stäben. Um die Wiederholung der Elemente bei großer Spannweite zu ermöglichen, wurde ein gleichseitiges Dreieck bei kreisbogenförmiger Abflachung des Daches gewählt.

Assembly hall/Salle de réunion/Versammlungshalle

19 Upper School, Desford, Leicestershire

Leicestershire Education Committee 1970

Planned to follow the contours of the south-sloping site on the outskirts of the village of Desford, this halfway house between school and college accommodates 900 children between the ages of 14 and 18 and is so planned that it can be readily extended to 1,400 places in the future. The design meets the client's requirement that it should be a community of young adults rather than of children, and the plan form was one of the first in the country to reflect its comprehensive schools policy.

There are three main elements: the administration and staff rooms with the adult centre directly approached from the road and the assembly, music, gymnasium group; the teaching areas both academic and specialist; and thirdly the upper level sixth form centre which connects the first and second groups.

Conçu pour se modeler au relief d'un terrain à la pente orientée vers le Sud, aux abords du village de Desford, cet établissement à mi-chemin de l'école et du collège peut recevoir 900 élèves âgés de 14 à 18 ans, et sa conception permet une extension ultérieure facile jusqu'à une capacité de 1.400 places. La conception reflète aussi l'objectif fixé par le maître d'ouvrage: que l'établissement constitue une communauté de jeunes adultes et non pas d'enfants, et le plan qui y répond a été l'un des premiers dans le pays à exprimer cette politique d'intégration intellectuelle.

L'école comprend trois éléments principaux: d'une part les pièces de l'administration et du personnel enseignant et le centre de cours du soir directement accessibles de la route, ainsi que le groupe salle de réunion, salles de musique, gymnase; d'autre part la zone réservée à l'enseignement; enfin les locaux des classes de première et de terminale qui font la liaison entre les deux premiers éléments.

Den Geländebewegungen des nach Süden abfallenden Grundstücks am Rande des Dorfes Desford folgend, kann diese Einrichtung, halb Schule, halb College, 900 Jugendliche im Alter von 14 bis 18 Jahren aufnehmen und ist so angelegt, daß sie leicht auf 1400 Plätze erweitert werden kann. Der Entwurf entspricht den Forderungen des Bauherrn nach einer Gemeinschaft von jungen Erwachsenen, nicht von Kindern. Der Grundriß gehört zu den ersten, welche die Gesamtschulpolitik des Landes zur Grundlage haben.

Die Anlage besteht aus drei Haupttrakten: Verwaltung, Räume für den Lehrkörper und Erwachsenenzentrum mit direktem Zugang von der Straße sowie Aula, Musiksaal und Turnhalle; allgemeine und spezielle Lehrbereiche und drittens dem Abschlußklassenbereich, der die erste und zweite Raumgruppe verbindet.

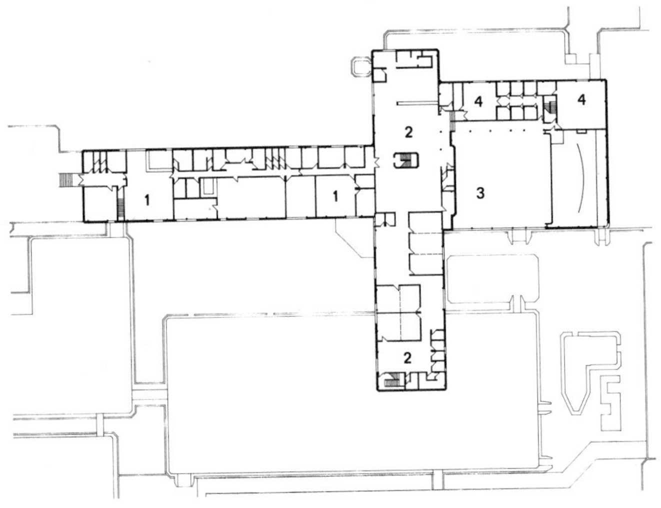

First floor plan
1. Administration department 2. Sixth form centre 3. Assembly hall 4. Music department

Plan du premier étage
1. Administration 2. Première et terminale 3. Salle de réunion 4. Salles de musique

Grundriß Obergeschoß
1. Verwaltung 2. Abschlußklassen 3. Aula 4. Musikabteilung

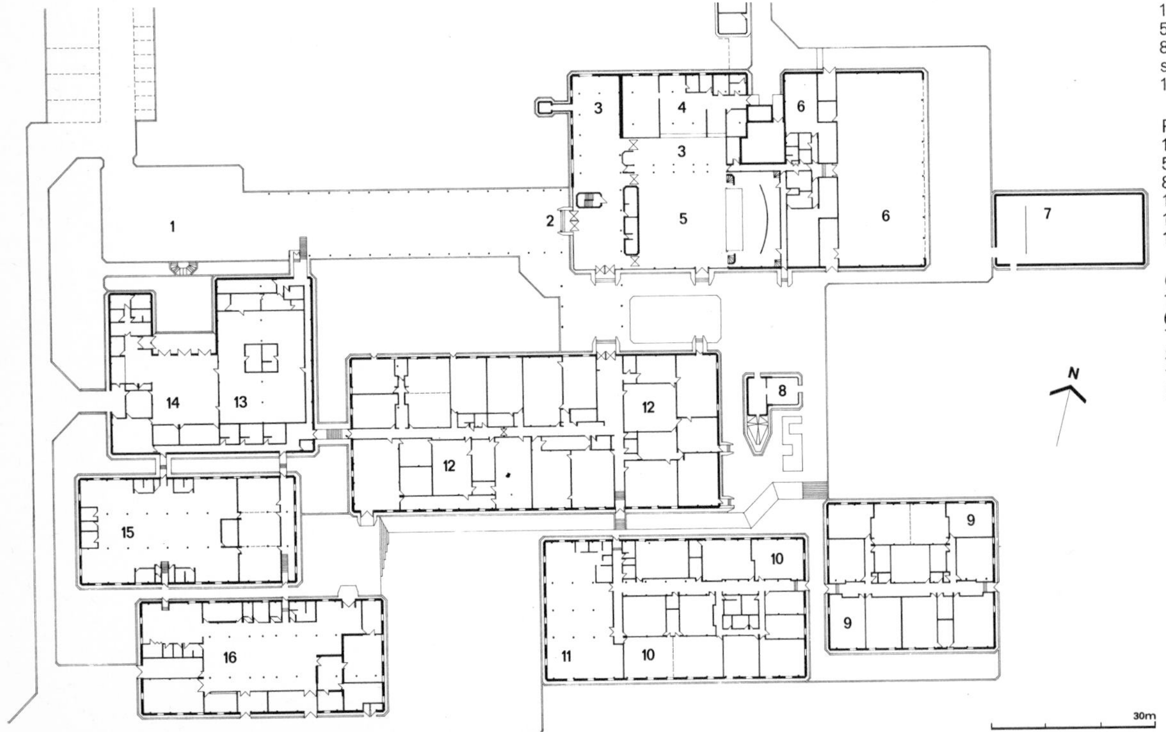

Ground floor plan
1. Terrace 2. Main entrance 3. Dining area 4. Kitchen 5. Assembly hall 6. Games hall and changing area 7. Gymnasium 8. Aviary and greenhouse 9. General teaching block 10. Liberal studies 11. Library 12. Science department 13. Housecraft 14. Youth centre 15. Arts and crafts 16. Practical studies

Plan du rez-de-chaussée
1. Terrasse 2. Entrée principale 3. Réfectoire 4. Cuisine 5. Salle de réunion 6. Hall de jeux et vestiaires 7. Gymnase 8. Volière et serre 9. Bloc d'enseignement général 10. Lettres 11. Bibliothèque 12. Sciences 13. Enseignement ménager 14. Club d'élèves 15. Activités artistiques et manuelles 16. Ateliers de travaux pratiques

Grundriß Erdgeschoß
1. Terrasse 2. Haupteingang 3. Eßbereich 4. Küche 5. Aula 6. Ballspielhalle und Umkleideräume 7. Turnhalle 8. Volière und Treibhaus 9. Allgemeiner Unterrichtstrakt 10. Freier Studienbereich 11. Bibliothek 12. Naturwissenschaften 13. Hauswirtschaft 14. Jugendzentrum 15. Kunst und Kunstgewerbe 16. Handwerkliche Fächer

20 International Airport Terminal, JF Kennedy Airport, New York

British Overseas Airways Corporation and Air Canada 1970

John F. Kennedy International Airport at New York has been developed on the unit terminal principle as, at the time of its conception in 1947, it was concluded that a decentralized layout would provide both the flexibility for handling the ever-increasing traffic and would permit the airlines to develop terminals particularly suitable for their differing methods of operation and their varied types of traffic. Originally, all the arriving international traffic had to make use of the centralized international arrivals building where the federal controls were based, the airlines' individual terminals being restricted to departing international passengers or domestic flights. In 1963, the federal authorities agreed, however, to decentralize their functions, thus making possible the design of the BOAC terminal capable of handling international arrivals as well as departures and Air Canada domestic flights. It is therefore the only individual airline terminal at Kennedy Airport designed from the outset to process international passengers through all federal controls, health, immigration, and customs.

The dominant architectural emphasis at JFK is the international arrivals building, which, with its formal landscaping in the central reservation, unifies the composition of the buildings of the various airline companies dispersed around the perimeter of the central area. Each of these buildings, in various idioms of contemporary architecture, seeks to express by its individuality the distinctiveness of the particular airline; it was therefore essential that the BOAC terminal be sufficiently strong in its individual architectural expression to hold its own against the other airline buildings whilst at the same time taking its place within the overall master plan.

L'Aéroport International John F. Kennedy à New-York applique le principe des unités terminales; à l'époque de sa conception, en 1947, on avait en effet conclu qu'un plan-masse décentralisé assurerait à la fois la flexibilité nécessaire pour pouvoir traiter un trafic en augmentation constante, et la faculté pour les différentes compagnies aériennes de construire des terminaux particulièrement adaptés à leurs méthodes opératoires propres et aux types de trafic variés qui sont les leurs. Initialement tout le trafic international « arrivées » était centralisé sur un seul bâtiment, où étaient installés les contrôles fédéraux; les terminaux propres aux différentes compagnies aériennes étaient réservés aux départs internationaux et aux vols intérieurs. En 1963 cependant les autorités fédérales acceptèrent de décentraliser leurs contrôles, rendant ainsi possible la conception d'un terminal de la BOAC capable d'assurer aussi bien les arrivées que les départs internationaux, ainsi que les liaisons USA–Canada d'Air Canada. C'est donc à l'Aéroport Kennedy le seul terminal propre à une compagnie aérienne qui ait pu être conçu dès l'origine en tenant compte du passage des voyageurs internationaux par les contrôles fédéraux, contrôle de santé, bureau de l'immigration et douane.

L'élément de l'Aéroport Kennedy qui domine par sa puissance architecturale est le bâtiment des arrivées internationales. Par sa position au centre même de la zone construite, il unifie la composition des bâtiments des différentes compagnies, qui sont dispersés tout le long du périmètre de la zone centrale. Ces différents terminaux, utilisant les modes d'expression variés de l'architecture contemporaine, essaient chacun d'individualiser les particularités de la compagnie aérienne qu'ils abritent. Il était donc essentiel que le terminal de la BOAC se distingue par une expression architecturale suffisamment forte pour « tenir dignement son rang » à l'égard des autres terminaux – tout en respectant la place qui lui était attribuée dans le plan-masse de l'aéroport.

Die Planung des internationalen Kennedy-Flughafens in New York beruht auf dem Prinzip der einzelnen Terminals, seinerzeit im Jahre 1947 der Auffassung folgend, daß eine dezentralisierte Anlage sowohl die notwendige Flexibilität für die Abfertigung des zunehmenden Verkehrs bieten als auch den Fluglinien den Bau eigener Terminals entsprechend den unterschiedlichen Methoden der Abfertigung und den verschiedenen Verkehrstypen ermöglichen würde. Ursprünglich mußte der gesamte internationale Anflugverkehr das zentrale internationale Empfangsgebäude benutzen, wo die Bundeszollkontrollen untergebracht waren, während die individuellen Terminals auf den internationalen Abflugverkehr oder Inlandflüge beschränkt waren. 1963 beschlossen die Bundesbehörden jedoch, ihre Funktionen zu dezentralisieren. Dadurch war es möglich, den BOAC-Terminal sowohl für internationale Anflüge als auch Abflüge und für Air Canada-Flüge zu planen. Er ist daher der einzige individuelle Terminal einer Fluglinie, der von Anfang an dazu vorgesehen war, internationale Passagiere durch sämtliche Bundesgesundheits-, -einwanderer- und -zollkontrollen zu schleusen.

Die architektonische Dominante des Kennedy-Flughafens ist das internationale Empfangsgebäude, das durch seine besondere Anordnung im zentralen Freibereich die Gruppe der verschiedenen, um diesen Umkreis verstreuten Gebäude der einzelnen Fluglinien vereint. Alle diese Gebäude suchen durch ihre Individualität in verschiedenen Idiomen der Gegenwartsarchitektur die Bedeutung ihrer jeweiligen Fluggesellschaft auszudrücken. Daher war es wichtig, dem BOAC-Terminal einen genügend starken architektonischen Ausdruck zu verleihen, damit er sich gegenüber den Bauten der anderen Gesellschaften behauptet und gleichzeitig seinen Platz in der Gesamtbebauung einnimmt.

BOAC
AIR CANADA

Departures/Départs/Abflug

Exterior detail/Détail extérieur/Detail, Außenwand

Departures concourse/Salle des pas perdus départs/
Erschließungsflur Abflug

The terminal, on a site some 10·5 hectares in area, lies on the north side of the airport and due to the necessity of being able to see from the control tower aircraft on the main taxiway system, was subject to a height restriction of 18 m on the south and 3 m on the north boundaries. It has some 32,500 m^2 of accommodation and has seven BOAC international aircraft stands to take a combination of Boeing 747s, Super VC10s, and supersonic airliners. There are also three Air Canada stands for DC9, DC8, and 'stretched' DC8 aircraft.

The prime considerations of shortness and directness of travel for passengers and simplicity and flexibility of administration, baggage handling, and services required that the building should be on two basic levels, with a mezzanine and an airside gallery which, wrapped around the concourse, allow aircraft to be brought directly up to the terminal. Outbound passengers use the upper level and inbound the lower; the mezzanine spans across the back of the main concourse and contains a restaurant, bars, first-class and VIP lounges, and the greater part of the administration. In the gallery are the gate-hold lounges with vertical separation for arriving and departing passengers and mechanical services for the aircraft fixed ramp services. Check-in and baggage acceptance are planned on the supermarket flow-through principle system, which pre-sorts both the passengers and their baggage by flight number; the baggage is then transferred by underfloor conveyors to the baggage hall, where it is mechanically sorted and loaded into containers.

Ce terminal est implanté sur un terrain de 10,5 hectares dans la partie Nord de l'aéroport, et la nécessité d'assurer à la tour de contrôle une vue complète de tout le système de pistes lui impose des limitations de hauteur qui vont de 18 m au Sud du terrain à 3 m à son extrémité Nord. La surface couverte des locaux est de 32.500 m^2 et il y a sept quais internationaux pour la flotte BOAC (Boeing 747, Super VC10 et avions supersoniques) et trois quais Air Canada pour DC9, DC8 et Super-DC8.

Les exigences primordiales de brièveté et d'évidence des parcours pour les passagers, de simplicité et de flexibilité de l'administration, de la manutention des bagages et des services, ont conduit à distribuer le bâtiment sur deux niveaux principaux, avec une mezzanine et une galerie extérieure qui entourent la salle des pas perdus, ce qui permet aux passagers d'aborder directement le terminal. Les passagers au départ utilisent le niveau supérieur et ceux qui débarquent le niveau inférieur. La mezzanine s'élargit en pont au dessus de l'arrière de la salle des pas perdus pour contenir un restaurant, des bars, les salons des premières classes et des personnalités, et la majeure partie de l'administration. Sur la galerie donnent les salles d'attente aux portes d'embarquement-débarquement, avec une séparation verticale entre arrivées et départs, et les installations mécaniques actionnant les rampes d'accès. Contrôle des billets et enregistrement des bagages s'effectuent d'après le système de « l'écoulement filtré » pratiqué dans les supermarchés, avec un tri préalable des passagers et de leurs bagages par numéro de vol; les bagages sont alors transférés par des convoyeurs en sous-sol au hall des bagages, où ils sont triés mécaniquement et chargés dans des containers.

Der Terminal liegt auf einem etwa 10.5 ha großen Gelände im Norden des Flughafens und unterlag, weil die Flugzeuge auf der Haupteinflugschneise vom Kontrollturm zu sehen sein müssen, einer Höhenbeschränkung von 18 m an der Süd- und etwa 3 m an der Nordseite. Er enthält etwa 32.500 m^2 Geschoßfläche und sieben Stände für BOAC-Überseemaschinen (Boeing 747, Super VC10 und Überschallflugzeuge). Außerdem sind drei Stände der Air Canada für DC9, DC8 und die längere DC8 vorhanden.

Die vordringliche Forderung nach kurzen und direkten Wegen für die Fluggäste und einfachem und flexiblem Ablauf von Verwaltung, Gepäckabfertigung und Service führte zu einem Gebäude mit zwei Hauptgeschossen und einem Zwischengeschoß sowie einer um den Bau geführten Galerie, die es ermöglicht, daß die Maschinen direkt an den Terminal herangeführt werden können. Abfliegende Gäste benutzen das obere Geschoß, ankommende das untere. Das Zwischengeschoß erstreckt sich über die Rückseite der Galerie und enthält ein Restaurant, Bars, Aufenthaltsräume für 1.-Klasse-Passagiere und für VIP sowie den Hauptteil der Verwaltungsräume. In der Galerie liegen die Flugsteige mit vertikaler Trennung der Abflug- und Anflugpassagiere sowie mechanische Einrichtungen für die Wartung der Maschinen an der Rampe. Check-in und Gepäckannahme sind nach dem Supermarket-System organisiert, das sowohl Passagiere als auch Gepäck nach Flugnummern vorsortiert. Das Gepäck wird auf Förderbändern unter dem Fußboden zur Gepäckhalle befördert, wo es mechanisch sortiert und in Container geladen wird.

Section
1. First-class lounge 2. Transit hold area 3. Departures road 4. Entrance 5. Departures concourse 6. Supermarket baggage and ticket check-in 7. Concession sales 8. Terrace 9. Observation deck 10. BOAC Departures hold lounge 11. Plant room 12. Arrivals corridor 13. Vehicle ramp to apron 14. Luffing bridges 15. Service road 16. BOAC baggage hall 17. Arrivals ramp from gallery 18. Immigration 19. Baggage claim 20. Customs 21. Arrivals lobby 22. Air Canada and precleared baggage claim 23. Exit 24. Arrivals road 25. Airport road

Section
1. Salon des premières classes 2. Zone de transit 3. Route d'accès des passagers au départ 4. Entrée 5. Salle des pas perdus départ 6. Contrôle des billets et enregistrement des bagages 7. Boutiques dédouanées 8. Terrasse 9. Terrasse d'observation 10. Salle d'attente des départs BOAC 11. Locaux techniques 12. Corridor des arrivées 13. Accès des véhicules à l'aire de stationnement des avions 14. Passerelles téléscopiques passagers 15. Route de service 16. Hall bagages BOAC 17. Descente des passagers à l'arrivée 18. Immigration 19. Livraison des bagages 20. Douane 21. Vestibule des arrivées 22. Air Canada et livraison des bagages du Canada 23. Sortie 24. Route de desserte des passagers à l'arrivée 25. Route de ceinture de l'aéroport

Schnitt
1. Wartesaal 1. Klasse 2. Wartesaal Transitpassagiere 3. Zufahrt Abflug 4. Eingang 5. Erschließungsflur Abflug 6. Gepäck- und Flugkarten-Check-in 7. Zollfreier Verkauf 8. Terrasse 9. Aussichtsterrasse 10. BOAC-Warteraum Abflug 11. Technikgeschoß 12. Erschließungsflur Ankunft 13. Fahrzeugrampe zum Vorfeld 14. Hubbrücke 15. Anlieferung 16. BOAC-Gepäckhalle 17. Zentraler Flur Ankunft 18. Paßkontrolle 19. Gepäckempfang 20. Zollkontrolle 21. Warteraum Ankunft 22. Gepäckempfang Air Canada und bereits abgefertigtes Gepäck 23. Ausgang 24. Zufahrt Ankunft 25. Flughafen-Ringstraße

Site plan
1. Boeing 747 gates 2. Apron drive telescopic jetways 3. VC10 gates 4. BOAC gallery 5. 150th Street 6. Common taxiway 7. Air Canada gallery 8. Stretched DC8 gate 9. DC8 gate 10. Departures road 11. Arrivals road 12. Airport road system 13. Car park 14. Taxi cab parking

Plan d'ensemble
1. Porte d'accès de Boeing 747 2. Rampe télescopique d'accès 3. Porte d'accès de VC10 4. Galerie de la BOAC 5. 150th Street 6. Pistes communes 7. Galerie d'Air Canada 8. Porte d'accès de Super-DC8 9. Porte d'accès de DC8 10. Route d'accès des passagers au départ 11. Route de desserte des passagers à l'arrivée 12. Route de ceinture de l'aéroport 13. Parc de stationnement autos 14. Station de taxis

Lageplan
1. Ausgang zu Boeing 747 2. Vorfeld-Finger 3. Ausgang zu VC10 4. BOAC-Galerie 5. 150th Street 6. Taxizufahrt 7. Air Canada-Galerie 8. Ausgang zu DC 8 9. Ausgang zur großen DC 8 10. Zufahrt Abflug 11. Zufahrt Ankunft 12. Flughafen-Ringstraße 13. Parkplatz 14. Taxistand

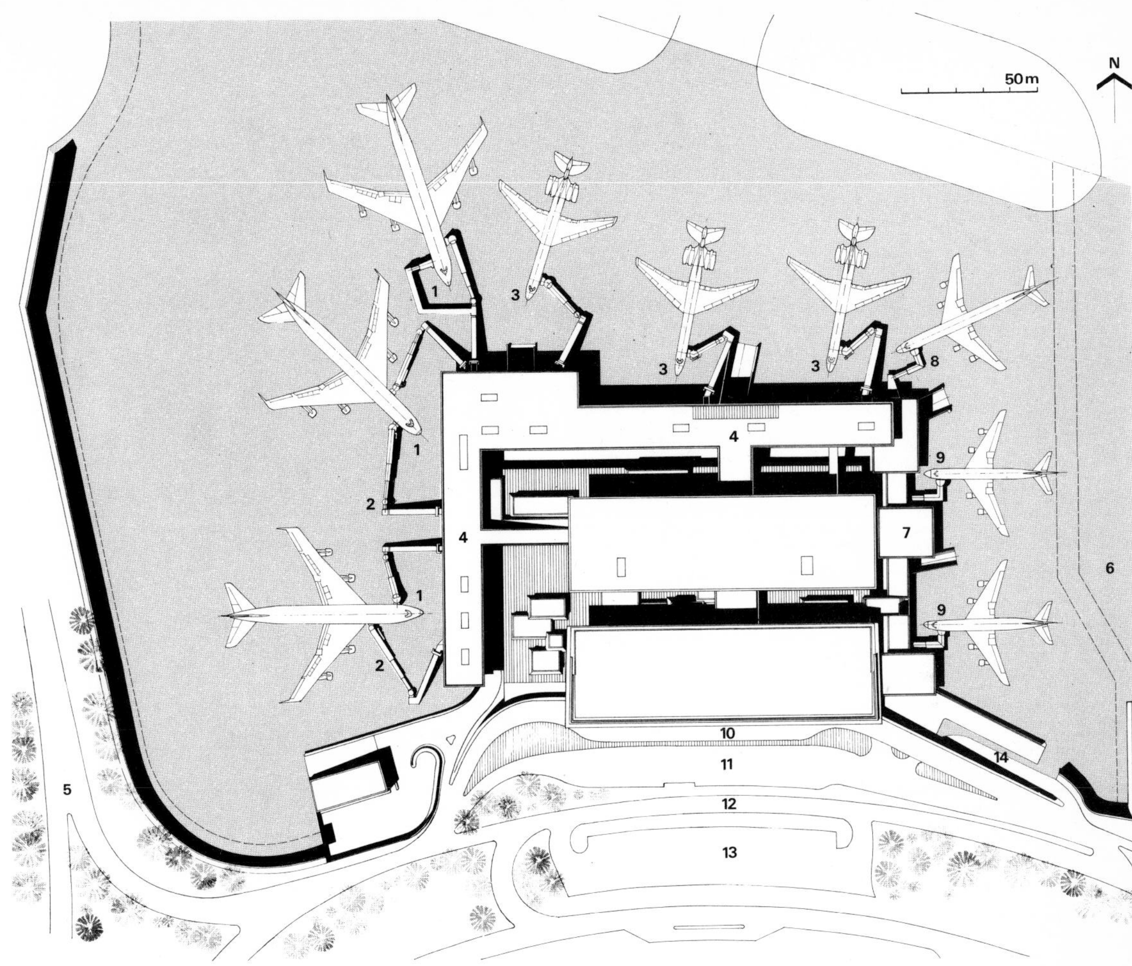

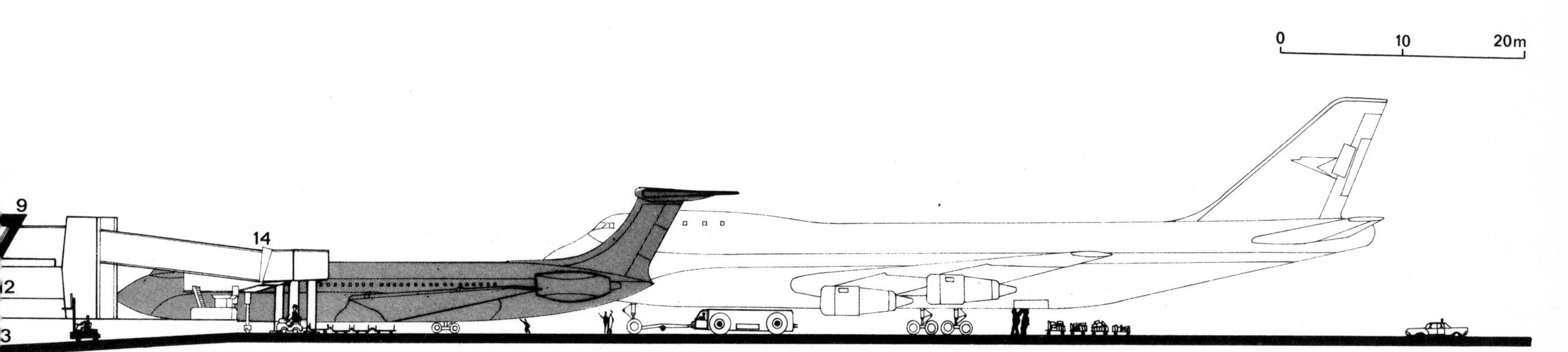

Service road/Route de service/Anlieferung

Departures concourse/Salle des pas perdus départs/
Erschließungsflur Abflug

21 Upper School, Syston, Leicestershire

Leicestershire Education Committee 1971

This school, planned for 1,440 girls and boys between the ages of 14 and 19, is on a 20 hectare- site in rural countryside on the outskirts of the village of Syston, near Leicester. It is on three floors with the classrooms and practical rooms grouped around a central core in which are, at ground level, the auditorium and, at first-floor level, the two-level main library/resource area. A self-contained sixth-form teaching and social/dining area opens off the main entrance foyer; two large physical education blocks adequate for badminton, basketball, and golf and cricket practice, are connected to the main building by a covered way.

The steel framed structure has 4 m deep lattice girders spanning from 15 m to 27 m; the external walls of pre-cast concrete units are faced with tiles.

Cet établissement, prévu pour 1.440 garçons et filles de 14 à 19 ans, est installé dans une région rurale sur un site de 20 hectares aux abords du village de Syston, près de Leicester. Les locaux se répartissent sur trois niveaux, les salles de cours et d'enseignement pratique entourant un noyau central qui comprend l'auditorium au rez-de-chaussée et au-dessus la « bibliothèque-centre de connaissances » installée sur deux niveaux. Du foyer de l'entrée principale on accède à la zone d'enseignement et d'activités sociales des classes terminales, qui forme une section indépendante; deux vastes bâtiments d'éducation physique permettant la pratique du badminton, du basketball, du golf et du cricket sont reliés par une allée couverte au bâtiment principal.

La structure métallique est constituée de poutres en treillis d'une hauteur de 4 m et dont la portée varie de 15 à 27 m; les murs extérieurs sont constitués de panneaux de béton préfabriqués recouverts de tuiles.

Diese Schule für 1440 Schülerinnen und Schüler im Alter von 14 bis 19 Jahren liegt auf einem etwa 20 ha großen Grundstück in ländlicher Umgebung am Rande des Dorfes Syston bei Leicester. Auf drei Geschossen sind die theoretischen und praktischen Unterrichtsräume um einen zentralen Kern gruppiert, in dem sich auf Eingangsniveau die Aula und im ersten Geschoß der zweistöckige Bibliotheks- und Erholungsbereich befinden. Ein unabhängiger Unterrichts- sowie Sozial-/Eßbereich der Abschlußklassen wird über die Haupteingangshalle erschlossen; zwei große Trakte für Leibeserziehung – nutzbar für Badminton, Basketball, Golf und Kricket – sind durch einen überdachten Gang mit dem Hauptbau verbunden.

Die Stahlrahmenkonstruktion besteht aus etwa 4 m langen Balken und überspannt eine Weite von etwa 15 bis 27 m. Die Außenwände aus vorgefertigten Betonelementen sind mit Fliesen verkleidet.

Site plan
1. Caretaker's house 2. Car park 3. Coach park 4. Main teaching block 5. Science wing 6. Art and craft area 7. Games hall 8+9. Sixth-form and adult centre 10. Future high school 11. Tennis courts 12. Gardening plots 13. All weather play pitch 14. Playing fields

Plan d'ensemble
1. Loge du concierge 2. Stationnement voitures 3. Stationnement cars 4. Bloc principal d'enseignement 5. Aile des Sciences 6. Travaux artistiques et manuels 7. Salle de jeux 8+9. Classes terminales et centre pour adultes 10. Futur lycée du premier cycle 11. Courts de tennis 12. Parcelles à jardiner 13. Terrains de jeux couverts 14. Terrains de jeux

Lageplan
1. Hausmeisterwohnung 2. Parkplatz 3. Busparkplatz 4. Allgemeiner Unterrichtstrakt 5. Naturwissenschaften 6. Kunst und Kunsthandwerk 7. Sporthalle 8+9. Abschlußklassen und Erwachsenenbildung 10. Geplante Oberschule 11. Tennisplätze 12. Gartenfläche 13. Überdachtes Sportfeld 14. Sportplätze

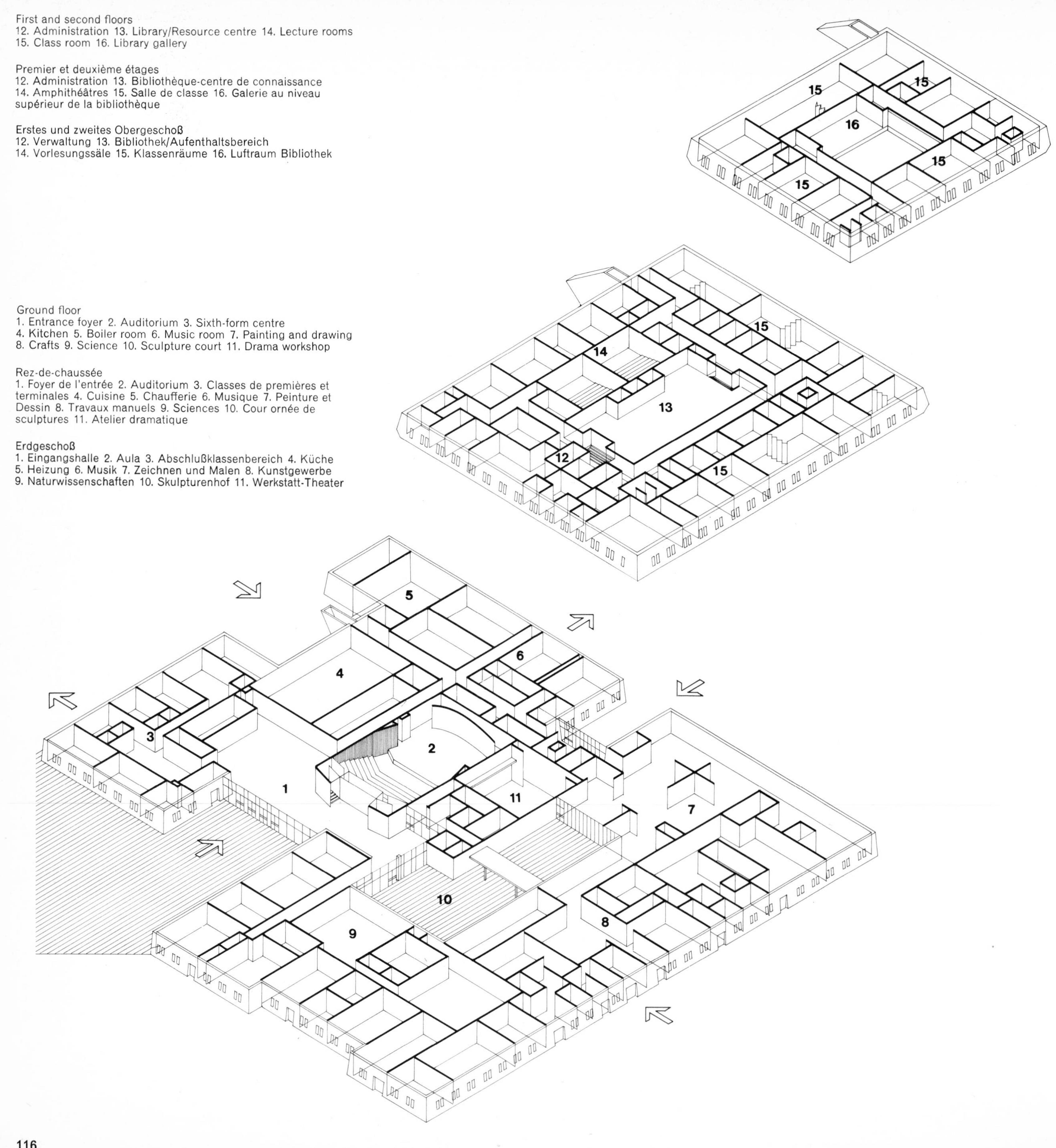

First and second floors
12. Administration 13. Library/Resource centre 14. Lecture rooms
15. Class room 16. Library gallery

Premier et deuxième étages
12. Administration 13. Bibliothèque-centre de connaissance
14. Amphithéâtres 15. Salle de classe 16. Galerie au niveau supérieur de la bibliothèque

Erstes und zweites Obergeschoß
12. Verwaltung 13. Bibliothek/Aufenthaltsbereich
14. Vorlesungssäle 15. Klassenräume 16. Luftraum Bibliothek

Ground floor
1. Entrance foyer 2. Auditorium 3. Sixth-form centre
4. Kitchen 5. Boiler room 6. Music room 7. Painting and drawing
8. Crafts 9. Science 10. Sculpture court 11. Drama workshop

Rez-de-chaussée
1. Foyer de l'entrée 2. Auditorium 3. Classes de premières et terminales 4. Cuisine 5. Chaufferie 6. Musique 7. Peinture et Dessin 8. Travaux manuels 9. Sciences 10. Cour ornée de sculptures 11. Atelier dramatique

Erdgeschoß
1. Eingangshalle 2. Aula 3. Abschlußklassenbereich 4. Küche
5. Heizung 6. Musik 7. Zeichnen und Malen 8. Kunstgewerbe
9. Naturwissenschaften 10. Skulpturenhof 11. Werkstatt-Theater

EXIT

Courtyard/Cour intérieure/Innenhof

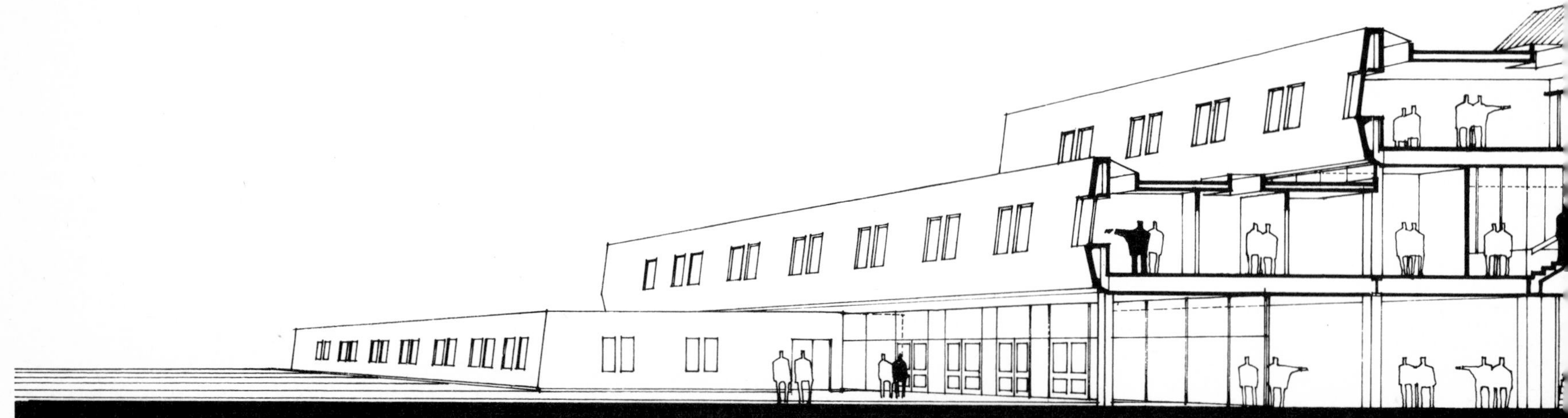

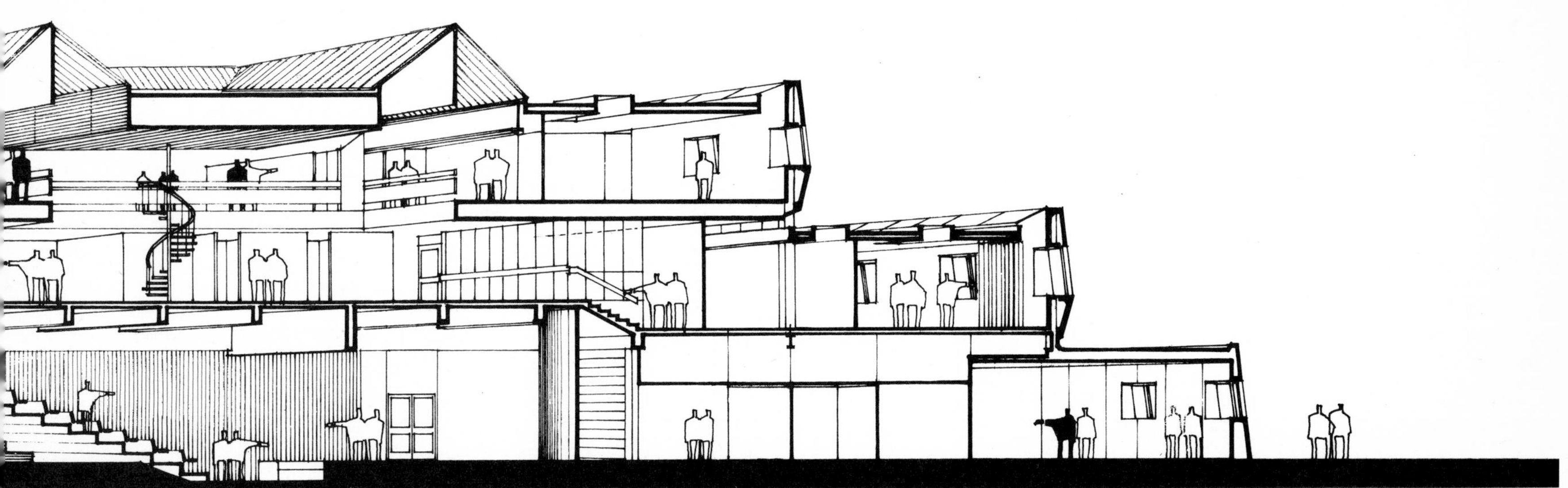

22 University of Sheffield

Biological Sciences 1971

This building, developed in three stages, completes the south-east corner of the rectangle of buildings envisaged in the original Edwardian plan for the university. The majority of the laboratories and ancillary rooms are in the eight-storey block facing Western Bank, and the lecture theatres and the department of human biology and anatomy form a square in plan building in the centre courtyard linked by corridor connexions to the north and south wings.

Construit en trois phases, ce bâtiment complète l'angle Sud-Est du rectangle de bâtiments prévu dans le plan original de l'Université établi à l'époque édouardienne. La majorité des laboratoires et de leurs dépendances sont installés dans le bâtiment de huit étages regardant la Western Bank, et les amphithéâtres ainsi que le département de biologie humaine et d'anatomie occupent un bâtiment de plan carré au centre de la cour intérieure, relié aux ailes Nord et Sud par des corridors.

Dieses in drei Baustufen entstandene Gebäude vervollständigt die Südostecke der rechteckigen Überbauung, die im ursprünglichen Plan aus der Zeit Edwards für die Universität vorgesehen war. Die Mehrzahl der Laboratorien und dazugehörigen Räume liegt in dem Western Bank zugewandten, achtgeschossigen Trakt. Die Hörsäle und die Abteilung für Humanbiologie und Anatomie befinden sich in einem quadratischen Bau im zentralen Hof. Sie sind durch Korridore mit den nördlichen und südlichen Trakten verbunden.

As both from University Court and Western Bank the building will always be seen in relation to the red-brick architecture of the original university, a similar brick has been used for facing the concrete framed structure. The south exposure and the considerable traffic noise from Western Bank required that there be no opening lights and a modified system of air conditioning with induction units has been adopted; the window-frames are bronze. The siting of the animal rooms and the greenhouse which do not require windows on the top floor allowed the brick band immediately below the coping to be exceptionally deep.

Comme les nouveaux bâtiments seront toujours vus, aussi bien de la Western Bank que de la cour intérieure de l'Université, en relation avec l'architecture de briques rouges de l'ancienne université, on a utilisé une brique semblable pour revêtir la structure de béton. L'exposition au Sud et le bruit considérable de la circulation dans la Western Bank exigeaient un vitrage sans ouverture et l'on a adopté un système particulier de conditionnement d'air utilisant des unités ozonair; les encadrements des fenêtres sont de couleur bronze. La localisation au dernier étage de l'animalerie et de la serre, qui ne nécessitent pas de fenêtres, a permis de donner une largeur exceptionnelle au bandeau de briques courant en dessous du toit.

Sowohl vom Universitätsgelände als auch von der Straße wird der Bau stets im Zusammenhang mit der roten Backsteinarchitektur der alten Universität gesehen. Daher wurde ein ähnlicher Backstein für die Ausfüllung des Betontragwerks verwendet. Die Südorientierung und der erhebliche Verkehrslärm vom Western Bank erforderten den Verzicht auf zu öffnende Fenster, dafür totale Klimatisierung mit Frischluftzufuhr; die Fenstereinfassungen sind aus Bronze. Die Situierung der Tierräume und des Gewächshauses, die keine Fenster benötigen, im obersten Geschoß ermöglichte den außergewöhnlich breiten Abschlußstreifen aus Backstein.

23 University Library Extension, Grange Road, Cambridge

University of Cambridge 1971

The existing library was opened in 1934 and contains 8,800 m² of accommodation for books and readers and 82,200 linear m of shelving, enough to accommodate two and a half million volumes. It was hoped in 1934 that this building would have enough capacity to accommodate new volumes for fifty years, but as a result of the increased rate of scholarly publications it became evident that it would become virtually full in the nineteen sixties. In 1951, therefore, the university authorized the planning of the extension, on which construction work started in 1968.

Sited immediately at the rear of the existing library, to which it is linked at all floor levels, the extension provides a storage capacity of just under 60,960 linear m adequate to accommodate a further two million books. In addition, on the first and third floors at each end of the bookstack which forms the main and central element of the plan are the double-storey height reading rooms and the lecture room, all of which have natural light. Beneath these rooms on the ground floor are the photographic and catalogue printing departments, and at first-floor level between the new bookstack and the main reading room of the original library is the new periodicals reading room.

The new stack, air-conditioned with full temperature and humidity controls, is planned on the principle of closed access, as it is largely for the storage of rarer books moved from the existing library which now has open access available to all readers. By introducing power-operated compact mobile bookstacks the ratio of books stored to a given floor area has been almost doubled on the lower floors, where the greater loads were more acceptable.

As further extensions are envisaged in the future the new building, which only represents Stage 1 of the total development, has been planned so that the principle of an artificially lit and air-conditioned central bookstack with naturally lit reading rooms on the perimeter can be extended in phases without fear of causing other than the minimum of inconvenience to the present users of the library.

La bibliothèque actuelle a été ouverte en 1934; elle a quelque 8.800 m² de surface utile et contient plus de 60.960 m linéaires de rayonnages, pouvant recevoir 2.500.000 volumes. On avait l'espoir en 1934 que ce bâtiment aurait ainsi une capacité suffisante pour recevoir les nouvelles acquisitions pendant cinquante ans mais avec l'accroissement du rythme des publications universitaires il devint évident que la bibliothèque serait pratiquement saturée vers la fin des années 60. C'est pourquoi l'Université admit en 1951 le principe d'une extension dont l'étude commença en 1968.

Située immédiatement à l'arrière de la bibliothèque existante, avec laquelle elle communique à tous les niveaux, l'extension assure une capacité de rangement supplémentaire de 60.000 m linéaires correspondant à deux millions de volumes de plus. En outre, au premier et au troisième étage de chaque côté des réserves de livres qui constituent l'élément principal et central du bâtiment, se trouvent des salles de lecture occupant deux niveaux et un amphithéâtre, tous bénéficiant d'un éclairage naturel. Au dessous de ces salles, au rez-de-chaussée, sont installés les départements de photographie et d'édition des catalogues, et au premier étage, entre les nouvelles réserves de livres et la salle de lecture principale de l'ancienne bibliothèque, se trouve la nouvelle salle de lecture des revues.

La conception de la nouvelle réserve, où l'air est conditionné avec contrôle complet de la température et de l'humidité, repose sur le principe qu'elle n'est pas accessible: on l'a en effet principalement utilisée pour y ranger les livres les plus rares, transférés de la bibliothèque ancienne dont l'accès est maintenant ouvert à tous les lecteurs.

En installant un système de rangement compact et mobile à commande électrique, on a pu pratiquement doubler le volume de livres à surface égale dans les niveaux les plus bas, c'est-à-dire là où des charges plus fortes étaient acceptables. D'autres extensions ultérieures étant envisagées, le nouveau bâtiment, qui ne représente que la première phase d'un développement plus vaste, a été conçu de telle manière que les phases suivantes puissent répéter ce principe d'une réserve centrale avec éclairage artificiel et air conditionné et de salles de lecture à éclairage naturel situées sur son périmètre – tout en ne causant pendant leur construction que le minimum d'inconvénients aux utilisateurs de l'actuelle bibliothèque.

Die vorhandene Bibliothek wurde 1934 eröffnet und enthält etwa 8.800 m² Nutzfläche für Bücher und Leser und etwa 82.200 laufende m Regale, ausreichend zur Unterbringung von 2½ Millionen Bänden. Im Jahre 1934 hoffte man, daß dieser Bau für 50 Jahre genügend Kapazität zur Aufnahme von neuen Bänden haben würde. Doch die wachsende Erscheinungsrate wissenschaftlicher Publikationen ließ erkennen, daß ihre Aufnahmemöglichkeit in den sechziger Jahren erschöpft sein würde. 1951 genehmigte die Universität daher die Planung der Erweiterung. Die Bauarbeiten begannen 1968.

Unmittelbar hinter der bestehenden Bibliothek situiert, mit der sie auf allen Ebenen verbunden ist, bietet die Erweiterung fast 60.960 laufende m Lagerraum zur Aufnahme von weiteren zwei Millionen Bänden. Außerdem liegen im ersten und dritten Obergeschoß an beiden Enden des Magazins, welches das zentrale Element des Grundrisses darstellt, die zweigeschossigen Lesesäle und der Vorlesungssaal, alle mit natürlicher Belichtung. Unter diesen Räumen im Erdgeschoß befinden sich die Foto- und Katalogdruckabteilungen. Im ersten Obergeschoß zwischen dem neuen Magazin und dem großen Lesesaal der alten Bibliothek liegt der neue Zeitschriftenlesesaal.

Das neue, klimatisierte, mit voller Temperatur- und Feuchtigkeitskontrolle ausgestattete Magazin ist nicht frei zugänglich, da es vorwiegend der Lagerung seltener Bände aus der alten Bibliothek dient, die jetzt für alle Leser zugänglich ist. Durch Einführung von energiebetriebenen, raumsparenden, mobilen Stapelelementen konnte die Zahl von gelagerten Büchern in den unteren Geschossen, wo größere Lasten akzeptabel sind, fast verdoppelt werden.

Da zusätzliche Erweiterungen in Zukunft vorgesehen sind, ist dieser Neubau, der nur die erste Stufe der geplanten Erweiterung darstellt, so geplant, daß das Prinzip des künstlich belichteten und klimatisierten zentralen Magazins mit natürlich belichteten Lesesälen im Außenbereichin Abschnitten weitergeführt werden kann, ohne daß mehr als nur minimale Unbequemlichkeiten den Benutzern der Bibliothek zugemutet werden müssen.

Reading room/Salle de lecture/Lesesaal

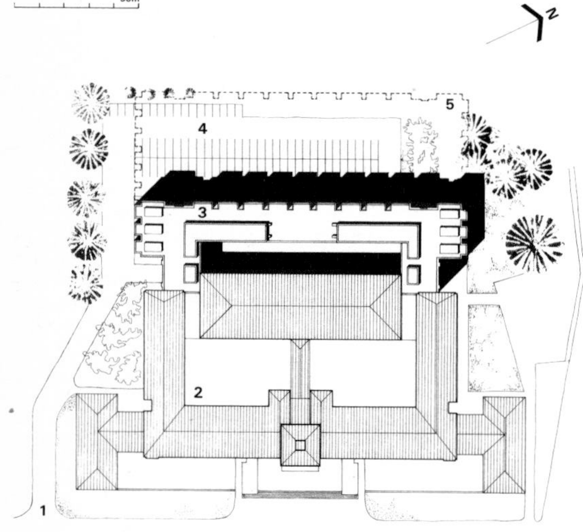

Site plan
1. Street entrance 2. Existing library 3. New library 4. Car park
5. Line of future extension

Plan d'ensemble
1. Entrée côté rue 2. Bibliothèque existante 3. Extension
4. Parc de stationnement autos 5. Tracé de l'extension ultérieure

Lageplan
1. Eingang von der Straße 2. Alte Bibliothek 3. Neue Bibliothek
4. Parkplatz 5. Geplante Erweiterung

24 Headquarter Offices, Stevenage, Hertfordshire

Manufacturers Life Insurance Company 1973

The site, near the centre of Stevenage New Town, has a frontage to St George's Way and is flanked on one side by St George's Church and on the other by the Fire Brigade Headquarters.

The office accommodation is on six similar floors above an extended ground floor where are the main and service entrances, the supply areas, and the kitchen and restaurant. The gross area is 8,120 m^2. The offset central core in which are three passenger lifts, two staircases and toilets, permits small offices on the narrow north side and deeper offices on the south. There is no basement and all plant rooms, boilers, and water storage are on the roof.

All floors are clad externally in class 'O' glass reinforced polyester panels which, on the upper floors, are 1·5 m wide by 3·5 m high and on the ground floor 3 m wide by 3·5 m high. The internal window wall lining, mullion casings, and induction unit covers are also of GRP, and the gasketed glazing of 6 mm clear bronze-tinted glass forms the junction between the inner and outer skins. The internal layout of the office floors occupied by Manulife is entirely open plan; to achieve the degree of acoustic privacy required, floors are carpeted, the core is lined with fabric-covered acoustic panels, and the curtains have both an acoustic and solar reflective value.

The ground floor structure of reinforced concrete columns is connected by a ring beam at first-floor level which supports on the upper floors mild steel-cased box section structural mullions at 3 m centres. The floors are of concrete coffered slabs and the core walls act as wind bracing.

Le terrain, proche du centre de la Ville Nouvelle de Stevenage, est en bordure de la St George's Way et est flanqué d'un côté par St George's Church, de l'autre par le quartier-général des pompiers.

Les bureaux sont répartis dans six étages identiques au dessus d'un rez-de-chaussée allongé comprenant les entrées principale et de service, les réserves de fournitures, les cuisines et le restaurant. La surface globale est de 8.120 m^2. Le noyau central (qui contient trois ascenseurs, deux escaliers et les toilettes) est décentré, ce qui permet d'avoir dans la partie Nord, étroite, de l'immeuble, de petits bureaux, et dans sa partie Sud des bureaux plus vastes. Il n'y a pas de sous-sol et tous les équipements techniques, la chaudière et les réservoirs d'eau sont sur le toit.

Tous les niveaux sont revêtus extérieurement d'un bardage de panneaux en fibre de verre renforcée de polyester de catégorie « O », mesurant 1,5 m de large sur 3,5 m de haut aux étages supérieurs et 3 m sur 3,5 m au rez-de-chaussée. Les dormants des fenêtres, trumeaux et grilles d'inducteurs sont aussi en fibre de verre renforcée de polyester, et le vitrage de 6 mm, à joints souples, coloré en bronze clair forme la jonction entre les parements interne et externe. Toute la surface affectée à des bureaux est traitée, à tous les niveaux, en plateaux paysagers: pour obtenir le niveau d'intimité acoustique nécessaire, les sols sont couverts de moquettes, le noyau central revêtu de panneaux acoustiques couverts de tissu et les rideaux ont une bonne valeur d'absorption des sons et des rayons solaires.

La structure du rez-de-chaussée faite de colonnes de béton armé est reliée au niveau du premier étage à une poutre de reprise qui supporte une structure de trumeaux espacés de 3 m. Ces trumeaux sont des profilés à froid fermés, en acier doux. Les planchers sont des dalles de béton en nid d'abeilles et les murs du noyau central jouent le rôle de contreventement.

Das Grundstück in der Nähe des Zentrums der neuen Stadt Stevenage liegt am St George's Way und ist an einer Seite von der Kirche St George's, an der anderen vom Hauptquartier der Feuerwehr begrenzt.

Die Büroräume liegen in sechs Geschossen mit gleichem Grundriß über einem ausgedehnten Erdgeschoß, in dem Haupt- und Anliefereingang, die Versorgungsbereiche, die Küche und das Restaurant untergebracht sind. Die Bruttogeschoßfläche beträgt 8.120 m^2. Der abgesetzte zentrale Kern, der drei Personenaufzüge, zwei Treppenhäuser und Toiletten enthält, ermöglicht die Anlage kleiner Büros an der schmalen Nordseite und tieferer Büros im Süden. Der Bau hat kein Untergeschoß, alle Maschinenräume, Kessel und Wasserreservoir befinden sich auf dem Dach.

Alle Geschoßdecken sind außen mit glasfaserverstärkten Polyesterplatten verkleidet, die in den Obergeschossen die Abmessungen 1,5×3,5 und im Erdgeschoß 3,0×3,5 haben. Die innere Verkleidung der Fensterwände, der senkrechten Verstrebungen sowie der Induktionselemente ist ebenfalls aus Kunststoff. Die abgedichtete, 6 mm starke, durchsichtige, bronzegetönte Verglasung bildet die Verbindung zwischen der inneren und der äußeren Haut. Die vom Bauherrn benutzten Bürogeschosse sind Großraumbüros. Zur notwendigen akustischen Abschirmung sind die Geschosse mit Teppichen ausgelegt, der Kern ist mit stoffbezogenen Akustikplatten verkleidet, die Vorhänge sind sowohl schall- als auch sonnenlichtreflektierend.

Die Konstruktion des Erdgeschosses aus Stahlbetonstützen ist auf Ebene des ersten Obergeschosses durch einen Ringbalken verbunden, der die stahlverkleideten, im Abstand von 3 m angeordneten Kastenquerschnitt-Stützen der oberen Geschosse tragen. Die Böden sind aus kassettenartigen Betonplatten, die Wände des Kerns wirken als Windaussteifung.

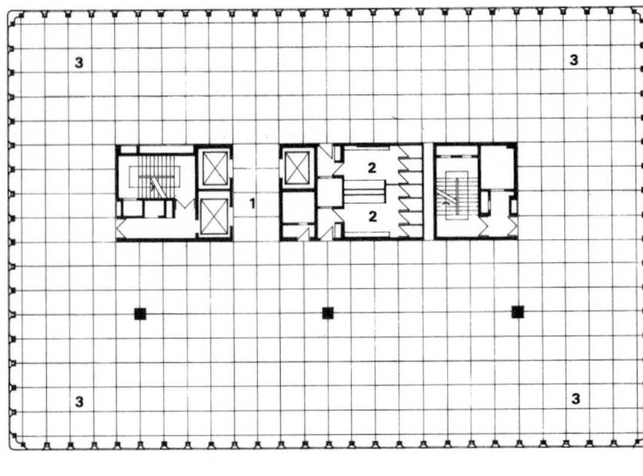

10m N

Typical floor plan
1. Lift lobby 2. WC 3. Office space

Plan-type d'étage
1. Vestibule des ascenseurs 2. WC 3. Espace de bureaux

Grundriß Normalgeschoß
1. Aufzugshalle 2. WC 3. Bürofläche

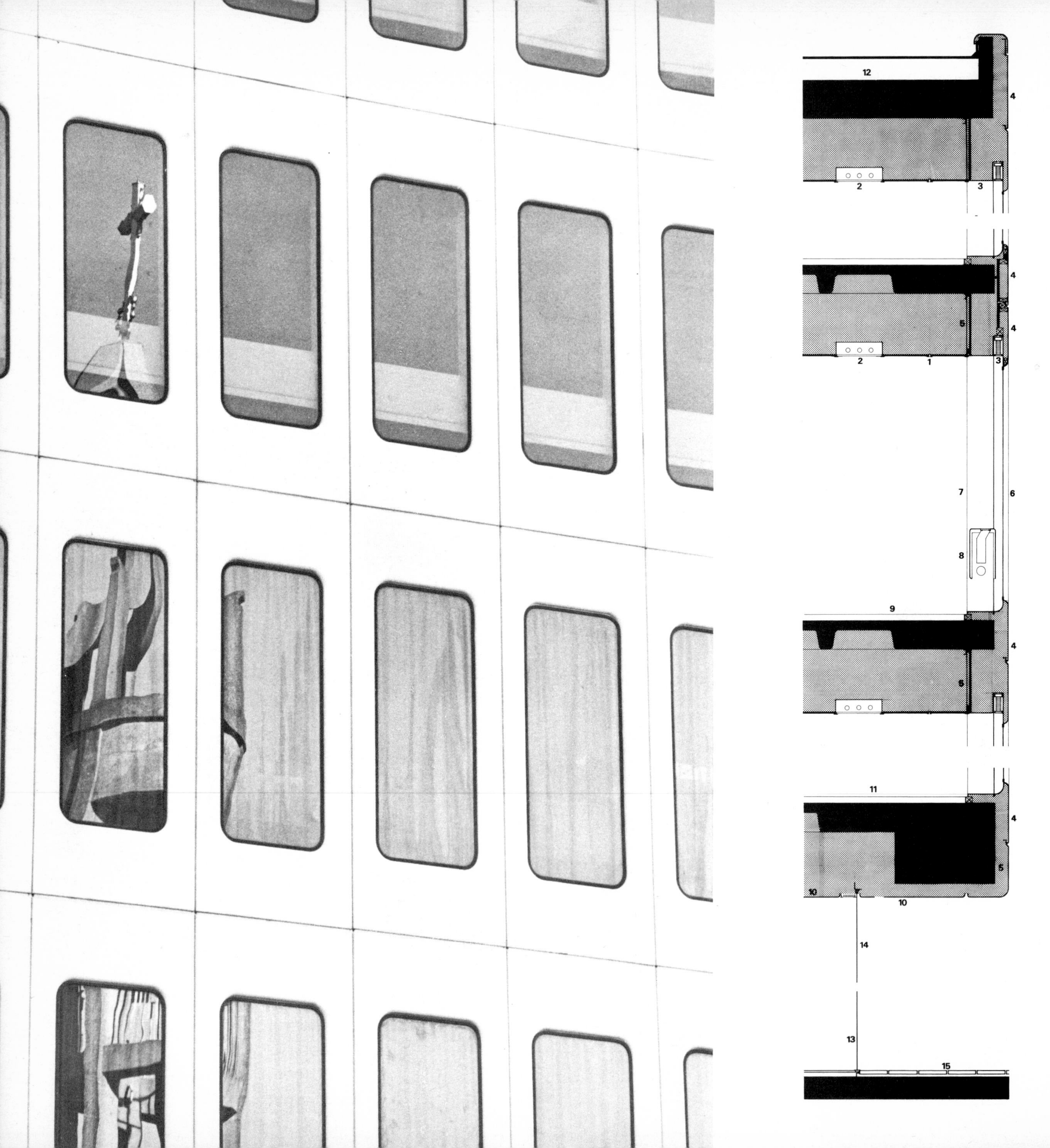

12
4
2
3
4
5
4
2
1
3
7
6
8
9
4
5
11
4
5
10
10
14
13
15

External wall details
1. Suspended ceiling 2. Light fitting 3. Blind box 4. Glass reinforced polyester panel 5. Fire break 6. Spectrafloat bronze glass 7. Glass reinforced polyester column casings 8. Induction unit 9. Typical office floor 10. Glass reinforced polyester soffit panel 11. First floor 12. Roof 13. Ground floor 14. Clear glass 15. 1200 mm Deep ring beam

Détails du mur de façade
1. Faux plafond 2. Appareil d'éclairage 3. Coffre de store 4. Panneau de verre renforcé de polyester 5. Coupe-feu 6. Verre réfléchissant teinté bronze 7. Habillage de poteau en verre renforcé de polyester 8. Unité d'induction 9. Étage-type de bureaux 10. Retombée habillée de verre renforcé de polyester 11. Premier étage 12. Toit 13. Rez-de-chaussée 14. Verre transparent 15. Poutre de reprise (épaisseur 1.200 mm)

Außenwanddetails
1. Abgehängte Decke 2. Beleuchtungskörper 3. Blinder Kasten 4. Glasfaserverstärkte Polyesterplatte 5. Feuerschutz 6. Reflektierendes Bronzeglas 7. Glasfaserverstärkte Stützenverkleidung aus Polyester 8. Klimaelement 9. Standard-Bürogeschoß 10. Glasfaserverstärkte Polyester-Unterseite 11. Erstes Obergeschoß 12. Dach 13. Erdgeschoß 14. Klarglas 15. 1200 mm breites umlaufendes Horizontalband

Entrance lobby/Vestibule d'entrée/Eingangshalle

25 Woking Centre Pool, Surrey

Woking Urban District Council 1973

The swimming pools form part of the new civic area complex at Woking which, when completed, will include the county library, two civic halls, the police station and magistrates court, and a number of administrative buildings for which the precise use has not yet been determined. The pools, which are the first of the group to be completed, lie at the extreme north-west corner of the area and are surrounded by the town centre relief road circuit. The close proximity of the Basingstoke Canal and the resultant high level of ground water precluded sinking the pools, and the pool surround is therefore at first-floor level where also are the male and female changing rooms and essential user services. The main pool with a 4·8 m springboard is 25 m long by 12·5 m wide, adequate for six racing lanes; on one side are tiered seats for 108 spectators. The teaching pool is 12·5 m long by 7·5 m wide with a maximum depth of 0·9 m and spectator seating for thirty.

At the upper level, with views over the main pool, are a self-service restaurant for forty and the administrative offices. At ground level there are a sauna suite, slipper baths and laundry and also the greater part of the mechanical plant both for the water treatment and air-conditioning installations. The ventilation system is designed to keep the pool halls at 28°C. in the daytime with eleven air changes per hour. The water treatment plant provides automatic backwashing of the filters approximately every seventy-two hours.

The structure, where exposed externally, is finished in a bush hammered white aggregate with pre-cast infill concrete panels of a similar texture. The non-openable steel windows are protected from the corrosive action of chlorine by a skin of dark grey mipolam; the double glazing is grey tinted.

Ces piscines constituent l'un des éléments du nouveau « complexe civique » de Woking qui, une fois achevé, comprendra la bibliothèque du comté, deux centres sociaux, le commissariat de police et le tribunal et un certain nombre de bâtiments administratifs dont la destination n'a pas encore été précisément déterminée. Les piscines, qui sont le premier élément du complexe à être achevé, sont situées à l'extrémité Nord-Ouest de celui-ci, et sont entourées par le circuit routier de dégagement du centre ville. La proximité immédiate du Basingstoke Canal et l'affleurement de la nappe phréatique qui en résulte ont interdit d'enterrer les bassins des piscines et le niveau des bordures de ces bassins est approximativement à la hauteur du premier étage; c'est aussi à ce niveau qu'on trouve les vestiaires hommes et dames, et les principaux services concernant les utilisateurs. Le bassin principal est équipé d'un plongeoir de 4,8 m; il mesure 25 sur 12,5 m et comporte six couloirs de course; sur l'un des côtés il y a des sièges en gradins pour 108 spectateurs. Le petit bassin mesure 12,5 sur 7,5 m, a une profondeur maximum de 90 cm et est bordé de trente sièges de spectateurs.

Au niveau supérieur, d'où l'on a vue sur l'ensemble de la piscine, il y a un self-service pour quarante personnes et les locaux administratifs. Au rez-de-chaussée il y a un sauna, des baignoires-sabots, une blanchisserie et la plus grande partie des équipements mécaniques concernant aussi bien l'épuration de l'eau que le conditionnement d'air. Le système de ventilation est réglé pour maintenir la température à 28° aux heures d'ouverture avec onze changements d'air par heure. Le système de traitement d'eau assure un nettoyage des filtres par remous automatiques toutes les soixante-douze heures environ.

La structure, là ou elle est visible extérieurement, est revêtue d'un agrégat blanc bouchardé et de panneaux de remplissage en béton préfabriqué d'une texture analogue. Les fenêtres non-ouvrables ont des encadrements d'acier enrobé de mipolam gris foncé pour les protéger de l'action corrosive de la chlorine; leur vitrage double est teinté en gris.

Das Schwimmbad in Woking ist Teil eines neuen Bürgerzentrums, das nach Fertigstellung eine Bibliothek, zwei Stadthallen, Polizeistation und Friedensgericht sowie eine Anzahl von Verwaltungsgebäuden, deren genaue Bestimmung noch nicht festgelegt ist, umfassen soll. Das Hallenbad, der erste ausgeführte Bau einer demnächst fertigwerdenden Gruppe von Bauten, liegt in der äußersten Nordwestecke des Bereiches innerhalb der das Stadtzentrum entlastenden Umgehungsstraße. Die Nähe des Basingstoke Kanals und der entsprechend hohe Grundwasserstand schlossen ein Tieferlegen des Schwimmbeckens aus. Die Becken liegen daher etwa auf Höhe des ersten Obergeschosses. Dort befinden sich auch die Umkleideräume für Männer und Frauen sowie die notwendigen Dienstleistungseinrichtungen. Das große Becken mit einem 4,8 m-Sprungbrett ist 25 m lang und 12,5 m breit und kann in sechs Wettkampfbahnen aufgeteilt werden. Auf einer Seite sind ansteigende Sitze für 108 Zuschauer angeordnet. Das Lehrschwimmbecken ist 12,5 m lang und 7,5 m breit mit einer Mindesttiefe von 90 cm und 30 Zuschauerplätzen.

Im Obergeschoß liegen, mit Blick auf das große Becken, ein Selbstbedienungs-Restaurant für 40 Personen sowie die Verwaltungsräume. Im Erdgeschoß sind die Sauna, Fußbäder und Wäscherei sowie der größte Teil der Technik – Wasseraufbereitung und Klimaanlage – untergebracht. Das Lüftungssystem hält die Schwimmhalle tagsüber bei 28 °C mit elf Luftumwälzungen pro Stunde. Die Wasseraufbereitungsanlage ermöglicht automatische Rückwaschung der Filter etwa alle 72 Stunden.

Die Konstruktion ist dort, wo sie sichtbar bleibt, sandstrahlbehandelter Beton mit hellem Zuschlag, die vorgefertigten Betonplatten der Ausfüllung haben ähnliche Struktur. Die nicht zu öffnenden Stahlfenster sind vor Korrosion durch Chlor durch eine Haut aus dunkelgrauem Mipolam geschützt; die doppelte Verglasung ist grau getönt.

Main pool/Bassin principal/Großes Becken

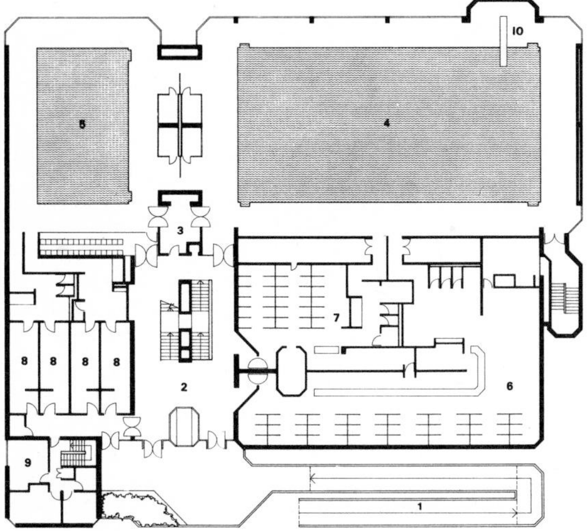

Centre pool main floor
1. Ramp 2. Entrance hall 3. First aid 4. Main pool 5. Teaching pool 6. Changing rooms male 7. Changing rooms female 8. Changing rooms children 9. Caretaker's flat 10. Springboard

Niveau principal du bassin central
1. Rampe d'accès 2. Hall d'entrée 3. Premiers soins 4. Bassin principal 5. Petit bassin 6. Vestiaires hommes 7. Vestiaires dames 8. Vestiaires enfants 9. Appartement du concierge 10. Plongeoir

Grundriß Hauptgeschoß (auf Ebene großes Becken)
1. Rampe 2. Eingangshalle 3. Erste Hilfe 4. Großes Becken 5. Lehrschwimmbecken 6. Umkleideräume Männer 7. Umkleideräume Frauen 8. Umkleideräume Kinder 9. Hausmeisterwohnung 10. Sprungbrett

26 Headquarter Offices, Fulham Road, London SW3

The Michelin Tyre Company

In 1970 the Michelin Tyre Company asked GMW to investigate the possibility of developing with good quality office accommodation their island site at the corner of Fulham Road and Sloane Avenue in Chelsea which they had acquired in 1902. Any scheme had to retain and remain in scale with the original existing listed building which fronts on to the Fulham Road and is faced with faïence tiling and coloured low-relief panels depicting exploits in Bibendum's life. It had also to take into account the restricted and awkward shape of the site and respect the predominantly residential character of the neighbourhood.

The gross office area of some 8,600 m^2 is partly in a four-storey tower and partly on the upper floor of the two-storey podium which extends over the whole area of the site. The ground floor of the podium, except for the entrance hall and a small showroom, is open. To relate the tower to the existing building the floors overlooking Fulham Road are, as they rise, cut back forming at each level large terraces available for landscaping; the elevational treatment repeats the idiom of the existing building with tile faced flat arches. The building is fully air-conditioned and has parking for seventy cars in the basement.

La Compagnie des Pneus Michelin demanda à Gollins Melvin Ward en 1970 d'étudier la possibilité de mettre en valeur l'ilôt qu'elle avait acheté en 1902 dans Chelsea à l'angle de Fulham Road et de Sloane Avenue, en y implantant des locaux de bureaux de qualité. Le projet devait conserver et rester à l'échelle du bâtiment classé qui donne sur Fulham Road et dont la façade est revêtue de carreaux de faïence et de panneaux de bas-reliefs en couleur retraçant les exploits de Bibendum; il devait aussi tenir compte des dimensions restreintes et malcommodes du terrain et respecter le caractère principalement résidentiel du voisinage.

La surface de bureaux (8.600 m^2) se répartit entre une petite tour de quatre niveaux et l'étage supérieur d'un podium de deux niveaux qui couvre tout le terrain. Le rez-de-chaussée du podium est resté libre, à l'exception d'un hall d'entrée et d'une salle d'exposition. Pour relier la tour au bâtiment ancien, les différents niveaux du côté de Fulham Road ont été prolongés par de larges terrasses qui pourront recevoir un décor de jardins; le traitement des façades répète le langage visuel du bâtiment existant, avec des arcades plates décorées de carreaux. Le bâtiment est entièrement climatisé et dispose au sous-sol d'un garage pour soixante-dix voitures.

Im Jahre 1970 wurden Gollins Melvin Ward von der Firma Michelin aufgefordert, die Möglichkeiten der Bebauung ihres 1902 erworbenen Grundstücks an der Ecke Fulham Road und Sloane Avenue in Chelsea mit modernen Büros zu prüfen. Der Entwurf mußte das vorhandene, unter Denkmalschutz stehende Gebäude am Fulham Road, das mit Fayencefliesen und bemalten Relieftafeln, die Heldentaten aus dem Leben des Bibendum darstellen, verkleidet ist, einbeziehen und im Maßstab dazu bleiben. Er mußte darüber hinaus die beschränkte und ungünstige Form des Grundstücks und den überwiegenden Wohncharakter des Gebietes berücksichtigen.

Die Bruttogeschoßfläche von etwa 8.600 m^2 ist teils in einem viergeschossigen Trakt, teils im Obergeschoß des zweigeschossigen Podiums untergebracht, das die gesamte Grundstücksfläche einnimmt. Das Erdgeschoß des Podiums ist, mit Ausnahme der Eingangshalle und einem kleinen Ausstellungsraum, offen. Um den Hochtrakt im Maßstab des alten Gebäudes zu halten, sind alle Geschosse am Fulham Road zurückgestaffelt, so daß große Terrassen entstehen, die sich zur Bepflanzung eignen. Die Fassade nimmt das Idiom des alten Hauses mit fliesenverkleideten, niedrigen Bogen auf. Das Gebäude ist vollklimatisiert und bietet im Untergeschoß Parkmöglichkeiten für 70 Wagen.

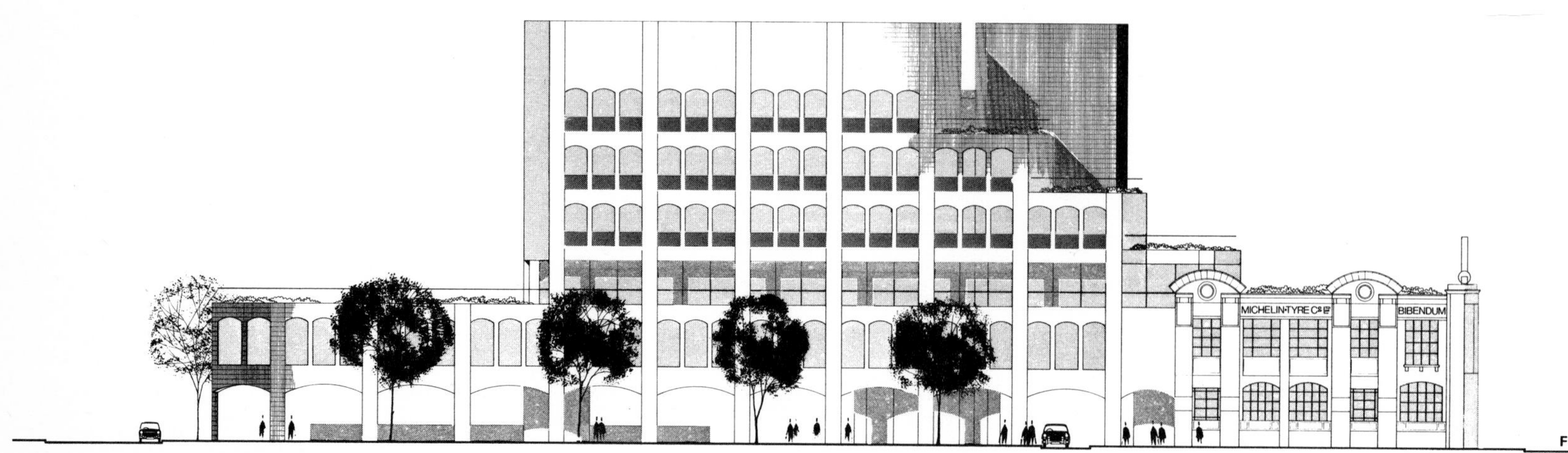

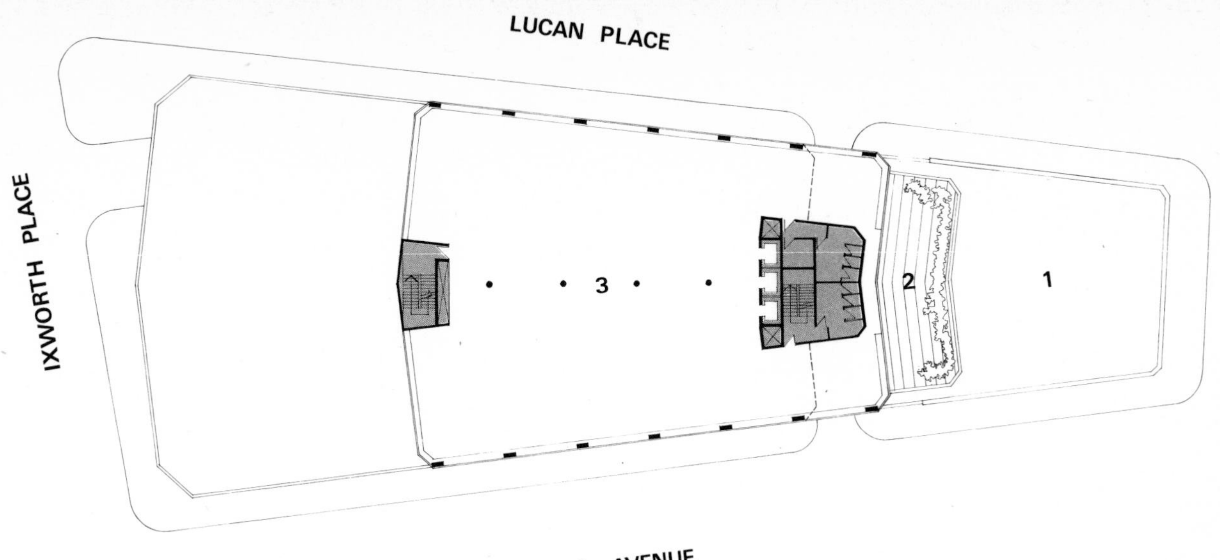

Third floor plan
1. Existing building 2. Landscaped terrace 3. Office space

Plan du troisième étage
1. Bâtiment existant 2. Jardins suspendus 3. Espace de bureaux

Grundriß drittes Obergeschoß
1. Altbau 2. Bepflanzte Terrasse 3. Bürofläche

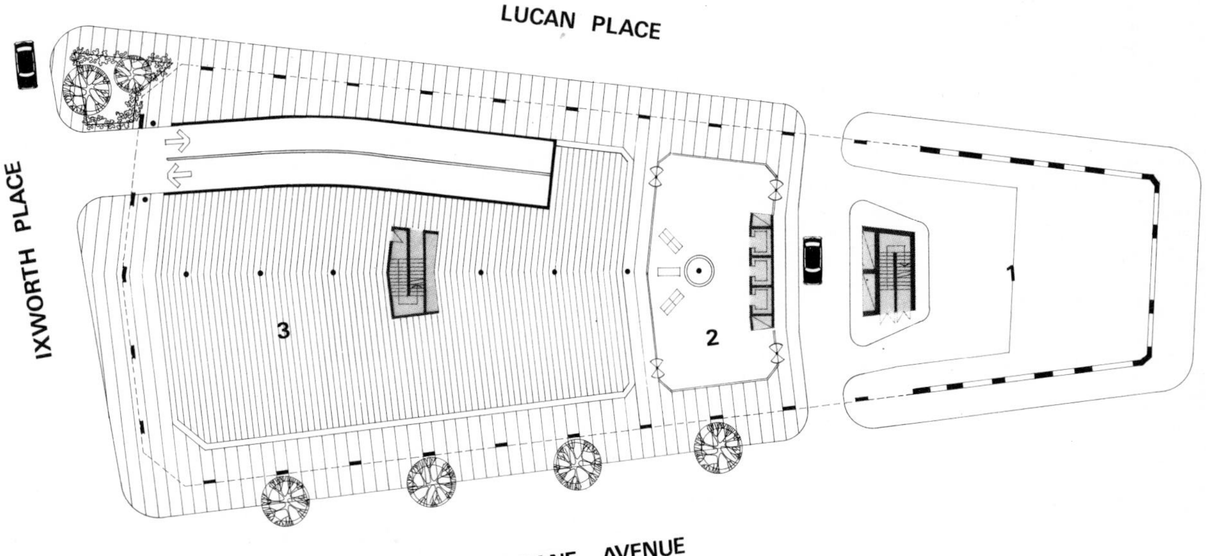

Ground floor plan
1. Existing building 2. Entrance hall 3. Sunken court

Plan du rez-de-chaussée
1. Bâtiment existant 2. Hall d'entrée 3. Cour en contrebas

Grundriß Erdgeschoß
1. Altbau 2. Eingangshalle 3. Tiefergelegener Garten

20 m

27 Munich 2 Airport, West Germany

Munich Airport Authority

Studiengruppe Luftfahrt, Aviation Consultants, in association with GMW and other aviation consultants, prepared a draft report feasibility study for the development of Munich 2 Airport in 1970. The principle of this concept is the complete physical separation of aircraft and passenger handling facilities. The linear concept of development in the future has been employed, but located in two separate functional areas of the airport. One of the prime advantages of this type of concept is that aircraft types may change and aircraft movements may increase, but future space requirements for both the parking apron and the terminal building will not conflict. The aircraft parking zone is essentially an open paved area not hemmed in by passenger buildings. Similarly, the terminal buildings are planned to expand unhindered in a linear direction along a transportation spine.

The link between the two functions must be flexible and during the early phases of the airport development it has been proposed that this should be by a rubber tyred transport vehicle carrying 100 seated passengers.

The master plan is sufficiently flexible to incorporate in the future stages of development sophisticated transportation systems (should they be available) in place of, or in addition to, the 'mobile lounges' currently proposed.

The passenger terminal consists of two basic parts which are separated by the access roads; a multistorey car park, and the passenger handling terminal proper. Both are closely related and interconnected to provide easy access between the two.

Passengers and friends park their cars on one of the seven parking floors and transfer via bridges to the departure floors for check-in. Moving passenger conveyors are provided within the bridges for arriving passengers and their baggage. It is anticipated that a computer-operated parking designation system will assist passengers in obtaining parking space adjacent to the bridge connection appropriate to their destination.

Une étude de factibilité d'un aménagement général de l'Aéroport Munich 2 a été établie en 1970 par le Studiengruppe Luftfahrt, consultants en matière de transport aérien, associé à GMW et d'autres consultants en problèmes aéroportuaires. La conception repose sur le principe d'une séparation physique complète entre les installations et équipements intéressant les avions et ceux concernant les passagers. On a retenu le concept d'un développement ultérieur linéaire, mais localisé dans deux zones fonctionnelles distinctes de l'aéroport. L'un des avantages majeur de ce type de conception est que les types d'avion peuvent évoluer, et le trafic aérien s'accroître sans qu'il y ait conflit entre les besoins d'espace tant pour le stationnement des avions que pour les bâtiments des terminaux. La zone de stationnement des avions est essentiellement une surface dallée ouverte, que ne cernent pas les bâtiments destinés aux passagers. Similairement, il est prévu que les bâtiments des terminaux puissent s'étendre sans obstacle d'une manière linéaire le long d'un axe affecté au transport.

La liaison entre les deux fonctions doit être souple. Pour les premières phases du développement de l'aéroport on a proposé que cette liaison soit assuré par un type de véhicule à pneus transportant cent passagers assis.

Le plan directeur est suffisamment souple pour pouvoir s'accommoder, à des phases ultérieures de développement, de systèmes de transport sophistiqués (à supposer qu'il s'en réalise), à la place ou en complément des « salles d'attente mobiles » actuellement proposées.

Le terminal des passagers comprend deux éléments constitutifs qui sont séparés par les routes d'accès; un parc de stationnement automobile à plusieurs niveaux, et le terminal des passagers proprement dit. Tous deux sont étroitement liés et interconnectés de manière à assurer un accès commode de l'un à l'autre.

Les passagers et leurs accompagnateurs parquent leurs voitures dans l'un des sept niveaux de parking et gagnent par des passerelles les étages des départs où a lieu l'enregistrement. Ces passerelles comportent des tapis roulants pour les passagers et leurs bagages. Il est envisagé qu'un système électronique de désignation de places de stationnement permette aux passagers de trouver une place voisine de la passerelle desservant les guichets de départ correspondant à leur destination.

Die Studiengruppe Luftfahrt, Berater für Flugverkehrsfragen, erarbeitete 1970 in Zusammenarbeit mit GMW sowie anderen Luftfahrtberatern ein Gutachten für die Bebauung des Flughafens München 2. Prinzip dieses Entwurfes ist die völlige Trennung der Einrichtungen zur Maschinen- und zur Passagierabfertigung. Das lineare Konzept für mögliche zukünftige Erweiterung ist in zwei separaten Funktionsbereichen des Flughafens angewandt. Ein entscheidender Vorteil dieses Konzeptes ist es, daß die Typen der Maschinen sich wandeln und der Flugverkehr zunehmen können, aber zukünftige Raumbedürfnisse des Vorfeldes einerseits und des Terminals andererseits nicht in Konflikt miteinander geraten können. Die Parkzone der Maschinen ist überwiegend ein offener Bereich mit fester Decke, der nicht durch Passagierbauten beeinträchtigt ist. Entsprechend sind die Abfertigungsgebäude so geplant, daß sie in horizontaler Richtung ungehindert entlang einer Transportachse erweitert werden können.

Die Verbindung zwischen beiden Funktionsbereichen muß flexibel sein. Für die ersten Phasen der Flughafenbebauung wird ein gummibereiftes Transportfahrzeug zur Aufnahme von bis zu 100 Passagieren vorgeschlagen.

Der Bebauungsplan ist flexibel genug, um in einem späteren Stadium ein hochentwickelteres Transportsystem zu integrieren (falls ein solches verfügbar ist).

Der Fluggastterminal besteht aus zwei Hauptelementen, die durch die Erschließungsstraße getrennt sind; einem mehrgeschossigen Parkhaus und dem eigentlichen Terminal. Beide stehen in enger Beziehung zueinander und sind miteinander verbunden, um leichten Zugang zu ermöglichen.

Passagiere und Begleiter parken ihre Wagen auf einem der sieben Parkgeschosse und gelangen über Brücken zu den Abfertigungsgeschossen. In den Brücken sind Förderbänder für Fluggast- und Gepäckbeförderung vorgesehen. Es ist geplant, daß eine elektronische Anlage den Fluggästen behilflich ist, Parkflächen an den entsprechenden Brükkenverbindungen zu finden.

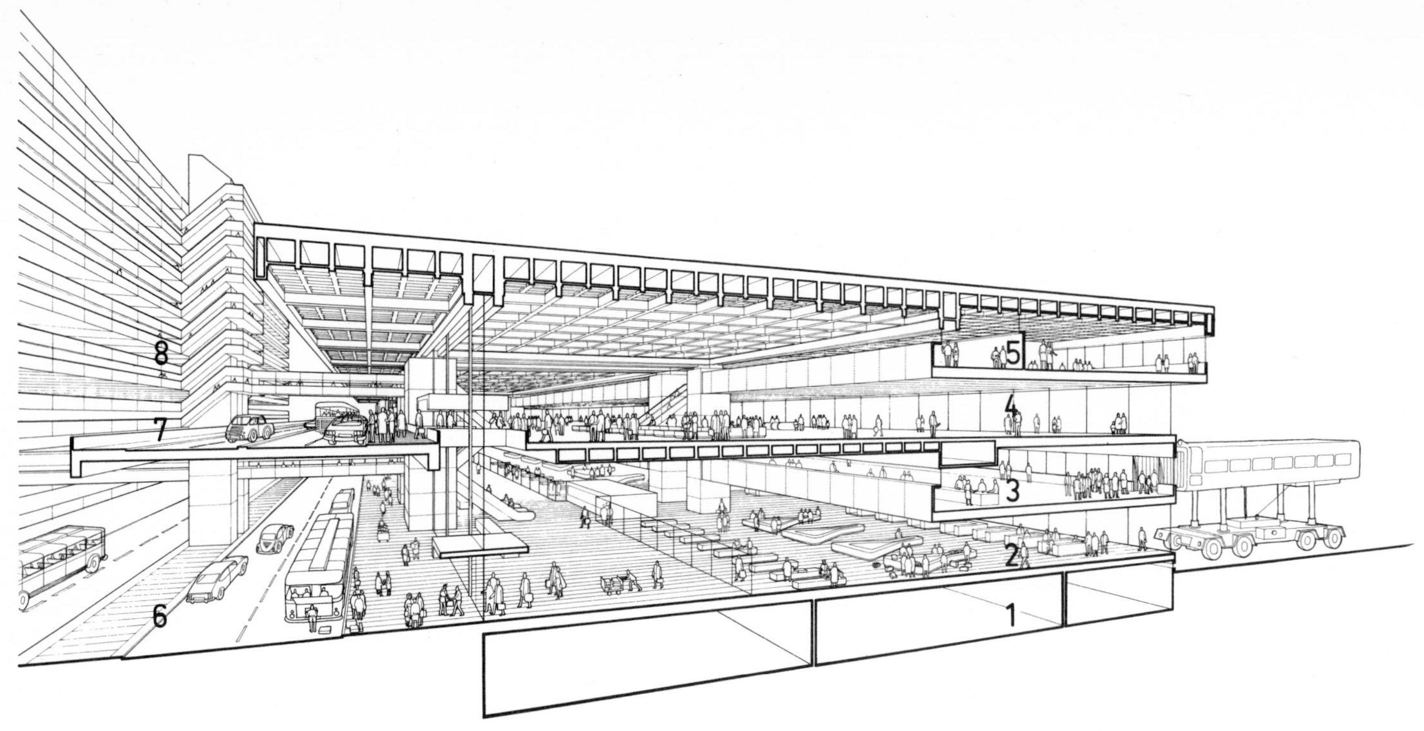

Section
1. Baggage hall 2. Baggage claim 3. Departures 4. Public concourse 5. Restaurant and administration 6. Arrivals road 7. Departures road 8. Parking

Section
1. Hall des bagages 2. Livraison des bagages 3. Départs 4. Salle des pas perdus 5. Restaurant et administration 6. Route de desserte des passagers à l'arrivée 7. Route d'accès des passagers au départ 8. Stationnement des voitures

Schnitt
1. Gepäckhalle 2. Gepäckempfang 3. Abflug 4. Schalterhalle 5. Restaurant und Verwaltung 6. Zufahrt Ankunft 7. Zufahrt Abflug 8. Parking

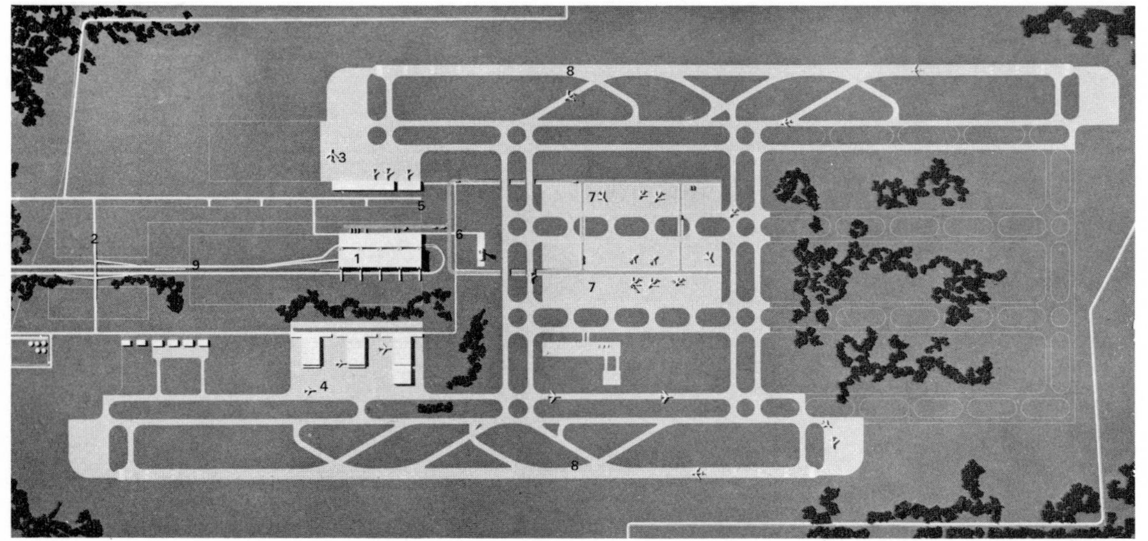

Site plan
1. Passenger terminal building 2. Airport ancillary buildings 3. Cargo 4. Aircraft service area 5. Mobile lounge road 6. Control tower 7. Aircraft parking 8. Runways 9. Road and rail access

Plan d'ensemble
1. Bâtiment terminal passagers 2. Bâtiments de service de l'aéroport 3. Chargement/déchargement fret aérien 4. Zone d'entretien des avions 5. Route de liaison pour le transport passagers 6. Tour de contrôle 7. Stationnement avions 8. Pistes d'envol 9. Accès routier et ferroviaire

Lageplan
1. Abfertigungsgebäude 2. Nebengebäude 3. Luftfracht 4. Maschinenwartung 5. Zubringerstraße 6. Kontrollturm 7. Maschinen-Standplätze 8. Rollfeldrampen 9. Erschließung Straße und Schiene

28 Mombasa Airport Development, Kenya, East Africa

The Government of Kenya

Studiengruppe Luftfahrt, Aviation Consultants, in association with GMW and other aviation consultants, prepared a draft report feasibility study for the development of Mombasa Airport in March 1971.

Investigations showed that a new main 3,350-m runway will be required to meet the types of operation of the current generation of large jet aircraft. A new terminal area will also be required with passenger terminal building, aircraft parking apron, and allied facilities.

The concept of the terminal building provides a multi-flexible series of spaces to accommodate current and future needs beneath a canopy roof. Primarily, protection has been provided from the sun and from the rain to give shade and shelter. Beneath this umbrella the terminal functions are arranged. Facilities are provided to process 500 passengers in a peak hour in both directions—arrivals and departures. The natural landscape forms part of this 'garden' terminal. Passenger functions are located under cover in garden courts as an extension of surrounding vegetation and landscapes. The building is open on all four sides and enclosures are only provided where required for security, protection from noise, and privacy. The terminal consists of two levels of accommodation. Main passenger handling activities are planned at the ground level, with public areas and administrative offices on the first floor.

Expansion may be obtained by expanding the passenger-handling accommodation on all sides of the terminal.

Une étude de factibilité d'un aménagement général de l'Aéroport de Mombasa a été établie en Mars 1971 par le Studiengruppe Luftfahrt, consultants en matière de transport aérien, associé à GMW et d'autres consultants en problèmes aéroportuaires.

Les enquêtes ont montré qu'une nouvelle piste d'envol de 3.350 m était nécessaire, pour correspondre aux besoins opérationnels de l'actuelle génération d'avions à réaction. Une nouvelle zone terminale sera également nécessaire avec un terminal passager, une zone-tablier de stationnement des avions et tous les équipements correspondants.

La conception du terminal retenue a été celle d'une série d'espaces « flexibles » et modifiables pouvant répondre aux besoins actuels comme à leur évolution future, distribués sous un large auvent dont la fonction essentielle est de fournir une protection contre le soleil et la pluie. Les équipements ont été prévus pour une capacité à l'heure de pointe de 500 passagers dans les deux directions (arrivées plus départs.) Le paysage naturel fait partie intégrante de ce « terminal-jardin ». Les différentes fonctions que doit remplir le terminal vis à vis des passagers sont en effet réparties sous l'auvent dans des cours-jardins qui paraissent une extension de la végétation et du paysage environnants. Le bâtiment est ouvert sur les quatre côtés et des clôtures ne sont disposées que là où l'exigent la sécurité, la protection contre le bruit ou le besoin d'intimité. Le terminal comprend deux niveaux. Les principaux services passagers sont installés au rez-de-chaussée, et les bureaux et les zones publiques au premier étage.

L'extension peut se faire facilement en prolongeant les services passagers sur tous les côtés du terminal initial.

Die Studiengruppe Luftfahrt, Berater für Flugverkehrsfragen, erarbeitete im März 1971 in Zusammenarbeit mit GWM sowie anderen Luftfahrtberatern ein Gutachten für die Bebauung des Flughafens Mombasa.

Untersuchungen ergaben, daß eine neue, 3.350 m lange Start- und Landebahn notwendig ist, die der gegenwärtigen Generation der großen Düsenflugzeuge entspricht. Auch wird ein neuer Abfertigungsbereich benötigt mit einem Terminal für Fluggäste, einem Vorfeld zum Abstellen der Maschinen und dazugehörigen Einrichtungen.

Der Entwurf des Abfertigungsgebäudes sieht eine Reihe von sehr flexiblen Räumen für gegenwärtige und zukünftige Bedürfnisse unter einem vorkragenden Dach vor. In erster Linie soll dadurch Schutz vor Witterungseinflüssen gewährt werden. Unter diesem Schirm sind die Funktionen des Terminals angeordnet. Einrichtungen zur Abfertigung von 500 Passagieren in Spitzenstunden in beiden Richtungen (Abflug und Ankunft) sind vorgesehen. Die natürliche Landschaft ist Bestandteil dieses „Garten"-Flughafens. Die Passagierräume sind in überdachten Gartenhöfen situiert als Erweiterung der umgebenden Vegetation und Landschaft. Das Gebäude ist nach allen vier Seiten offen, abgeschlossene Räume sind nur dort vorgesehen, wo sie aus Sicherheitsgründen oder zum Schutz vor Lärm und wegen der Privatheit notwendig sind. Das Gebäude hat zwei Ebenen: alle Aktivitäten zur Passagierabfertigung sind im Erdgeschoß untergebracht, öffentliche Bereiche und Büros im Obergeschoß.

Eine Erweiterung der Anlage ist durch Ausdehnung der Abfertigungsräume für Fluggäste an allen vier Seiten des Gebäudes möglich.

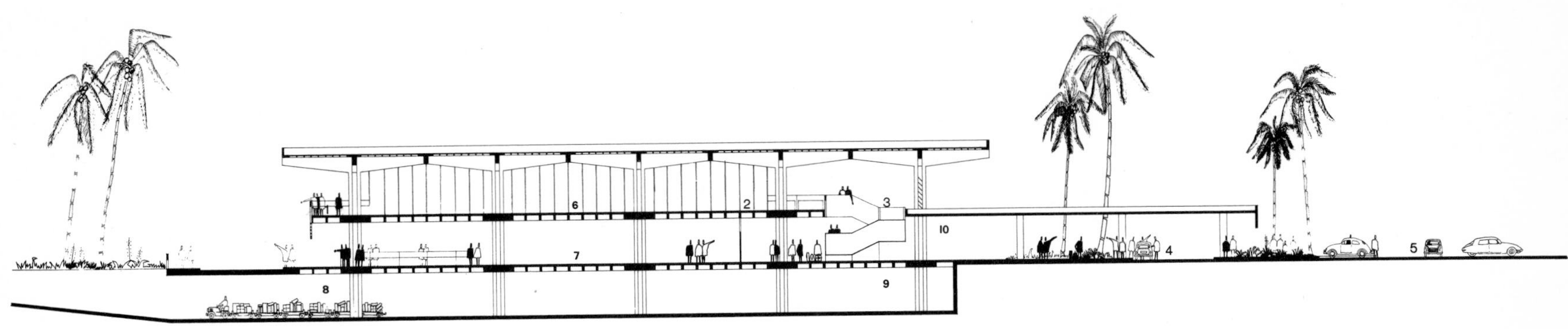

Section
1. Terrace 2. Staff canteen 3. Public access 4. Terminal set down road 5. Public car park 6. Restaurant 7. Departure lounge 8. Tunnel 9. Departure baggage hall 10. Public concourse

Coupe
1. Terrasse 2. Cantine du personnel 3. Accès du public 4. Route de débarquement au terminal 5. Stationnement public des voitures 6. Restaurant 7. Salon d'attente départs 8. Galerie couverte 9. Hall des bagages au départ 10. Salle des pas perdus

Schnitt
1. Terrasse 2. Mitarbeiterkantine 3. Zufahrt 4. Tiefergelegte Erschließungsstraße 5. Öffentlicher Parkplatz 6. Restaurant 7. Warteraum Abflug 8. Tunnel 9. Gepäckhalle Abflug 10. Schalterhalle

29 Holiday Resort and Hotel, Cesme Peninsula, Turkey

The Shell Company of Turkey

In 1970 Transport and Tourism Technicians Limited and the Gollins Melvin Ward Partnership were asked by the Shell Company of Turkey to select a number of sites in Turkey for development as holiday resorts. The scheme illustrated is a hotel at Ekmeksiz, an undeveloped bay on the Cesme Peninsula some fifty miles west of Izmir, comprising 150 bedrooms for guests, twenty-five bed/living rooms for the sixty staff, and the normal entertainment, public, and administrative rooms.

It was accepted as essential that the architectural idiom should be in sympathy with the existing natural environment and the design solution was a fragmented plan of individual units linked to a central communal complex; long travel distances are avoided and ease of extension is ensured. The principal materials are stone and timber.

The administrative and reception areas and the lounges and dining rooms are on three levels in the central complex, the main reception being at the intermediate level thus avoiding the need for lifts. The bedrooms are single-storey elements linked to the central complex by a main corridor at the intermediate level and overlap in a raking formation on the hills around the bay. Large terraces and sliding folding window units serve to enlarge the living spaces and horizontal sunblinds over the balconies provide shade and privacy.

En 1970 la compagnie Shell de Turquie demanda au bureau d'études Transport and Tourism Technicians Limited et la Gollins Melvin Ward Partnership de sélectionner en Turquie un certain nombre de sites pour y développer des centres de villégiature. Le plan donné ici représente le projet d'un hotel à Ekmeksiz, baie déserte de la péninsule de Cesme, située à 80 km à l'Ouest d'Izmir. L'hôtel comprend 150 chambres pour clients, vingt-cinq chambres-séjours pour un personnel de soixante personnes et l'ensemble normal d'équipements de distraction, de locaux publics et administratifs.

Il avait été jugé essentiel que le parti architectural s'harmonisât avec l'environnement naturel existant et la solution retenue a été un plan fragmentant l'hébergement en petites unités individualisées reliées à un complexe hôtelier central; on a évité les longs parcours et ménagé des possibilités d'extension. Les matériaux de construction sont la pierre et le bois.

Les zones administrative et de réception ainsi que les salons et salles à manger sont réparties sur trois niveaux dans le complexe central, la réception principale étant au niveau intermédiaire – ce qui évite les ascenseurs. Les chambres sont réparties dans des éléments sans étage reliés au niveau intermédiaire du complexe central par un corridor principal – éléments qui forment des bandes se superposant partiellement sur les collines encadrant la baie. De vastes terrasses et des baies à panneaux coulissants rabattables élargissent l'espace intérieur des chambres, et des stores horizontaux au dessus des balcons assurent ombre et intimité.

1970 wurden die Firma Transport and Tourism Technicians Ltd und Gollins Melvin Ward von der Türkischen Shell AG aufgefordert, eine Reihe von Grundstücken in der Türkei für die Bebauung als Ferienzentrum zu prüfen. Der dargestellte Entwurf ist für ein Hotel in Ekmesiz, einer unverbauten Bucht auf der Halbinsel Cesme, etwa 80 km von Izmir entfernt, und sieht 150 Gästeräume, 25 Schlaf-/Wohnräume für 60 Angestellte sowie die üblichen Unterhaltungs-, Publikums- und Verwaltungsräume vor.

Es wurde als wichtig erachtet, die Architektur der vorhandenen natürlichen Umgebung anzupassen. Die Lösung ist eine Addition individueller Einheiten, verbunden mit einem zentralen gemeinschaftlichen Komplex. Lange Fahrdistanzen sind vermieden und Erweiterung auf einfache Weise gesichert. Die Hauptmaterialien sind Naturstein und Holz.

Der Verwaltungs- und Empfangsbereich sowie die Aufenthalts- und Eßräume sind in drei Geschossen im zentralen Komplex untergebracht. Die Hauptrezeption liegt im Zwischengeschoß, dadurch wird die Notwendigkeit eines Fahrstuhls umgangen. Die Schlafräume sind eingeschossige Elemente, die durch einen Korridor im Zwischengeschoß mit dem zentralen Komplex verbunden sind und zu den die Bucht umgebenden Hügeln ansteigen. Große Terrassen und Faltschiebefenster dienen als Erweiterung der Wohnfläche, horizontale Sonnenblenden über den Balkons gewähren Schatten und Privatheit.

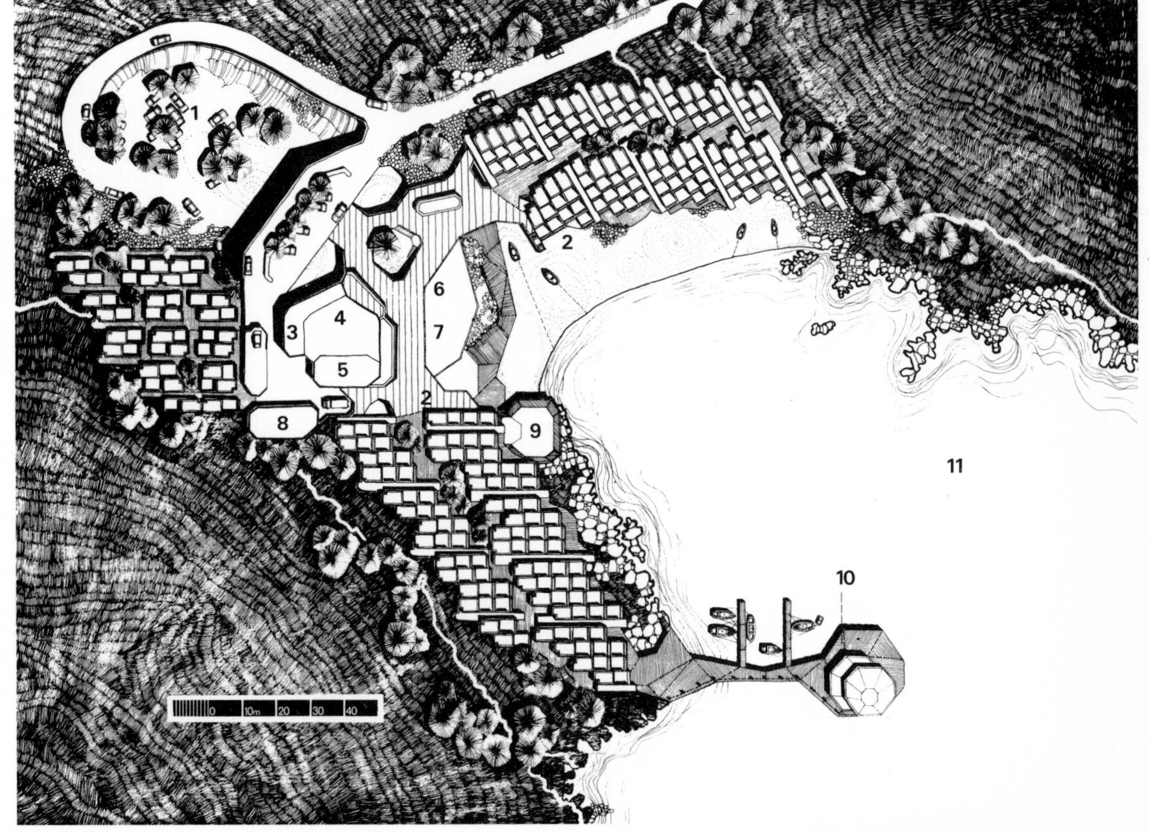

Site plan
1. Parking 2. Bedroom units 3. Administration 4. Kitchen 5. Laundry 6. Reception 7. Lounge 8. Plant 9. Swimming pool 10. Entertainment 11. Aegean Sea

Plan d'ensemble
1. Stationnement automobile 2. Unités d'hébergement 3. Administration 3. Cuisine 5. Blanchisserie 6. Réception 7. Salon 8. Locaux techniques 9. Piscine 10. Installations récréatives 11. Mer Egée

Lageplan
1. Parkplatz 2. Schlafraumeinheiten 3. Verwaltung 4. Küche 5. Wäscherei 6. Rezeption 7. Halle 8. Technik 9. Schwimmbecken 10. Unterhaltungsbereich 11. Ägäisches Meer

30 Westminster City School, Nine Elms, London SW8

Planned on three levels, the main access to the school is at the middle level which contains the upper school academic accommodation and is connected by means of a bridge, to a separate sports complex. At the upper level the first- and second-year facilities are planned as a self-contained unit with open teaching spaces as well as arts, crafts, and general science. Subject departments for other years are planned on the 'race-track' principle with the library/resource core in the centre and are linked vertically to the lower school. Science, arts and crafts, and technical studies departments for the upper school are located at ground level.

To assist the transition from open planned and more freely socially orientated primary schools, the junior section at Westminster is largely a general teaching social area with a shared resource, general science, and technical studies departments. Here, a limited number of traditional classrooms are provided. Even these are multi-use and, with the exception of one fitted out for audio visual aids, may be used for any subject.

The upper school has subject departments surrounding the library/resource core. All non-technical activities are, therefore, central to the information core. This also contains the normal library activities, tutorial, seminar, remedial rooms, a lecture theatre, and perhaps most important, a direct link to the lower school resource area immediately above. This forms an educational and administrative continuity between the two schools.

A separate sixth-form centre is also provided at Westminster containing social and tutorial spaces which is connected to but separate from the remainder of the school.

L'école est distribuée sur trois niveaux, l'accès principal se faisant au niveau intermédaire contenant les locaux d'enseignement général du second cycle qui est relié par un pont à un complexe sportif constituant un bàtiment indépendant.

Au niveau supérieur, on a conçu les installations pour le premier cycle comme une unité indépendante, comprenant des espaces d'enseignement ouverts aussi bien que des locaux affectés aux lettres, sciences ou travail manuel. Les départements des différentes disciplines concernant les autres années ont été disposés selon le principe de la double circulation, entourant le noyau central occupé par le « centre de connaissances » qui est relié verticalement à l'unité du premier cycle. Les locaux des disciplines scientifiques, des lettres, des travaux manuels et des études techniques du second cycle sont situés au rez-de-chaussée.

On a cherché à faciliter la transition aux enfants venant de classes primaires où il n'y a pas de locaux spécialisés et où les allées et venues comme les relations sociales entre élèves sont plus libres. C'est pourquoi la zone affectée au premier cycle à Westminster a été conçue comme un vaste espace ouvert à l'enseignement et aux relations sociales où sont communs les départements des disciplines scientifiques générales et techniques et le centre de connaissances. On n'a prévu qu'un nombre restreint de classes traditionnelles, et même celles-ci sont polyvalentes, à l'exception d'une classe équipée pour l'enseignement audiovisuel.

Dans le second cycle, les départements des différentes disciplines entourent le noyau de la bibliothèque – centre de connaissances. Toutes les activités non techniques sont donc orientées vers le noyau du centre d'information. Celui-ci contient les activités normales d'une bibliothèque, les salles de cours particuliers, de groupes (séminaires), de cours supplémentaires et, ce qui est peut-être plus important, une liaison directe avec le « centre de connaissances » du premier cycle situé immédiatement au-dessus. Ceci assure un lien administratif et éducatif entre les deux cycles.

Les classes de terminale sont aussi constituées à Westminster en un centre indépendant comprenant des espaces d'activités sociales et de cours individuels – qui est relié au reste de l'établissement tout en étant distinct.

Der Haupteingang des dreigeschossigen Schulgebäudes liegt auf der mittleren Ebene, welche die Unterrichtsräume der Oberstufe enthält und von der aus eine Brücke zu einem separaten Sporttrakt führt. Im Obergeschoß liegen die Einrichtungen für das erste und zweite Schuljahr als unabhängige Einheit mit offenen Lehrbereichen sowie Räume für Kunsterziehung, Werken und Naturwissenschaften. Die Fachklassen für die anderen Jahrgänge umschließen den Bibliotheks-/Erholungskern und sind vertikal mit den unteren Schulbereichen verbunden. Kunsterziehung und Werken sowie die Abteilungen für technische Fächer der Oberstufe sind im Erdgeschoß situiert.

Um den Übergang vom Großraum und der freier organisierten Grundschule zu erleichtern, ist die Unterstufe in Westminster vorwiegend ein allgemeiner Lehr-/Sozialbereich mit einem von allen benutzten Aufenthaltsraum sowie Abteilungen für allgemeine und technische Fächer. Hier ist eine beschränkte Anzahl von traditionellen Klassenräumen vorhanden. Seibst diese sind Vielzweckräume. Mit Ausnahme von einem, der für AV ausgestattet ist, können sie für jedes Fach genutzt werden.

Die Oberstufe hat Fachklassen, die um den Bibliotheks-/Erholungsbereich angeordnet sind. Alle nicht-technischen Aktivitäten sind zentral im Informationskern angeordnet. Dazu gehören auch die üblichen Bibliotheksaktivitäten, Tutoren-, Seminar-, Krankenzimmer, ein Vorlesungssaal und, das vielleicht wichtigste, eine direkte Verbindung zum unmittelbar darunterliegenden Aufenthaltsbereich der Unterstufe. Sie stellt das pädagogische und verwaltungsmäßige Bindeglied zwischen beiden Schulen dar.

Ein getrennter Abschlußklassenbereich ist ebenfalls vorhanden. Er enthält Sozial- und Unterrichtsräume, die zwar mit Verbindung zur übrigen Schule, doch separat angeordnet sind.

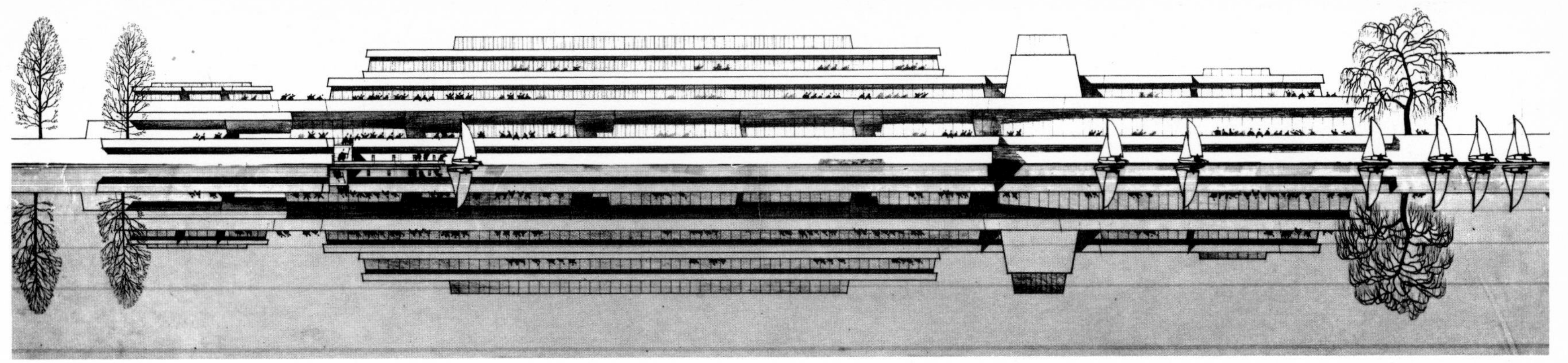

Site plan
1. River Thames 2. Sixth-form centre 3. Main teaching accommodation 4. Play deck 5. Bridge 6. Sports complex 7. Hard play areas 8. Caretaker's house

Plan d'ensemble
1. Tamise 2. Centre des terminales 3. Locaux principaux d'enseignement 4. Préau (jeux) 5. Pont 6. Complexe sportif 7. Terrains de jeux "en dur" 8. Conciergerie

Lageplan
1. Themse 2. Abschlußklassen 3. Allgemeiner Unterrichtsbereich 4. Spieldeck 5. Brücke 6. Sporttrakt 7. Hartplatz 8. Hausmeisterwohnung

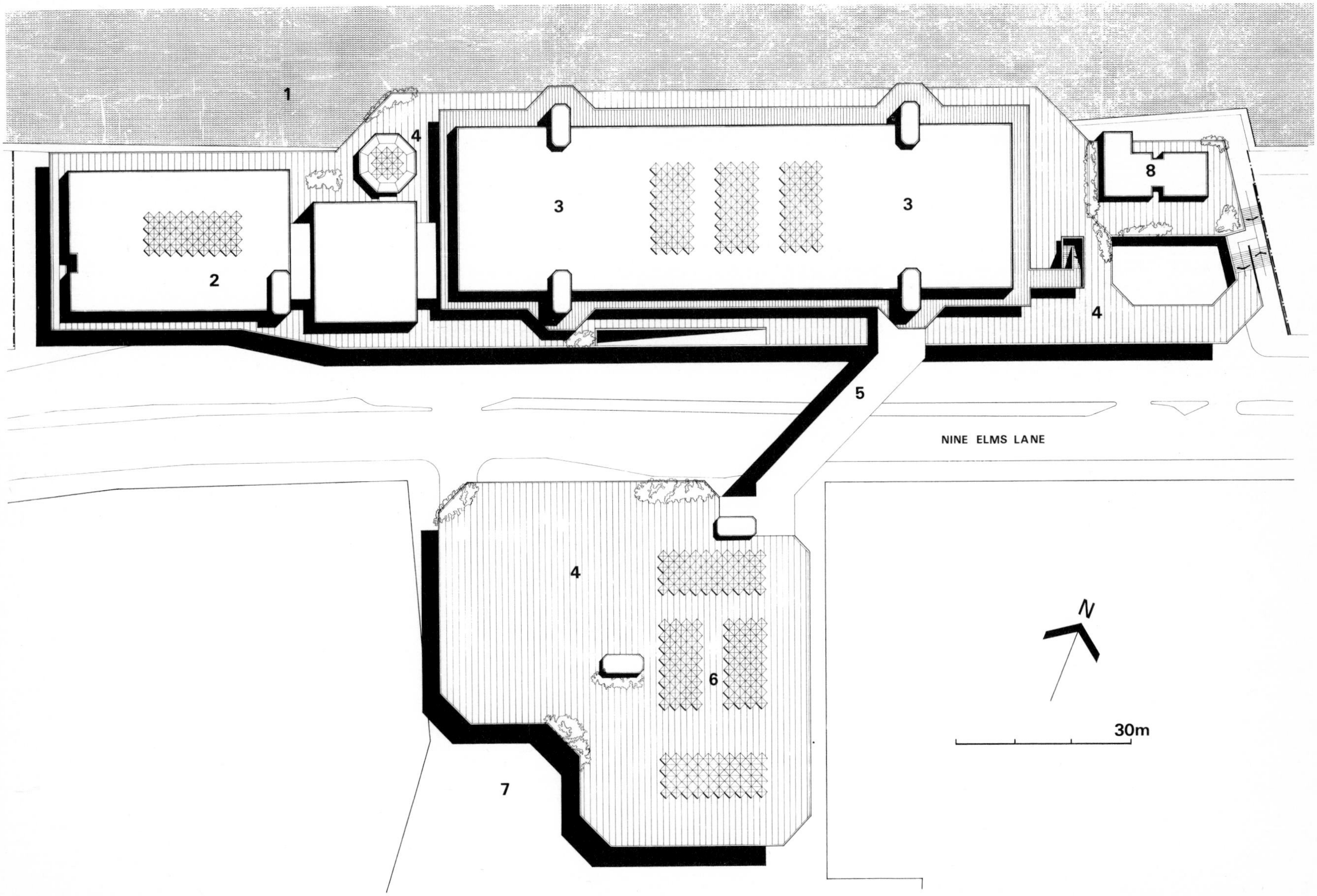

31 Headquarter Offices, Brighton, Sussex

American Express International Banking Corporation

American Express first opened offices in Brighton in 1967; these have been rapidly outgrown and in 1972 they authorized the preparation of plans for a new headquarters building of some 28,500 m^2 on a sloping site near the sea in Edward Street. The very natural concern of the Brighton Corporation that the particular character of the city should not be hazarded made the light angles and height restrictions critical. The six-storey tower is over a three-storey podium set well back from the main street and forms a large landscaped court to which the public has access.

The accommodation is entirely air-conditioned and the structure is *in situ* reinforced concrete on a 7·2-m grid; the projecting coffered floors are clad externally in white glass reinforced polyester and the glazing throughout is a reflective blue glass.

Peter Wood and Partners were in association.

L'Americain Express a ouvert ses premiers bureaux à Brighton en 1967. Ceux-ci-devinrent rapidement trop exigus, ce qui conduisit en 1972 à préparer les plans d'un nouveau siège social d'environ 28.500 m^2 sur un site en pente, près de la mer, donnant sur Edward Street. Le souci très naturel de la société de ne pas compromettre le caractère très particulier de la ville de Brighton se traduisait par des contraintes très sévères de prospect et de limitation de hauteur. Une tour de six étages s'élève au dessus d'un podium de trois niveaux. L'ensemble est suffisamment en retrait de la rue principale pour ménager une vaste cour-jardin à laquelle le public a accès.

Les locaux sont entièrement climatisés. La structure est en béton armé coulé en place selon une trame de 7,2 m; le revêtement extérieur des étages coffrés en porte-à-faux est de verre blanc renforcé de polyester et le vitrage en verre bleuté réfléchissant.

L'Agence Peter Wood et Associés a participé à ce travail.

Nachdem American Express im Jahre 1967 sein Büro in Brighton eröffnet hatte, erfolgte eine schnelle Expansion, die 1972 die Erstellung von Plänen für ein neues Verwaltungsgebäude mit etwa 28.500 m^2 Nutzfläche auf einem abfallenden Gelände nahe dem Strand in der Edward Street rechtfertigte. Das berechtigte Anliegen der Stadtverwaltung von Brighton, den besonderen Charakter der Stadt zu wahren, ließ die Vorschriften für Bauabstände und Höhenbeschränkungen kritisch werden. Der Entwurf sieht eine sechsgeschossige Scheibe über einem dreigeschossigen Podium vor, das von der Straße zurückgesetzt ist und eine große Grünfläche freiläßt, die öffentlich zugänglich ist.

Das Gebäude ist vollklimatisiert und die Konstruktion besteht aus am Ort gegossenem Beton auf einem 7,2 m-Modul. Die vorkragenden Deckenfelder sind außen mit weißem, glasfaserverstärktem Polyester verkleidet, die durchgehende Verglasung besteht aus reflektierendem, blauem Glas.

Peter Wood and Partners waren am Entwurf beteiligt.

32 Royal Opera House, Covent Garden, London WC2

The Royal Opera House

The removal of London's main fruit and vegetable market from Covent Garden in 1974 has enabled plans to be prepared to provide much needed extensions to the Royal Opera House to replace the present grossly inadequate backstage facilities and to improve the public amenities.

Provision is also made for the opera and ballet schools, at present located at some distance from the Royal Opera House, and for a second auditorium to seat 1,200 with its own appropriate backstage and dressing facilities. The existing auditorium will remain unaltered.

The extensions will restore the traditional relationship of the Royal Opera House to the central market piazza originally designed by Inigo Jones in 1633, thus re-establishing it in its historical context.

La relocalisation en 1974 des Halles aux fruits et aux légumes de Londres, en libérant le site de Covent Garden, a permis de dresser les plans des extensions, depuis longtemps réclamés, de l'Opéra Royal, visant à remplacer tout le dispositif, singulièrement inapproprié, des coulisses actuelles et à améliorer les installations destinées au public.

Les extensions abriteront en outre les écoles d'opéra et de ballet, qui sont actuellement installées à une certaine distance de l'Opéra, et une seconde salle de 1.200 places munie de son propre appareil de loges, cintres, dessous, coulisses et dégagements. La salle d'opéra existante restera inchangée.

Ces extensions rétabliront la relation architecturale qui existait à l'origine entre l'Opéra Royal et la « piazza » du marché central, dessinée en 1633 par Inigo Jones, qui sera ainsi restituée dans son contexte historique.

Die Verlegung des größten Londoner Obst- und Gemüsemarktes aus Covent Garden im Jahre 1974 hat die Planung der dringend benötigten Erweiterung des Opernhauses als Ersatz für die gegenwärtig völlig unzureichenden Bühnenanlage und zur Verbesserung der Zuschauereinrichtungen ermöglicht.

Außerdem sind Räumlichkeiten für die Opern- und die Ballettschule vorgesehen, die beide zur Zeit auswärts untergebracht sind, und für einen zweiten Zuschauersaal mit 1.200 Plätzen, eigenen Bühnen- und Umkleideeinrichtungen. Der vorhandene Zuschauerraum soll unverändert bestehen bleiben.

Die Erweiterung wird die traditionelle Beziehung des Opernhauses zum zentralen Marktplatz von Inigo Jones aus dem Jahre 1633 wiederherstellen und es damit wieder in seinen historischen Kontext einbeziehen.